DISCARDED

What Kind of Liberation?

The publisher gratefully
acknowledges the generous
support of the Anne G. Lipow
Endowment Fund for Social Justice
and Human Rights of the University
of California Press Foundation,
which was established by
Stephen M. Silberstein.

WHAT KIND OF LIBERATION?

WOMEN AND THE
OCCUPATION OF IRAQ

Nadje Al-Ali and Nicola Pratt

Foreword by Cynthia Enloe

UNIVERSITY OF CALIFORNIA PRESS

BERKELEY   LOS ANGELES   LONDON

Half of author royalties will go to the following two nongovernmental and nonpartisan organizations:

Knowledge for Iraqi Women Society (K41WS) provides services for women and children, including a clinic, illiteracy classes, small grants for income generation projects, and medical services, as well as organizing relief work. Contact Dr. Rashad Zaydan, Dr.R.Zaydan @almaarefa.org, or Aldawodi Post Office, P.O. Box 28058, Postal Code 12631, Baghdad, Iraq.

The Women's Human Rights Centre (WHRC) works to empower Iraqi women in a variety of fields to ensure their full participation in society and to build a free and democratic Iraq on the basis of equality between men and women. Contact dwrc_sc@yahoo.com, or H. no. 9, St. 39/208, Diwaniya, Iraq.

University of California Press, one of the most distinguished university presses in the United States, enriches lives around the world by advancing scholarship in the humanities, social sciences, and natural sciences. Its activities are supported by the UC Press Foundation and by philanthropic contributions from individuals and institutions. For more information, visit www.ucpress.edu.

University of California Press
Berkeley and Los Angeles, California

University of California Press, Ltd.
London, England

Library of Congress Cataloging-in-Publication Data

Al-Ali, Nadje Sadig.
    What kind of liberation? : women and the occupation of Iraq / Nadje Al-Ali and Nicola Pratt ; foreword by Cynthia Enloe.
        p.   cm.
    Includes bibliographical references and index.
    ISBN 978-0-520-25729-0 (cloth : alk. paper)
    1. Women—Iraq—Social conditions.   2. Women's rights—Iraq.   3. Women in politics—Iraq.   4. Iraq War, 2003—Women.   I. Pratt, Nicola Christine. II. Title.
HQ1735.A66   2009
305.48'8927567090511—dc22   2008025291

Manufactured in the United States of America
18 17 16 15 14 13 12 11 10 09
10 9 8 7 6 5 4 3 2 1
The paper used in this publication meets the minimum requirements of ANSI/NISO Z39.48–1992 (R 1997) (Permanence of Paper).

To the women of Iraq

Contents

Foreword

Cynthia Enloe

It's happening. The country, the complex, dynamic society that is Iraq, is becoming "Iraq," just as the complex, dynamic society that is Vietnam has become merely "Vietnam." Starting as early as the late 1970s, one began to hear people casually saying, for instance, "Vietnam should have taught us a lesson" or "That song was popular during Vietnam." As if Vietnam—with its history of Chinese and French colonizations, its poetry, its rice and rubber economies, its ethnic tensions between highlands and low country, its women activists' fascination with the heroic Trung Sisters and the rebellious George Sand—as if Vietnam could be reduced to "Vietnam," merely a brief late-twentieth-century American (and Australian and Filipino and Korean) wartime experience.

Today, as this terrific book is going to press, a similar shrinkage is being imposed on Iraq. Iraqis are being shrunken down to a narcissistic "Iraq." Listen, and you will hear Americans and British men and women say things such as "Iraq should teach us a lesson" or "Iraq is the reason he killed his wife." As if Iraq—with its history of ancient civilizations' achievements, British colonial rule, multiethnic marriages and lively urban neighborhoods, prolific writers and filmmakers, Communist and Ba'thist parties' competitive courtings of activist women, a disastrous war with Iran—as if Iraq would be squeezed into "Iraq," a newly blown small glass bottle of American and British angst.

One sure way to release Vietnam from its imprisoning "Vietnam" and Iraq from its currently hardening confines of "Iraq" is to start paying close, detailed attention to Vietnamese and Iraqi women's long histories of theorizing, debating, alliance-making, organizing, and campaigning. By taking seriously the historical and contemporary political lives—and ideas—of women, we can inoculate ourselves against the temptation to treat any society simplistically or, worse, narcissistically. I've found that when we observe carefully the twists and turns of women's relationships with men, with each other, with the state, and with international allies and invaders, it becomes impossible to imagine that society to have ever been merely frozen in a timeless "tradition" or dominated by a monolithic elite. Instead, by taking any country's diverse women seriously, over not just five years but over generations, we are compelled to come to grips with the crucial watersheds, disparate movements' and state officialdoms' failures and successes, as well as the sources of pride, ambivalence, contradiction, and fissure that shape any society and fuel its ongoing dynamism.

We are now building up a substantial body of literature on Vietnamese women, much of it researched and written by Vietnamese women scholars. It is becoming available, however, at the very time when most non-Vietnamese readers aren't paying much attention to Vietnamese affairs and even less to the ideas and activist strategizing of Vietnamese women. They have already become content to think of Vietnam as "Vietnam."

Yet here in Nadje Al-Ali and Nicola Pratt's groundbreaking book we do have a chance, before our alarmingly short attention spans turn elsewhere, before we consign Iraq to "Iraq," to engage with Iraqi women's continuously evolving political lives.

By doing so, we can not only throw sand into the works of the shrinkage machine, but we also can make ourselves smarter about larger puzzles with which so many of us today are struggling:

- When has a nationalist campaign been liberating for women and when, conversely, has it become mainly a movement to refurbish patriarchy?
- What strategies employed by women's advocates have the best chance of narrowing the formidable class, ethnic, religious, generational, and rural-urban gulfs separating women from each other?
- What are the most effective ways for local women's rights activists to have an impact on neocolonial powers' decision-makers, without opening themselves up to cooptation?

- What erroneous assumptions made by well-meaning mid-level women in an occupying bureaucracy allow them to be unwitting tools of their patriarchal superiors?
- What criteria distinguish a pawn from a genuinely transnational feminist effort?
- What will it take to make the historic passage of UN Security Council Resolution 1325—calling on all member states to insure women's meaningful participation in peace accord negotiations and post-accord nation rebuilding—a practical tool for dismantling masculinized political cultures and practices?
- When are political party–based competitive elections not empowering for most women?
- How exactly does decision-makers' fixation on "ethnic reconciliation" and "ethnic balance" marginalize women and silence feminists?
- Why should feminists become constitutional experts?
- When do patriarchal officials find the discourses of "women's liberation" useful for their own patriarchal ends?
- How integral are masculinized politics to the perpetuation of militarism?
- And, of course, what does the process of authentic democratization really look like?

Yes, this is a tall order. But, as I read and then reread these rich chapters (there is something to learn on literally every page here), I found myself nudged by Nadje Al-Ali and Nicola Pratt to think of their implications for answering each one of these important questions. That is what such a sophisticated one-country feminist case study, such as *What Kind of Liberation?*, does: it helps us craft answers to questions we are asking elsewhere.

Acknowledgments

A book about the role of women in the "new Iraq" would not have been possible without the many Iraqi women living inside and outside Iraq who generously shared with us their time, observations, analyses, and often quite painful experiences. Although we cannot name all of them here, we would like to express our deep gratitude to them for spending time with us and encouraging us to pursue the project for this book. Our views might not correspond to those of all the women we interviewed, but we hope that we managed to present everyone's views and experiences fairly. Both Nicola and Nadje would like to thank in particular Sundus Abass, Souad al-Jazaeiri, and Hanaa Edwar for sharing their insights and contacts continuously over the period of our research. We would also like to thank everyone else we interviewed in Erbil, Sulaymaniya, Amman, Washington, D.C., San Diego, and London.

We are both particularly grateful to our wonderful interpreters Hedy in Erbil (Hawler) and Sheelan in Sulaymaniya—both cities in Iraqi Kurdistan. They greatly facilitated our visits by helping with language and logistics, and we enjoyed their company and the opportunity to learn from them about their daily lives and life in general in Iraqi Kurdistan.

Nadje and Nicola would also like to thank the many friends and colleagues who read drafts of one or more chapters and gave us their invaluable feedback: Mike Bowker, Ellen Cantarow, Richard Crockatt, Jean Davis, Shirouk Dillaa, Mark Douglas, Catherine Eschle, Lesley Grahame, Virginia Greasley, John Greenaway, Joost Hiltermann, Claire Hynes, Brian

Katulis, Kim Longinotto, Lee Marsden, Maysoon Pachachi, Chris Parker, Glen Rangwala, Maha al-Sakban, Heather Savigny, Robert Springborg, and Nira Yuval Davis.

We have both been inspired by Cynthia Cockburn, Cynthia Enloe, Deniz Kandiyoti, Shahrzad Mojab, and Spike Peterson, whose writings and interventions have shaped and influenced our own thinking and analysis. Cynthia Enloe and Spike Peterson read the whole manuscript on a short deadline and provided invaluable comments and suggestions. Thank you so much!

The cover image and images inside the book were kindly shared by Eugenie Dolberg, whose Open Shutters project we greatly admire. We were deeply moved and impressed by the photos taken by Antoinette, Dima, Lulua, Raya, Sarab, Umm Mohamed, and Zeinab.

The research for this book would not have been possible without the financial support of the British Academy. We are especially grateful for their flexibility and understanding when we had to change our research plans because of the worsening security situation inside Iraq. Once the research was under way, we were supported by our editor Niels Hooper, whose encouragement and enthusiasm for the project helped us to produce this book in good time. We also thank Jane Clarke for administrative support.

Nadje would like to express her thanks and deep gratitude to her friends from Act Together: Women's Action for Iraq, whose presence and continuous support have made a huge difference over the years. She is also grateful to Kawther Ibraheem for her help in finding an interpreter in Erbil and to Ali Mandalawi for helping facilitate her trip to Iraqi Kurdistan in spring 2007. Aysha Dennis Pachachi lent a miraculous helping hand over the summer of 2007 as the chaos in Nadje's study was threatening to seep into her thinking. Finally, Nadje would like to thank her husband, Mark Douglas, and her daughter, Alhena, for providing a safe and loving home in the midst of the violence and destruction inside Iraq that have profoundly affected not only Iraqis living inside the country but also many of us living outside.

Nicola would like to thank several people who provided crucial help to her in the course of her research: Michele Dunne, Hala Ghosheh, Joost Hiltermann, Brian Katulis, Abeer Mohammad, Brenda Oppermann, Zainab Shakir, Sherzad Sherif, Shkow Sharif, and (Canadian) Liz Williams. She expresses her deep gratitude to Agnieszka Pacynzska and her wonderful family, who housed and entertained her while she was conducting research in Washington, D.C. She thanks Cassandra Cavallaro and Hilary Cornish for their excellent research assistance; the School of Political, Social and International Studies at the University of East Anglia for granting her research leave in the autumn of 2007, which enabled her to finish the book manuscript on time; and, last but not least, (British) Liz Williams for vital administrative support. Most of all, she feels fortunate to have been able to spend time with so many interesting and inspiring people in the course of this research.

Acronyms

CASI	Campaign against Sanctions on Iraq
CIPE	Center for International Private Enterprise
CPA	Coalition Provisional Authority
CSIS	Center for Strategic and International Studies
DFI	Development Fund for Iraq
DFID	(U.K.) Department for International Development
GFIW	General Federation of Iraqi Women
IBWA	Iraqi Business Women's Association
ICP	Iraqi Communist Party
IGC	Iraqi Governing Council
IIG	Iraqi Interim Government
IMIE	International Mission for Iraqi Elections
INA	Iraqi National Accord
INC	Iraqi National Congress
IWF	Independent Women's Forum
IWW	Iraqi Women's Will
KDP	Kurdistan Democratic Party

MEPI	Middle East Partnership Initiative
NCCI	NGO Coordinating Committee in Iraq
NDI	National Democratic Institute
NGO	nongovernmental organization
ORHA	Office for Reconstruction and Humanitarian Assistance
OWFI	Organization for Women's Freedom in Iraq
PUK	Patriotic Union of Kurdistan
SCIRI	Supreme Council for the Islamic Revolution in Iraq
SIGIR	Special Inspector General for Iraq Reconstruction
SIIC	Supreme Islamic Iraqi Council
TAL	Transitional Administrative Law
TNA	Transitional National Assembly
UIA	United Iraqi Alliance
UNAMI	United Nations Assistance Mission for Iraq
UNDP	United Nations Development Programme
UNESCO	UN Educational, Scientific and Cultural Organization
UNFAO	UN Food and Agriculture Organization
UNHCHR	UN High Commissioner for Human Rights
UNHCR	UN High Commissioner for Refugees
UNICEF	UN Children's Fund
UNIFEM	UN Development Fund for Women
UNMOVIC	UN Monitoring, Verification and Inspection Committee
UN-OCHA	UN Office for the Coordination of Human Affairs
UNSC	UN Security Council
UNWFP	UN World Food Programme
USAID	U.S. Agency for International Development
USIP	U.S. Institute for Peace
WAFDI	Women's Alliance for a Democratic Iraq
WFFI	Women for a Free Iraq

INTRODUCTION

During International Women's Week in 2004, a year after the invasion of Iraq, President Bush gave a speech to 250 women from around the world who had gathered at the White House. "The advance of women's rights and the advance of liberty are ultimately inseparable," he began. Supported by his wife, Laura, who praised the administration's success in achieving greater rights for Afghan women, the president continued, "The advance of freedom in the greater Middle East has given new rights and new hopes to women there." Of women leaders in Afghanistan and Iraq he added that they had displayed "incredible courage" (White House Office of the Press Secretary 2004).

Today, several years down the line, *liberty, freedom, women's rights,* and *hope* are not words anyone would associate with Iraq—even advocates of the U.S. invasion and of Bush. Much has been written concerning the possible causes of the disastrous and continuously deteriorating situation in Iraq. These range from failed policies to poor strategies, from reckless incompetence to evil scheming (see, among others, Diamond 2005; Dodge 2005; Hashim 2006; Herring and Rangwala 2006; Phillips 2005).[1] This book examines the reasons why military intervention and occupation have failed to liberate Iraqi women and why they have instead produced a deterioration in women's circumstances and position.

Our book tells how women in Iraq have fared since the fall of the Ba'th regime in 2003. Official rhetoric puts Iraqi women at center stage, but we show that in reality women's rights and women's lives have been exploited

1

in the name of competing political agendas. We also challenge the widespread view—even among progressive antiwar and peace activists—that something inherent in Muslim, Middle Eastern, or Iraqi culture is responsible for the escalating violence and systematic erosion of women's rights. We argue that it is not Islam or "culture" that has pushed Iraqi women back into their homes. Instead we blame specific and rapidly changing political, economic, and social conditions as well as a wide range of national, regional, and international actors. A closer look at Iraqi women's historical participation in public life, their achievements in education, their contribution to the workforce, and the overall social climate shows that in many ways conditions were actually better for women in the past than now.

Yet far from being passive victims, Iraqi women continue to negotiate the challenges of the war and occupation and to find strategies for resisting and adapting to events as these unfold. Through interviews with women's rights activists and women doctors, lawyers, teachers, members of nongovernmental organizations (NGOs), politicians, and parliamentarians, we document Iraqi women's rich and varied involvement in political transition, reconstruction, and attempts at shaping "the new Iraq." We move beyond simplistic representations of Iraqi women either as victims or as heroines. They are both, and a lot more besides. Some women have greater opportunities to survive, adapt, and resist than others. We are suspicious of sweeping statements like "Iraqi women think . . ." or "Iraqi women want . . ." Like women anywhere else in the world, Iraqi women are not all the same. Moreover, they differ in more than being Shi'i, Sunni, or Christian, Arab or Kurd. Aside from the fact that there are many other religious and ethnic groups in Iraq, differences derive much more from social class, educational and professional background, place of residence, experiences of the previous regime, political orientation, and attitude toward religion.

For Iraqi women's worsening circumstances we find multiple culprits in discriminatory policies, oppressive practices, and violence. Much of the debate and literature about the occupation reduces to polarized political positions. Antiwar activists and critics of the Bush administration stress the atrocities committed by the occupation and portray Iraqi women as the victims of American and British imperialist ambitions, neocolonial modes of thinking, and military aggression. Pro-Bush supporters and proponents of military intervention condemn the threats and dangers posed by al-Qaeda, Islamist insurgents more generally, and remnants of the previous Ba'th regime. However, Iraqi women are exposed to discriminatory practices and policies as well as to violence from a range of sources—political parties, militarized groups, and the occupation forces. These sources of abuse and violence are often interlinked. In a situation where women are caught between occupation, Islamist extremists, remnants of the former regime, and Mafia-type criminals, those opposing the occupation find that "the enemy of my enemy is not my friend" (Al-Ali 2006).

Questions arise from the polarized positions of pro- and antiwar forces: Can we ask for women's rights in the context of a military occupation? Or in the struggle against war and occupation must women's rights take a back seat? For many antiwar and antioccupation activists the latter appears to be the case. We examine this question in greater detail while simultaneously asking whether the struggle for women's rights means abandoning criticism of imperialism. In the course of our research and our antiwar activism, we have come across international and Iraqi feminists who shy away from critically engaging with the neoliberal notion of "empowerment." They also avoid openly criticizing the Bush administration's military intervention and its failure to provide security and reconstruction, let alone democracy and freedom. Perhaps, the dependency of some women's rights activists on U.S. or U.K. funding for various projects works to silence them. But more often their silence springs from the perception that between the American and British occupation and the increasing threat of conservative and extremist forces, the former is the lesser of two evils.

Many books could and should be written about the various ways women's lives have been affected by the lack of security, escalating violence, lack of reconstruction, and devastating humanitarian crisis in light of widespread poverty, unemployment, a collapsed infrastructure, and a lack of state services. In this book, we cite evidence of Iraq's deteriorating living conditions, but we focus more on women's roles in the postinvasion political process and reconstruction efforts and on how women have been "instrumentalized" as part of these processes.

Finally, our book addresses the importance of a gendered analysis of political processes in a context of war, conflict, reconstruction, and political transition.[2] As we try to show throughout, putting gender on the agenda is not merely a matter of discussing women's political participation and attitudes toward the occupation. War and violence affect men and women differently. Gender, while appearing to be the most natural of differences existing in society, is a significant ordering principle of political, social, economic, and cultural institutions. Gender roles, relations, and identities do not simply exist within domestic and national lives. As the feminist scholar of international relations Spike Peterson has written (1998: 42), "Gender is a structural feature of the terrain we call world-politics." It shapes the way political power is deployed and resisted, the way money, property, and other resources are distributed, and the way individual men and women and different groups of men and women interact (C. Cockburn 1999). The "gendering" of international relations has led feminist scholars in the field to make women visible by focusing on processes and actors beyond the interactions of statesmen and politicians. "Nonstate, antistate and trans-state actors" must be included (Peterson and Runyan 1993: 113), and writers must show how global processes like economic restructuring, war, and migration have different impacts on women and men (see, e.g., Enloe 1990; Tickner 1992; Peterson 2003).

THE UNITED STATES AND THE "WAR ON TERROR"

In many ways, the story of what happened to Iraq after 2003 began on September 11, 2001. Speaking on national television a few hours after the attacks, George Bush announced that America and its allies would "stand together to win the war against terrorism" (Bush 2001). The most visible aspect of this new foreign policy approach was the use of military force to combat terrorism. Within one month the United States, with international support, launched attacks on Afghanistan to topple the Taliban regime, which had been harboring al-Qaeda. Not content to stop at Afghanistan, neoconservative figures who had earlier formed the think tank they named the Project for the New American Century called on George Bush to launch a preemptive strike against Iraq as an integral part of a strong U.S. national security policy: "Any strategy aiming at the eradication of terrorism and its sponsors must include a determined effort to remove Saddam Hussein from power in Iraq. Failure to undertake such an effort will constitute an early and perhaps decisive surrender in the war on international terrorism" (Project for the New American Century 2001).

Throughout 2002, U.S. and U.K. government officials attempted to set the stage for an attack on Iraq. They alleged that Iraq, despite UN resolutions demanding disarmament, continued to possess weapons of mass destruction and that these constituted a direct threat to the safety and security of the United States and its allies. They also tried to demonstrate a connection between Saddam Hussein and al-Qaeda and claimed that Iraq had secretly purchased yellowcake uranium for the production of nuclear weapons. At the same time, an antiwar movement slowly emerged in many countries of the world to counter the claims of the U.S. and U.K. governments (which were subsequently proved untrue; see, e.g., Zunes 2006) and to oppose a military attack on Iraq.

The 2003 war on Iraq should be seen not only as a result of 9/11 and neoconservative political agendas but also as linked to U.S. ambitions following the end of the Cold War. The Gulf War of 1990, which aimed to expel Iraqi military forces from Kuwait, marked a new era of U.S. hegemony within the Middle East, unchallenged by the Soviet Union. Despite the obviously unrivaled position of the United States during the 1990s, and its successes in enhancing its military presence in the Gulf region and opening up new Middle Eastern markets to U.S. capital, the end of the Cold War did not usher in an uncontested Pax Americana, as illustrated by several countries' opposition to the continuation of the sanctions imposed on Iraq (Hinnebusch 2003: 234). In the face of an unraveling multilateral containment policy, U.S.-led regime change in Baghdad became the preferred policy option for foreign policy "hawks" in Washington (Pollack 2002). The events of 9/11 made that policy more acceptable (Cox 2004: 597).

We would agree with those who argue that the wars on Iraq and on Afghanistan, under the banner of the so-called War on Terror, represent the latest phase of U.S. empire building (see, e.g., Colás and Saull 2005). Empire is not only about the "control" of other countries and their resources through military intervention and occupation. It is about the reconfiguration of relations of power both within and between the United States, its allies, and its "opponents" for the purpose of ensuring U.S. hegemony. It is about U.S. domination through economic power, moral and cultural leadership, and military might and armed force. The U.S. empire uses coercion where necessary, but its success is its ability to universalize its worldview—to use its "soft" power to co-opt its allies and dominate its opponents (Colás 2007: 166–68).

The discourses of democracy promotion, human rights, and women's empowerment have been seen by many as a smokescreen for U.S. empire building. After all, the U.S. record with regard to these values is far from unblemished (Eisenstein 2004). Yet we argue that the notions of democracy promotion, human rights, and women's empowerment are not merely a way of duping well-intentioned people into supporting military intervention; they are integral to empire building. These notions construct an "us versus them" mentality that underpins and helps to perpetuate the War on Terror. Within the discourse of U.S. officials as well as other Western politicians, democracy, human rights, and women's rights distinguish the United States and its Western allies from the "rest." They are used as markers of "civilization" as well as reasons for "civilizing" others. As Jean Bethke Elshtain, a just-war theorist turned defender of the "War on Terror," argues, it is "disparate views of women's place in society that most dramatically separates us from radical Islam" (2003: 27). After the 9/11 attacks, George Bush announced, "America was targeted because we're the brightest beacon for freedom and opportunity in the world" (Bush 2001). As some have noted, the claim that al-Qaeda attacked the United States because of its supposed support for women's rights or other liberal values is unfounded (Sjoberg 2006: 168).

This "us versus them" dichotomy reflects the claim of Samuel Huntington's influential article (later to become a book) entitled "The Clash of Civilizations?" (1993). Huntington argues that in the post–Cold War era conflicts will take place not along ideological fault lines but between different "civilizations" along cultural lines. The dearth of empirical evidence for this theory has been widely documented (see, e.g., Said 2001; Sen 2006). Huntington assumes that there are discrete blocs of civilizations ("Western," "Muslim," "Hindu," and "Sinic," among others) with which people identify themselves and their interests. This completely ignores both the interdependency of cultures and the struggles that take place *within* so-called civilizations—for economic resources, political power, women's rights, human rights, and democracy, and over interpretations of religion and its role in the public sphere, among other issues. This applies to the so-called Muslim civilization as much as to the so-called West. Across the Middle East, civil society actors lobby their governments, advocate for greater rights, and debate the concept of democracy (Pratt 2007). Meanwhile, George Bush's administration wages war on American women—cutting welfare, threatening reproductive rights, and employing in government positions individuals who deny the gender pay gap and minimize the incidences and significance of violence against women (see Flanders 2004).

The War on Terror is not only a war waged in "uncivilized" lands. It is also a war at home that empowers governments at the expense of individuals. Following 9/11, the U.S. Congress passed the PATRIOT Act. The U.K. government had already passed the Terrorism Act of 2000. However, after 9/11 and particularly after the bombings of July 7, 2005, new legislation granting far-reaching powers to the police was introduced. The erosion of civil liberties in the name of protecting democracy and human rights is a grotesque contradiction. Yet because of their fear of terrorism, many people are passive in the face of this attack on our democratic rights. While George Bush and his U.K. ally have been at pains to stress that the War on Terror is not a war on Islam, it constructs a conflict implicitly based on religious/cultural difference. Some authors have even argued that Islamophobia is representative of a "new" racism that substitutes cultural differences for racial ones (Runnymede Trust 1997). While this argument is problematic (see, e.g., Malik 2005), so-called antiterror legislation echoes "crime prevention" measures that have disproportionately targeted people of color through racial profiling and police stop-and-search powers. Antiterror legislation allows foreign nationals to be detained or deported without trial, enables racial profiling, and is accompanied by crackdowns on asylum seekers (see, e.g., Human Rights Watch 2006, 2007b). In Guantánamo Bay, "unlawful combatants"—not prisoners of war and not criminals—are kept in inhumane conditions and without charge or trial. The construction of a category of prisoner called "unlawful combatant" and deprived of rights represents an extreme form of dehumanization of "the other." The practice of extraordinary rendition demonstrates the degree to which the United States and its allies operate beyond international law in the name of fighting terrorism.

In this context, the War on Terror has contributed to the emergence of new justifications for racism within the United States and Europe. In public discourse, fears of terrorist attacks have become displaced onto migrants and citizens of color, particularly male South Asians and Middle Easterners. Since 9/11, American Arabs, Muslims, and those perceived to be Arab or Muslim have been subjected to hate crimes, discrimination, and official harassment (Cainkar 2002). In the United Kingdom, increasing numbers of public officials and intellectuals have launched a covert attack on British Muslims through their attacks on multiculturalism (Allen 2007).[3] As in the War on Terror abroad, the targeting of Muslims and Arabs focuses on women in these communities, who are generally portrayed as victims of "barbaric" or "backward" religious/cultural practices, such as the wearing of the veil, arranged marriages, and honor killings.

WOMEN ARE THE KEY

The discourse of democracy, human rights, and women's rights is not only a means of drawing the boundaries between "us" and "them," of building U.S.-led coalitions to wage war, or of buttressing the power of governments at home. Neoconservatives, building on the "democratic peace thesis" that democracies do not go to war with one another, argue that the promotion of democracy and women's empowerment is a solution to terrorism. In a speech at the National Endowment for Democracy in November 2003, George Bush stated: "Sixty years of Western nations excusing and accommodating the lack of freedom in the Middle East did nothing to make us safe—because in the long run, stability cannot be purchased at the expense of liberty. As long as the Middle East remains a place where freedom does not flourish, it will remain a place of stagnation, resentment, and violence ready for export. And with the spread of weapons that can bring catastrophic harm to our country and to our friends, it would be reckless to accept the status quo." Already, in December 2002, then–U.S. Secretary of State Colin Powell announced the Middle East Partnership Initiative (MEPI), which provides funds for projects supporting political, economic, and educational reforms and women's empowerment, as a means of building "a more peaceful and prosperous Middle East" (U.S. Department of State n.d.).

"Women's empowerment," as the U.S. administration calls it, is seen as essential to "democratization" and "peace building." Through channels such as MEPI, millions of dollars are allocated to projects targeting women not only as a humanitarian or developmental concern but also as a "U.S. foreign policy imperative" (Dobriansky 2005). The U.S. secretary of state has appointed a "senior advisor for women's empowerment" (U.S. Department of State 2006), and George Bush has stated: "There's no doubt in my mind, empowering women in new democracies will make those democracies better countries and help lay the foundation of peace for generations to come" (America.gov 2006). Concerns for "women's empowerment" go beyond neoconservative circles. Democratic Congressman Tom Lantos (2002), a member of the House International Relations Committee, asserted a link between countries where al-Qaeda recruits and these countries' practice of "gender apartheid." "Empowering women," he observed, "is critical to promoting democracy, which is imperative if we are to defeat terrorism."

Some have argued that the Bush administration's rhetoric about "women's empowerment" is a "strategic co-optation of women's rights" to justify the War on Terror and to obscure its devastating effects, particularly for women (Hunt 2002: 117, 118). Yet much thinking about the link between gender, violence, and peace originates within feminist thinking—paradoxically, perhaps, for the antifeminist neoconservatives and their supporters. Many feminists have identified a link between patriarchy (i.e., a political, economic, social, and cultural system based on the subordination of women by men) and the use of violence ranging from war to domestic abuse (see, e.g., Reardon 1985). In the run-up to wars, men are enjoined to be "real men" by protecting their country or community and their families or womenfolk through resort to violence. Meanwhile, women, who are often represented as symbols of community identity, are often specifically targeted by enemy men, particularly through rape, as a means of attacking the masculinity of that community's men. Since women have a direct interest in overturning patriarchy, several feminist scholars have therefore argued that women play a key role in ending violence and challenging dominant conceptions of masculinities and femininities (gender stereotypes), which underpin militarism. For this reason many peace groups throughout history and around the world have been women's or feminist groups (C. Cockburn 2007; Enloe 2001; Yuval-Davis 1997).

Some feminist writers have argued that women's experience of motherhood is a powerful resource for peace building (Ruddick 1989). Indeed, there are plenty of examples of how women have used the symbolism of motherhood to protest against wars, violence, and other injustices, including the Mothers of the Plaza de Mayo in Argentina, the Greenham Common women's peace camp in the United Kingdom in the 1980s, and Mothers Against War, founded in the United States in 2006. Other feminists have strongly argued against essentializing women's roles in this way, as it may be counterproductive in challenging the gender stereotypes that underpin the war system (see, e.g., Richards 1990). Still, in reality women make up a disproportionate number of caregivers, and this fact alone has an impact on defining women's interests. As Ann Tickner argues (1992: 61), "When more resources go to the military, additional burdens are placed on women as public sector resources for social services shrink."

Despite a tradition of feminist concern to end violence and conflict, we agree with those writers who have criticized the Western feminist or women's movement for being blind to the role of imperialism in giving rise to war and conflict and perpetuating women's oppression. As far back as 1984, Valerie Amos and Pratibha Parmar underlined the latent racism of the British women's movement toward women in the Third World and the assumptions that the West is better than the Third World with respect to women's rights. Unfortunately, we still find such beliefs in some women's and feminist groups, as illustrated in the U.S.-based Feminist

Majority Foundation's campaign to stop gender apartheid in Afghanistan. As Ann Russo argues (2006: 558): "While the FMF's campaign has brought public attention to some of the realities of women's lives under the Taliban since the mid-1990s, it does so from a framework of 'imperial feminism' that ultimately serves to bolster US world hegemony and empire." Indeed, the U.S. administration's championing of women's empowerment through military intervention may be seen as part of a long history of "imperial feminism" within Western nations.

Not all feminists in the West subscribe to "imperial feminism." We locate ourselves within a feminist approach to theory and action that has developed as a result of criticisms by black and Third World feminists. This approach recognizes the significance of imperialism, racism, class inequalities, and sexual orientation, and not only gender, in shaping the experiences of different women. Such an approach emphasizes the way power relations operate across national boundaries, or "transnationally," and focuses on international issues of war and global justice as well as women's oppression and struggles in different parts of the world. In the context of Iraq, certain feminist organizations are transnational in some of the ways they operate, such as having transnational membership and using the Internet extensively for campaigns, yet they are not necessarily transnational in their politics, working with imperialist, neoliberal, and militaristic government agendas. On the other hand, some transnational feminist activists and organizations not only advocate for Iraqi women's rights but also oppose the U.S.-led invasion and occupation of Iraq and the exploitation of the country's resources by foreign corporations.

It is also useful to distinguish between "transnationalism from above" and "transnationalism from below" when exploring feminist networks and campaigns. The United Nations, social democratic governments in the North, and well-endowed private foundations play an important role in facilitating interaction and cooperation among feminist and women's organizations around the world. Many feminist or women's NGOs, particularly in countries of the South, rely on funds from these sources. This has contributed to processes of professionalization and bureaucratization, which some argue have led to a "depoliticization" of women's movements (see, e.g., Jad 2004; El-Kassem 2007; Mojab 2007) and their distancing from their social bases (Brenner 2003; Thayer 2000). On the other hand, international funding has created new political debates in women's movements of countries of the South concerning what is "authentic culture" and what is "cultural encroachment" and how to maintain independence from foreign agendas and neocolonial domination without becoming co-opted by authoritarian regimes (Al-Ali 2000; Pratt 2007).

RESISTANCE TO U.S. EMPIRE IN THE MIDDLE EAST

Resistance to foreign domination has a long history in the Middle East. With the onset of European colonialism in the region, from the mid–nineteenth century onwards, indigenous movements emerged to oppose colonial rule and demand independence. Resistance to colonialism and, after independence, neocolonialism/imperialism was articulated mostly through secular-oriented ideologies—particularly that of Arab nationalism. For example, the Suez Crisis in 1956, in which Britain, France, and Israel attacked Egypt, was met with massive opposition in Egypt and across the Arab world, unified under the banner of Arab nationalism and led by Egyptian president Gamal Abdel-Nasser. However, the failure of Arab nationalist regimes to bring about sustained socioeconomic development and to prevent the expansion of the state of Israel after the 1967 war helped generate support for Islamist movements (for more details, see Ayubi 1991).

Anti-imperialist sentiments (in terms of opposition to foreign domination, as well as Israel's occupation of Palestine) characterize much of the political spectrum in the Middle East, including Marxist, nationalist, liberal, and Islamist. All these groups oppose or criticize U.S. domination of the international system, including economic exploitation, human rights abuses, and military interventions. However, they differ in their understanding of the reasons for this domination, ranging from the nature of global capitalism to U.S. economic greed and immorality.

The decline of secular forces in the Middle East has led to a focus on Islamist resistance to U.S. empire. Islamists articulate their resistance in terms of opposition to "inauthentic," secular political systems and the "corrupting" cultural influences of the West, as well as a variety of injustices perpetrated by countries in the West against Muslim countries. Islamist resistance includes both nonviolent resistance, such as the Egyptian Muslim Brotherhood, and what some call "armed resistance" or others call "terrorism." The United States and many of its allies label groups such as al-Qaeda, Hamas, and Hizbullah as terrorist organizations. However, many, including respective members themselves, would make a distinction between Hamas and Hizbullah on the one hand and al-Qaeda on the other. Hamas and Hizbullah see themselves as national movements engaged in a legitimate struggle against Israeli occupation, and both have distanced themselves from al-Qaeda in terms of political thinking as well as tactics.

Gender remains an understudied but crucial element in all these movements. In the past, secular-oriented movements and regimes promoted women's participation in education, work, and politics as both a symbol and a generator of modernization, which in turn was seen as a means of resisting Western influence and ensuring national sovereignty. We discuss this in chapter 1 with regard to the revolutionary movement in the 1950s and 1960s as well as the early phase of the Ba'th regime in Iraq. Islamist movements have also made women key symbols in terms of their role in building a strong nation and Islamic community and countering Western influence. However, Islamists have recast conceptions of gender roles and relations. Islamist doctrines focus on the regulation of public morality, and an important part of this is defining how women should behave—in their dress and their interactions with men—and supporting strict gender roles. However, Islamist groups differ on issues such as whether women should hold public office, go out to work, or get educated. Al-Qaeda is against women's public participation, while groups such as Hamas, Hizbullah, and the Muslim Brotherhood support women's roles within the public sphere so long as these do not contravene their ideas about women's domestic duties and the gender hierarchy.

Throughout this book we discuss how Iraqi women have been affected by the range of Islamist opinions on gender roles and relations. More significantly, a context in which the United States uses women's rights as part of its strategy of empire building and Iraqi political parties and militia use notions of Iraqi women's "proper" roles as a means of resisting U.S. occupation makes it very difficult to speak about women's rights and to build transnational solidarity in support of women—as we have experienced in the context of the global antiwar movement.

THE ANTIWAR MOVEMENT AND THE MIDDLE EAST

Like any social movement, the antiwar movement in the West that emerged to protest the invasions of Afghanistan and Iraq is made up of a wide variety of individuals and groups in Europe and North America, including leftists/socialists/anarchists, liberals, self-identifying Muslims, and peace activists. These different groups and individuals have mobilized under a common demand for an end to U.S.-led military action, principally under national umbrella groups, such as the U.K. Stop the War Coalition, the U.S.-based ANSWER, and the Canadian Peace Alliance.

In addition, the North American and U.K. antiwar movements have spearheaded the building of coalitions with Muslims, both at home and abroad. At home, they have been active in identifying and opposing Islamophobia. Simultaneously, they have participated in international conferences with Islamist groups, as well as secular forces, in the Middle East. In particular, the Cairo Conference against U.S. Imperialism and Zionism, held annually since December 2002, has provided the most important forum for the building of transnational alliances of antiwar and anti-imperialist secular and Islamist groups.

The Cairo conferences have demonstrated the possibility of building a transnational front against U.S. empire, irrespective of political or ideological beliefs or religious or national affiliation. However, some groups and individuals who are critical of U.S. military intervention are concerned that the unity of leftist and Islamist forces may come at the expense of human rights and women's rights. For example, at the 2007 Cairo Conference a young Egyptian leftist declared: "When I sit with a member of the Muslim Brotherhood, I shouldn't talk about the things that divide us, such as our attitude towards the veil. Rather we should focus on the things that unite us" (see also Pratt 2007: 175–82). In other words, maintaining a united front against U.S. empire may marginalize the struggle for women's rights. This problem is compounded by the claims of the United States and other Western governments to be promoting women's rights.

BACKLASH AGAINST WOMEN'S RIGHTS

One of the many consequences of the "clash of civilizations" rhetoric and military interventions linked to the War on Terror is a backlash against women's rights in predominantly Muslim societies. Throughout the Middle East as well as the wider Muslim world, the resistance to U.S. imperialism and Western cultural encroachment is symbolically articulated through gender ideologies and relations. "Our women are different from your women!" has been a phrase used in the context of communal and nationalist tensions and struggles throughout history and cross-culturally.[4] However, the Western media's obsession with women's oppression and symbols of Islam, such as different forms of veiling, and pronouncements of Western governments, most notably the U.S. administration, that make the liberation of Muslim women and women's rights a central focus of their justification for military intervention have created a situation where these markers of difference have become much more significant than they were historically.

The more President Bush talks about "women's rights" while his troops are occupying Iraq, the greater the backlash for women within the country. Unfortunately, many Iraqi women's rights organizations and women activists are discredited and accused of being stooges of the West as their demands appear to overlap with those of the Bush administration. Throughout the history of colonialism and imperialism, local women's groups and activists have frequently been discredited for aping the Western occupiers. Yet many Iraqi women activists with whom we talked stress the long history of local women's rights struggles inside the country and declare that Iraqi women never needed a Western woman or man to identify social injustice or certain inequalities. Indeed, activists throughout the world resist the U.S. government's attempted appropriation of human rights and women's rights as well as democracy. Listing the vast array of human rights abuses as well as undemocratic practices and policies within "the West" and by "the West" is one way of challenging the notion that "the West" has a monopoly on these terms. In practice, of course, Western rhetoric is often far from actual policies, which are frequently based on pragmatic and strategic compromises rather than a set of ethical and moral principles. Around the globe, women's rights are often the first to be sacrificed for issues that are perceived to be priorities, such as federalism, the distribution of oil revenues, and the status of Kirkuk in the Iraqi context.

INTERNATIONAL SUPPORT FOR WOMEN'S PARTICIPATION IN POSTCONFLICT PROCESSES

While the transnational movement against U.S. empire appears to have made the issue of women's rights secondary to the need to resist imperialism, the transnational women's movement has raised the demand for women's inclusion in all aspects of international peace and security. Years of international lobbying by women's groups and other peace groups have led to a recognition of women's efforts in peace building and their particular needs in conflict in the form of UN Security Council Resolution 1325 on Women, Peace, and Security, passed in 2000. In many ways, Resolution 1325 builds on feminist understandings of the links between gender, peace, and violence that we briefly discussed above. It also responds to the marginalization of women in official peace-building and conflict-resolution processes and forums, despite their significant grassroots role in rebuilding communities and mediating conflicts in countries around the world. It seeks to mainstream an official sensitivity to gender within UN institutions, as well as the decision-making processes of all governments, with regard to conflict resolution, peacekeeping, and peace building. It provides an important advocacy tool for women's groups and others to ensure their inclusion in postconflict planning and to unite women activists in different countries (e.g., the work of the Women's International League for Peace and Freedom).

However, Resolution 1325 does not condemn war and the war system (C. Cockburn 2007: 147; Cohn 2008). It leaves intact the whole international security architecture in which the use or threat of violence is perceived as legitimate. It focuses on getting women into relevant decision-making bodies once war and conflict are already a fact. It assumes that women will be able to moderate and mediate between "warlords" and other powerful political leaders, who are often supported by foreign countries in line with those countries' strategic interests. It assumes that women necessarily promote "women's interests" and that these are self-evident. In this book we demonstrate how the assumptions of Resolution 1325 are rendered hollow by the security concerns of the United States and its allies, the competing political agendas of different Iraqi politicians, and the fact that not all women support the same agenda.

OUR RESEARCH METHODS

The research for this project took place over a period of three years, from May 2004 to September 2007. We originally intended to spend time in different cities inside Iraq to engage in qualitative and quantitative in-depth research about the gendered impact of political transition and the scope and content of Iraqi women's activism. But we soon realized that the security situation was deteriorating to such an extent that we felt unable to travel to central and southern Iraq. In early 2004, one of Nadje's cousins, thirteen-year-old Mustafa, was kidnapped. Although he was released after one week for a hefty ransom, Nadje's family, who were at the time still living in Baghdad, felt it was too dangerous for her to visit. In fact, it might have made her family even more of a target for Mafia-type gangs, as the visit of a relative from abroad is associated with Western currency. Around the same time, foreign journalists and NGO workers were also being kidnapped and assassinated, so Nicola felt it would be too risky for her to travel to Iraq. However, we both visited Iraqi Kurdistan in the spring of 2007 and interviewed women active in public life (in civil society, the media, and/or politics) in Erbil and Sulaymaniya.

The other sites of our research were Amman (Jordan), Cairo (Egypt),

Washington, D.C., Detroit, San Diego (United States), and London (United Kingdom). In Amman and London, we spoke to Iraqi women who were still living inside Iraq and had traveled outside the country to attend conferences, seminars, or training sessions, engage in advocacy activities, or visit friends and relatives. In Washington, D.C., Detroit, and San Diego, we interviewed Iraqi diaspora women who had close links with Iraq and were involved in transnational feminist activities. We generally pursued a division of labor: Nicola focused her research primarily on policy makers, NGO workers, and people working in international organizations and funding institutions, while Nadje mainly concentrated on Iraqi women activists. However, at times our respective research crossed over when one of us had access to particular people whom the other wanted to interview.

In addition to interviewing over one hundred individuals, we consulted available reports and statistics from various international organizations and academic sources to document relevant economic, social, and political trends and phenomena. We also drew upon relevant articles and reports from newspapers, magazines, and the Internet. We have interpreted our data through a "gendered lens": that is, we have paid attention to understanding the differential impact on women and men of political and social processes unfolding since the invasion of Iraq.

Since much of the information we obtained is politically sensitive and since Iraqi women's rights activists face so many threats and risks, we have tried to protect the anonymity of our respondents by using pseudonyms throughout the book and, in some cases, not revealing the name of an interviewee's organization. Occasionally we use actual names when people we interviewed encouraged us to do so. A pseudonym is identifiable by our use of a letter for the surname (e.g., "Hala K."). However, we spell out the full name when we use actual names. We also use actual names for information and quotes obtained from written and electronic sources that are already published.

Our Own Subject Positions

How we see ourselves and how others see us (our "subject positions" or "positionalities") necessarily affect our relationships to those whom we interviewed for this research, as well our audiences and readership. Much has already been written about the myth of objectivity in research and the various ways a researcher's gender, class, religion, sexuality, political orientation, nationality, ethnicity, age, and so on may influence the research process. It has also been recognized that a researcher's "positionality" is not fixed but shaped by the subject of the research, the wider environment in which the researcher operates, and the multiple interactions between researcher, interviewees, and audience. In the case of this research, one factor that has particularly shaped each of our respective subject positions is that of perceived belonging to a national community, amplified by perceived cultural/religious belonging.

Nicola feels that many interviewees and audiences of this research have seen her primarily as white, British, non-Muslim, and non-Arab and have ascribed a certain authority to her research on that basis. Some have perceived her as "other" because of her assumed cultural/religious belonging (and government officials in the United States and United Kingdom have perceived her as "other" because she is an academic). Her "outsider" status has brought advantages and disadvantages. As noted by others, people may tell a stranger information that they would not tell friends or family (Simmel 1921). In the context of this research, where all interview respondents are aware of the political stakes involved in what they say, outsider status may be equated with the status of "neutral" observer. In addition, people often perceived Nicola in terms of common assumptions about academics—as engaged in a positivist enterprise of "independent" and "objective" seeking of the "truth." Consequently, some respondents may have seen it as politically important to grant her access so that she could record their versions of "the truth," thereby ensuring that they would play a role in producing knowledge about Iraq. On the other hand, Nicola was sometimes discredited by her perceived outsider status. Because she is not Iraqi, or even Arab nor Muslim, some people implied that she had no authority to speak about women in Iraq. Nevertheless, there were interviewees with whom Nicola shared an empathetic bond based not on nationality, religion, or other ascribed characteristics but on shared ideological outlooks, common concerns, or simply mutual respect as individuals.

Nadje's Iraqi "origins" have mostly opened up doors in the context of fieldwork among Iraqi women in the diaspora and have also increased her credibility and expert status in the West. Despite this, she has frequently felt uncomfortable with the way she is considered "Iraqi" by the Western media, academics, and Iraqi women alike. There appears to be something simplistic about attaching this label, given that her mother is German and that Nadje herself grew up in Germany and subsequently lived in the United States, Egypt, and the United Kingdom. However, Nadje has experienced a shift in her sense of self and belonging—"feeling

Iraqi"—less because of her father's birth country and "her blood" than because of the political developments inside Iraq and her political and emotional involvement in them.

Like Nicola, Nadje has encountered situations in which her views, analyses, and assessments have been discredited by Iraqi women and men on the basis of her Western and feminist background. It is very hard to argue against opinions that are based on "I have lived it and you have not" and that thereby discredit any view perceived not to be "authentic" and "experiential." Although we find such a position problematic intellectually, we feel humbled by people's personal experiences inside Iraq and acknowledge that some dimensions of "truth" and experience cannot be grasped if not lived personally.

Another set of tensions in terms of Nadje's positionality is related to her dual roles as researcher and activist. She is a founding member of a London-based women's organization called Act Together: Women's Action for Iraq. The group, consisting of Iraqi, British, and other international women activists, has aimed to raise the awareness about the impact of economic sanctions, dictatorship, wars, and occupation on women and gender relations inside Iraq. She has sometimes found it difficult to engage with women in her research whose political views she considers extremely problematic. Yet encounters with different women activists and organizations in the context of this research have made her realize possibilities for common ground in political activism despite widespread perceptions of unbridgeable differences, and the realization of these possibilities has prompted her to organize joint actions and events with other women's organizations.

Approaches to Our Research

We want to stress that although our respective "identities" and backgrounds have influenced the research process, the ways our interviewees perceived us, and people's willingness to share information with us, our political positioning as transnational feminists and peace activists has had the most significant impact on our approach, analysis, and interpretation. At the core of transnational feminism is the concept of "intersectionality": we cannot address the issue of patriarchy and women's rights without talking about imperialism and racism, as well as issues related to class, economic exploitation, and struggles for a more just distribution of resources. Both of us also position ourselves against simplistic notions of either supporting U.S. intervention in the name of women's rights or promoting all forms of resistance to the United States and, in the name of fighting imperialism, issuing a blanket condemnation of all policies, programs, and projects that support women's rights.

In terms of our different disciplinary backgrounds—anthropology and politics—we are hoping that the interdisciplinary nature of our work contributes to the growing body of literature in political science and international relations that addresses the gendered nature of international politics (e.g., Enloe 1990; Peterson 1992; Peterson and Runyan 1993; Sylvester 1994; Tickner 1992). Political science has traditionally focused on "high politics" of elites, formal institutions, and power politics. Already, the majority of books on the postinvasion period in Iraq fall within the "high politics" category (e.g., Dodge 2005; Hashim 2006; Herring and Rangwala 2006). Despite some recent work on the significance of gender in postwar transformation (Chinkin and Paradine 2001; C. Cockburn 1998; C. Cockburn and Zarkov 2002), social anthropological approaches to gender in the context of war and reconstruction are rare. In this book, we combine traditional political science approaches to conflict and political transition with the bottom-up approaches more characteristic of anthropology.

Feminists' recognition that political institutions are linked to social relations necessarily implies a challenge to the perceived separation between public and private spheres and an expansion of what has traditionally been considered to constitute politics and political activism (Pateman 1989). Our analysis of women's political activism encompasses activities that take place in formal organizations, such as political parties, various ministries, and parliaments, and activities that take place in informal organizations, such as grassroots women's groups and networks based on interpersonal relationships.

ABOUT THIS BOOK

This introduction has provided a context for the remainder of the book by posing the questions that we think are important, establishing our positions in relation to the events that have unfolded since 2003, and identifying the principal trends shaping those events and responses to them. In chapter 1, we provide a historical overview of gender roles, relations, and identities in Iraq prior to the 2003 overthrow of the Ba'th regime. We describe attempts by the Iraqi women's movement to reform women's rights and gender relations from the early part of the twentieth century onwards; examine so-called state feminism under the Ba'th regime in the

1970s; and document the impact of wars, repression, and sanctions on different groups of women from the late 1970s until the invasion of 2003. Chapter 1 identifies the ways in which political and economic developments have changed women's lives and their opportunities for participation in public life. In addition, the chapter shows how sectarianism, secularism, and religion, rather than being immutable characteristics of Iraqi society, have changed over time, with particular consequences for women.

Chapter 2 moves to the period of the U.S.-led invasion and occupation of Iraq. We describe the efforts of the U.S. and U.K. governments, as well as other international agencies, to address Iraqi women through aid and humanitarian assistance. Despite the rhetoric of the United States and its allies about empowering Iraqi women in the reconstruction process, this chapter highlights how women's lives have been negatively affected by the U.S.-led occupation because of the failure of reconstruction, the absence of security, the dismantling of the state, and the prioritization of U.S. security objectives.

Chapter 3 looks specifically at women's involvement in emerging political structures following the fall of the Ba'th regime, including the Iraqi Governing Council (IGC), the interim government, the elections of January and December 2005, the drafting of the constitution, and the national parliament. Despite the enthusiasm of many women for democracy, we argue that the United States has helped create political institutions rooted in corruption, nepotism, and communal political agendas that have marginalized women's voices and contributed to fueling violence.

Chapter 4 documents the varied activities, strategies, and demands of Iraqi women activists both inside and outside Iraq and discusses the tensions and political rifts between them. We evaluate the obstacles and challenges facing women since 2003, arguing that the future of the women's movement in Iraq has become inextricably linked to the future of Iraq and an end to the occupation and the violence tearing the country apart.

Our final chapter draws out the implications of the preceding chapters for thinking about the relationship between women's rights and military intervention in general. We address the roles of religion and culture, militarism, and imperialism in shaping women's rights. We also explore possible ways of promoting women's rights in the context of war and occupation—from the point of view of the international community as well as from the point of view of transnational social movements such as the antiwar and women's movements. Finally, we attempt to describe what peace would mean for Iraqi women and, on this basis, to contribute to an anti-imperialist, democratic, and feminist politics for peace.

ONE

IRAQI WOMEN BEFORE THE INVASION

A few days after Laura Bush's visit to Afghanistan in March 2005, Nadje was invited to speak about the situation of Iraqi women on National Public Radio in the United States. Also live on the air was Charlotte Ponticelli, then senior coordinator for the International Women's Issues Office within the State Department. Ponticelli spoke about Laura Bush's visit and the great achievements of both Iraqi and Afghani women since their respective liberations. Her very positive account of the situation of Afghan women differed drastically from the stories we had heard from friends and colleagues who had traveled to Afghanistan and reported that not much had changed for women since 2001. However, when it came to Iraqi women, the extent of Ponticelli's misconceptions became even more obvious when she stated that people were generally unaware that Iraqi women, just like their Afghan counterparts, had been prevented by Saddam Hussein from entering schools and universities.

When it was her turn to be interviewed, Nadje tried to dispel this extreme misrepresentation of past realities: while there was no doubt about the numerous atrocities and horrors committed by the previous regime, Iraqi women were until quite recently among the most educated in the region and had been actively involved in Iraq's labor force until economic sanctions destroyed Iraq's economy.[1] Nadje argued at the time that Saddam Hussein and the Ba'th regime had committed uncountable crimes while in power—crimes that should be addressed and recognized—but that with respect to women the picture was much more complex.

During the past years, as we have given numerous talks at universities, bookstores, and community centers in the United States, the United Kingdom, and various European countries, we often came across the perception of the passive, oppressed Iraqi woman who had been deprived of all rights including those of education, work, and freedom of movement. Often our audiences' views were based on stereotypes and generalizations about Islam and Muslim societies. In this chapter, we challenge these misconceptions and generalizations and provide a historical context for the current situation in Iraq by examining women's active involvement in political life prior to the fall of the previous regime in 2003. We show how prevailing gender ideologies and relations have been shaped by and, in turn, have shaped the evolution of political, economic, and social structures and state policies. We begin with a description of early reformists and feminists in the beginning of the twentieth century, particularly in connection to the revolutionary movement in the 1950s and early 1960s, before examining "state feminism" under the initial period of the Ba'th regime. We then explore the turn toward greater social conservatism during the 1980s and 1990s as a result of wars (1980–88 Iran-Iraq War, 1991 Gulf War) and economic sanctions (1990–2003). In addition, we highlight the changing nature and significance of secularism, religion, and sectarianism within Iraqi society, challenging both primordialist accounts of the violent and fragmented "nature" of Iraqi society and glorifications of harmonious multiculturalism that gloss over tensions and violent state policies of exclusion.

THE FIRST REFORMISTS

Like the women's movements in other Middle Eastern countries, Iraqi women's rights activism emerged in the context of modernist discourses about the Iraqi nation and its "new women" (Efrati 2004; Kamp 2003). Male reformers such as the poets Jamil Sidqi al-Zahawi (1863–1963) and Ma'ruf al-Rusafi (1875–1945) were inspired by the Egyptian reformist and champion of women's rights Qasim Amin and called for the education of women and an end to veiling, seclusion, and forced marriages (Efrati 2004: 155). Women were seen to be central to the project of progress and modernizing the country.

The first women's organization in Iraq, the Women's Awakening Club (Nadi al-Nahda al-Nisa'iyya, was founded in 1923 by a group of secular Muslim, educated, middle- and upper-middle-class women, many of whom were married to male political leaders and intellectuals. One of the sixty or so members, Naʿima al-Said, stated at one of the group's early meetings: "It is clear that a nation cannot achieve progress unless men and women cooperate, and women can not help men unless they are educated. . . . Some people in the east mistakenly consider women to be incapable of undertaking any useful projects. . . . I hope we can prove by the success of this Club the fallacy of such thinking" (Ingrams 1983: 93). Projects aiming at women's "awakening" involved literacy courses, lectures on health, hygiene, and housework, and discussions on political, social, and economic issues. Elite women from upper-class backgrounds were the main beneficiaries of these educational programs while lower-class women became mainly recipients of charity. However, members of the Women's Awakening Club stressed the importance of education and organized classes for orphaned and illiterate girls. While male reformers and traditionalists were engaged in a fierce debate about "the veil," with reformists arguing that unveiling was a necessary step in the context of modernization, Iraqi women activists focused their efforts more on wider issues related to women's rights, education, suffrage, and entry into the labor force.

Under British occupation and later British mandate, Iraqi women participated in the nationalist independence struggle in the 1920s and 1930s. Although Iraq received its formal independence in October 1932, British meddling continued until the revolution in 1958, which transformed Iraq from a monarchy to a republic. Like their sisters in other colonized countries such as Egypt, Iraqi women gained political and social spaces through their commitment to their nation's independence (Efrati 2004: 164). Charitable organizations proliferated in the 1930s to deal with the main social ills at the time: poverty, illiteracy, and disease (166). These organizations stepped in where the state had failed to provide and established health centers, shelters for orphans, schools for the blind, and mother and child care centers. Women became actively involved in both gender-mixed organizations, such as the Red Crescent Society (Jamʿiyyat al-Hilal al-Ahmar), and women-only groups, such as the Women's Union Society (Jamʿiyyat al-Ittihad al-Nisaʾi) (Efrati 2004: 166).

During the 1940s, these charitable organizations gained momentum while new religiously based groups and organizations with more political and feminist orientations emerged as well (Efrati 2004: 166–67). The Women's League against Nazism and Fascism (Jamʿiyyat Mukafahat al-Naziyya wa-l-Fashiyya) supported democratic ideas and dedicated most of its efforts to eradicating women's illiteracy. It also published a magazine called *Woman's Liberation* (Tahrir al-Marʾa) and attempted to raise women's cultural and social awareness (Efrati 2004: 168). After the end of World War II and the defeat of the Nazis in Germany, the organization was renamed the Women's League Society (Jam'iyyat al-Rabita al-Nisa'iyya) before it was suspended in 1947 by the government as part of a crackdown on leftist organizations and activities.

The Iraqi Women's Union, founded in 1945, was the most important feminist organization at the time. It was inspired by a major women's conference in December 1944 organized by the Egyptian Feminist Union (which had been founded by Huda Sharawi) (Efrati 2004: 169). The Iraqi Women's Union had been active throughout the 1940s and 1950s, not only in charity work, but also in women's education and networking between the various women's organizations inside Iraq and across the Arab world. Most significantly, however, members of the Iraqi Women's Union had addressed previously taboo issues such as prostitution, divorce and child custody, women's working conditions, and property rights (Efrati 2004: 169). But members were largely affiliated with the political establishment under the monarchy and did not share the revolutionary spirit of many of the younger women, who later became involved in the Iraqi Women's League (Rabitat al-Mar'a al-'Iraqiyya).

WOMEN AND POLITICAL PARTIES

From the late 1940s onwards, resentment against the established political regime grew. The major opposition force in the 1940s and 1950s was the Iraqi Communist Party (ICP), founded in 1934. Notions of social justice, egalitarianism, class struggle, anti-British Iraqi nationalism, and secularism were appealing to an intellectual elite as well as impoverished workers and peasants, shantytown dwellers, and students. Not officially licensed by the government, members of communist-led organizations had to work underground and were regularly subjected to repression and persecution. Nevertheless their numbers grew.

In 1952, mass demonstrations initiated by student discontent, known as the Intifada (Uprising), resulted in martial law, increased repression, and mass arrests of political leaders. Many of the older women we talked to had become politicized in the context of the student movement in the late 1940s before they joined the ICP. Soraya K., who has been living in exile in London for over three decades, remembers with great enthusiasm the days of her political activism: "I was initially recruited by fellow students when I was at the university in the late forties. We were all politicized. After I graduated I started to become involved in the Communist Party. We would spend a lot of time in the countryside talking to poor peasants, helping them out with food and medicines but also educating them and trying to get them to support our struggle." Not all women were attracted to communism. Some slightly younger women Nadje spoke to found it generally quite hard to admit that they had been initially involved with the Ba'th Party as part of their Arab nationalist orientation and admiration for the pan-Arab leader Nasser in the 1950s.[2] Women who had initially been attracted to the Ba'th Party were careful to stress the difference between the ideology of pan-Arabism rooted in Arab heritage and regional solidarity and the way political leaders, such as Saddam Hussein, had implemented it and acted when coming to power. Mona F., who became an outspoken critic of Saddam's regime in the eighties and nineties, said:

> At that period, in 1959, I joined the Ba'th Party. All my friends and my sister were in the Ba'th Party. This was my life, my teenage years. I was so much involved. I put all my passion, all my love into the party. My parents did not know about it. My mother once told me that someone told her that I went to someone's house. She was very angry with me. My father heard that I went to demonstrations. He took my hand and for the first time he told me: "My whole family honour is in this hand. Please protect it. I respect you. And I don't want to question you. I trust you, but please protect our family honour." I was attracted to the Ba'th because of Arab nationalism and Nasser. My sister brought home lots of Ba'th Party literature. She was a librarian and she had access to books. She was highly educated. She had a strong personality and was very dominating, so I would do anything she would say. (Al-Ali 2007: 81–82)[3]

Different political orientations existed even within one family. What seems to have united the generation of young educated people across a range of middle-class backgrounds was their politicization rather than a specific political orientation. Mona and her elder sister left the Ba'th Party shortly after the first Ba'th coup d'état in 1963 in protest against the arrest and torture of their brother, who had been a leading member of the ICP:

> My brother was moved from one prison to another. He was tortured, despite my sister's connection in the Ba'th Party. We both left the party and that was the end of my political career. But I have no regrets. It made me read a lot. It made me think on a much higher level than what is usual for an ordinary teenager. I was thinking about the world, about the needs of people. The experience in the party formed my personality and made me grow up a lot. But leaving the party and knowing what I knew about the party was devastating. I suffered from depression for the first time in my life. I escaped into the world of books. (Al-Ali 2007: 84)

Both of the main political orientations at the time—communism and Arab nationalism—were essentially secular, and religious ideology did not play a significant role. Political ideology also cut across ethnic and religious backgrounds. Ba'thism promoted an Arab nationalism based on the idea of Arab "brotherhood" and attracted Iraqi Arabs of all religious backgrounds, including some middle-class secular Shi'i and Christians, especially during the initial period of economic expansion (Davis 2005: 149). The Ba'th political leaders, including Presidents Hassan al Bakr (1968–79) and Saddam Hussein (1979–2003), were convinced of the superiority of Sunni Arabs (Tripp 2000: 195), but to secure support of other religious and ethnic groups they placed a few token Christian and Shi'i in powerless positions (Davis 2005: 148) and stressed Iraq's Mesopotamian heritage as a means to unify Iraqis of all backgrounds. Yet more Iraqi Kurds and Shi'i were attracted to the more inclusive and egalitarian Iraqi nationalism promoted by the ICP.

THE WOMEN'S MOVEMENT IN REVOLUTIONARY TIMES

Several women who had been involved in the student movement also became active in an emerging women's organization that was closely linked with the ICP, initially called Rabitat al-Difa'an Huquq al-Mar'a (League for the Defense of Women's Rights), later changed to Rabitat al-Mar'a al-'Iraqiyya (Iraqi Women's League). One of the founders of the league was the famous pioneer Dr. Naziha al-Dulaymi, who inspired thousands of young women to join in the struggle for women's legal rights. Dr. al-Dulaymi, who passed away as we were finishing this book in the fall of 2007, also played an important role in her profession as a medical doctor, where she was instrumental in improving public health in Iraq, and has been credited as the first woman in the Arab world to become a cabinet minister (she became minister of municipalities in 1959).

Soraya K., who has been in the midst of debates and campaigns revolving around changes in women's legal rights, feels proud about the achievements at the time: "The most important thing we did in the Rabitat [Iraqi Women's League] is the Qanun al-Ahwal al-Shakhsiya (personal status laws). We had a group of women lawyers working in the Rabitat. What we ended up achieving was not complete, but it was the best we could do. In the media and in the mosque, we were accused of not caring about religion. But our friends and family were happy and they appreciated the changes. Reactionary people and Ba'thists attacked it" (Al-Ali 2007: 90). Despite widespread opposition and protest by conservative social forces, the revolutionary regime of ʿAbd al-Karim Qasim did take women's demands for increased legal rights and equality seriously and passed one of the most progressive family laws in the region in 1959. A unified code replaced the previously differential treatment of Sunni and Shiʿi women and men with respect to legal rights in marriage, divorce, child custody, and inheritance. Although still based on shariʿa (Islamic law), the personal status code of 1959 was relatively progressive in interpretation and entailed some radical changes to previous laws: women were given equal inheritance rights, polygamy and unilateral divorce (i.e., on the part of the man) became severely restricted, women's consent to marriage became a requirement, and women's right to *mahr* (bride-price) was stressed (Efrati 2005). Although these legal changes would not have been possible without the support of the male political leadership, it was women activists' lobbying, campaigning, and participation in the legislative processes in the context of drafting a new constitution that led to the new more progressive personal status code.

THE SOCIAL CLIMATE IN REVOLUTIONARY TIMES

While the political establishment prior to the revolution was largely dominated by Sunni Arabs, largely because of the legacy of the Ottoman Empire and the choices of the British mandate authorities, the government of ʿAbd al-Karim Qasim (1958–63) was much more inclusive of the various ethnic and religious groups. Sectarian divisions did not significantly dominate Iraqi politics and social lives prior to and in the years following the 1958 Revolution. Social class and political and intellectual orientation, much more than ethnic or religious background, influenced people's social circles. More than being Sunni, Shiʿi, Kurd, Christian, Mandean, or Yazidi, or, until the early 1950s, Jewish, social class was the main marker of differences and commonalities. Most older Iraqi women we talked to stressed the sense of intercommunal contacts, coeducation of students of different religious and ethnic backgrounds, and the sharing of religious celebrations and everyday lives. As Hana N., a woman of Shiʿi origin, put it: "We grew up with all the ethnic and religious groups. We went to school with Jews and Christians. And we celebrated all holidays together" (Al-Ali 2007: 65).

Many contemporary commentators argue that Arab nationalism has not been appealing to the majority of the Shiʿi population, who feel alienated by a movement that is dominantly Sunni. However, rather than thinking of themselves as Shi'i or Sunni, in the past people would think of themselves as Arab, or alternatively Iraqi, before anything else. Once the state of Israel was established, xenophobic attitudes toward minorities were most tragically in evidence with Iraq's Jewish population, but later on they also targeted the Kurds and increasingly the Iraqi Shi'is. However, only after the Ba'th coup in 1963 did sectarianism deepen and become institutionalized (Davis 2005: 85).

Prior to the revolution in 1958, there was a wide rift between social classes: the majority of girls and women belonging to impoverished classes had no access to education or adequate health care facilities, and tribal and traditional patriarchal values circumscribed their lives, whereas educated young women activists of largely middle-class backgrounds experienced revolutionary changes and relatively liberal social values and norms. Soraya M., who had been a political activist since her high school years, told Nadje that as a young woman growing up in Baghdad she had never felt restricted or oppressed:

> From the late 1940s, when we were students, we used to wear sleeveless shirts and shorts. We would go to the club, swim and play tennis or ping pong. Nobody would say: "Don't go out!" I would just inform my parents that I was going out. We had lots of freedom. I would be home by ten. And all activities were mixed. We used to listen to classical music together, both Arabic and Western. We read a lot. I would borrow books from my elder brothers and sisters. During holidays I would read all day. Sometimes we would go to the cinema. (Al-Ali 2007: 100)

Despite some incidents of prejudice and sectarianism, most of the urban middle-class women Nadje interviewed said they had lived in relatively multicultural and to some extent cosmopolitan environments that encouraged education, travel abroad, and cultural appreciation. However, the majority of Iraqis, especially girls and women, did not have access to education and were struggling to survive under harsh economic conditions. Social injustice and exploitation led to social unrest and later on to the revolution, but there was also an increasingly politicized class of educated young people who wanted total independence from Britain, the former colonizer, and a more just social system.

BA'THISTS CHALLENGING THE REVOLUTION

Tensions between Arab nationalists and communists heightened after the revolution, often resulting in street demonstrations and marches in support of or opposition to the government. Some of these ended up in violence and also brought out ethnic, sectarian, intertribal and economic antagonisms (Tripp 2000: 156). Throughout his rule, 'Abd al-Karim Qasim maintained an ambiguous relationship with the ICP, needing its support against increasingly disgruntled pan-Arab nationalists but also fearing its influence. The appointment of Dr. Naziha al-Dulaymi and two known communist sympathizers to ministerial posts had been an attempt to bind the party closer to the regime while keeping it in check (Tripp 2000: 175). Yet by the end of 1960 Dr. al-Dulaymi, who was also the head of the Iraqi Women's League, was dismissed, as were the two other ministers. This was in the context of an increasing crackdown on the ICP, as Qasim feared their influence among the population. Most significantly, the government closed down the main associations linked with the ICP, including the Iraqi Women's League, which had to operate underground once again (Al-Ali 2007: 91).

'Abd al-Karim Qasim was struggling at home with Kurdish political leaders of the Kurdistan Democratic Party (KDP) as well as regionally. Already tense relations with Egypt worsened after Iraq's failure to recognize Kuwait's sovereignty, and Iraq became more isolated from its neighbors (Abdullah 2003: 163–64). Arab nationalist forces within Iraq, especially members of the Ba'th Party, became convinced that the only way to bring the country back out of its isolation within the Arab world and to stop the influence of communists once and for all was to overthrow Qasim's government. Yet when a coup was staged in 1963 by Ba'thist and Arab nationalist officers, it did not trigger support from significant numbers of the population. On the contrary: masses of people poured out onto the streets expressing their support for Qasim and fiercely resisting the coup, especially in the poorest neighborhoods.

The level of violence in the immediate aftermath of the coup is described by many Iraqi women as a turning point in the modern history of Iraq. Within only one week of the coup, about three to five thousand communists and sympathizers with the Qasim government were arrested, tortured, and killed. Soraya M., who had been a known figure in both the communist movement and the Iraqi Women's League, managed to escape: "I put on the *abaya* and hid in the house of relatives. I hid there with my children for about ten days. My husband was arrested and tortured. It was a terrible experience for all of us" (Al-Ali 2007: 92). Ibtesam K., who had been living in Najaf, remembers the violence and atrocities committed by the Ba'th National Guard (al-Haris al-Qawmi), which not only arrested, tortured, and killed many communists but also was responsible for raping many young women (Al-Ali 2007: 93).

Widespread resentment against the thuggish and brutal National Guard linked to the Ba'th Party, as well as deep divisions within the party itself, eventually allowed the non-Ba'thist officer 'Abd al-Salam 'Arif to install a military government in November, dissolve the National Guard, and arrest a number of leading Ba'thists. According to most women we talked to, the violence and repression receded dramatically once 'Arif had managed to contain the Ba'th and especially the National Guard. Lamia K., a writer and retired journalist, described the brief period between the two Ba'th coups of 1963 and 1968: "Although it was still a military regime, things started improving again after 'Arif took over. There was less violence and the rule of law started again. Many of us had great hopes of 'Abd al-Rahman al-Bazzaz,[4] who was a civilian and became prime minister in '65" (Al-Ali 2007: 94). Although dependent on the patronage and military support of President 'Arif, al-Bazzaz tried to ensure the respect of civil liberties and introduce some democratic structures into the state (Farouk-Sluglett and Sluglett, 2003: 98). However, President 'Arif tried hard to present himself as a pious president to appease Sunni and Shi'i religious leaders, who were outraged by some of the socialist laws and measures put in place after the revolution. For women activists, the most devastating measure was the amendment to the progressive personal status code, which introduced some changes regarding polygamy and inheritance and revoked the more progressive interpretation of 1959 (Efrati 2005: 581).

Meanwhile, the Ba'th Party had reorganized itself after the crackdown following the coup of 1963, allowing a faction controlled largely by members of Tikrit to take control. The Arab-Israeli defeat of 1967 weakened the pro-Nasserist Arab nationalists and left them in disarray and on the defensive while strengthening the Ba'th camp of Arab nationalism. In July 1968, three military officers together with their Ba'thist allies staged another coup, arrested the cabinet, put President 'Arif on a plane out of the country, and installed Hassan al-Bakr as president (Tripp 2000: 191). His kinsman Saddam Hussein controlled the various security apparatuses and key intelligence services and played a dominant role within the Ba'th Party before he became president of Iraq in 1979. The coup of 1968 started a dictatorial, repressive, and fascist regime that was based less on the political ideology of Ba'thism than on tribal and family connections as well as the whims of Saddam Hussein and his close entourage.

STATE FEMINISM OF THE EARLY BA'TH REGIME

In the 1970s and early 1980s, a relatively large segment of the Iraqi population enjoyed high living standards in the context of an economic boom and rapid development, which were a result of the rise in oil prices and the government's developmental policies. Oil prices had shot up after the oil crisis in 1973, and oil-producing countries started to become aware of their bargaining power related to Western countries' dependence on oil. These were the years of a flourishing economy and the emergence and expansion of a broad middle class. State-induced policies worked to eradicate illiteracy, educate women, and incorporate them into the labor force (Al-Ali 2005: 744). Many women Nadje interviewed remember this first decade of Ba'th rule with great nostalgia and think of it as "the days of plenty."

In the context of the rise in oil prices and an expanding economy, labor was scarce. While the other oil-producing Gulf countries started to look for workers outside their national boundaries, the Iraqi government mainly tried to tap into the country's own human resources: women. Less motivated by egalitarian principles than by pragmatic economic calculations, the Iraqi government encouraged women to get an education and become part of the labor force. Another factor to be taken into account was the state's attempt to indoctrinate its citizens, whether male or female. A great number of party members were recruited through their workplaces. Obviously it was much easier to reach out to and recruit women when they were part of the so-called public sphere and visible outside the confines of their homes (Al-Ali 2005: 754).

Through the party's modernist and developmental rhetoric evident in political speeches, newspaper articles, and radio and TV broadcasts, the "good Iraqi woman" was constructed to be "the educated working woman." Not only rhetoric but concrete measures and legislation were introduced to encourage women's labor force participation. For example, in 1974 a government decree stipulated that all university graduates—men or women—would be employed automatically. Subsequently, working outside the home became for women not only acceptable but prestigious and normative.

Many Iraqi women, although extremely critical of the Ba'th regime, especially with respect to its political repression, human rights abuses, and engagement in a series of wars, stress some positive policies regarding women. Several women Nadje talked to gave accounts of the various ways the ideal of the "working mother" was not only widely accepted but encouraged by the state and society at large. Dr. Rashad, for example, a pharmacist working in a Muslim charity organization in Baghdad, told Nadje:

> I have four children. Two girls and two boys. We have to tell the truth. Not everything was bad under Saddam. We got maternity leave with full salaries. But the manager had to agree and sign. When I got my first boy, my boss called and said that they had no one to cover for me in the pharmacy. I asked my boss: "So where shall I put my child?" He said: "I will solve that problem." I was working in the pharmacy of a factory at an oil refinery in the south. My boss got me one of the Bangladeshi workers of the oil refinery to look after my baby. He got me a small bed for my son. I told him: "You must be joking!" But he was serious, and this is how we solved the problem. The worker would make the bottle, feed my baby, look after it while I was giving out medicine to the patients. I worked two shifts and took the baby with me both times. After about four months, there were other women with children, so they opened a nursery in the factory. (Al-Ali 2007: 133–34)

Free child care, generous maternity benefits, and transportation to and from schools as well as workplaces were all part of the regime's attempt to modernize and develop Iraq's economy and human resources. Despite the difficulties of juggling both child care and work, or even a career, middle-class women generally benefited from the double support of extended families and state provisions.

Hala R., whose family suffered from severe political repression by the regime, recalls:

> We were always afraid of the government. But despite the fact that the Ittihad [General Federation of Iraqi Women] was a branch of the Ba'th, they did some good things. Everyone remembers the phrase "Rasheed yazra" [Rasheed is planting]. They taught peasant women how to read and write with examples from their own society. It was obligatory for all women of all ages to attend literacy classes. There were branches all over Iraq, including the countryside. They also opened large sewing centres all over. They taught women how to sew and they also bought them sewing machines so that they could make a bit of income. But in their ideas and ideology the Ittihad [GFIW] was Ba'thi. Women would have accepted them more if they would not have tried to get women to join the party. (Al-Ali 2007: 136–37)

Whatever the government's motivations, Iraqi women became among the most educated and professional in the whole region. Indeed, the Iraqi government won an award from the UN Educational, Scientific and Cultural Organization (UNESCO) in 1982 for its achievements in illiteracy eradication.[5] How far this access to education and the labor market resulted in an improved status for women is a more complex question. As in many other places, conservative and patriarchal values did not automatically change because women started working (Al-Ali 2005: 745). The impact of state discourse and policies on Iraqi women was rather different depending on the class background of the woman, her place of residence (rural versus urban), and her family's attitudes toward religious and traditional values and norms. Moreover, even at its most revolutionary the regime remained ambiguous at best or even conservative where changes in traditional gender ideologies and relations within the family were concerned (Farouk-Sluglett 1993; Rassam 1992).

THE GENERAL FEDERATION OF IRAQI WOMEN

Although Iraqi women have a history of political participation and activism prior to Saddam Hussein's regime, their autonomous political participation came to an end in the 1970s. Women were encouraged to join the Ba'th Party and to run for the rubber-stamp parliament. The major vehicle for women's participation was the General Federation of Iraqi Women (GFIW), founded in 1968 shortly after the Ba'thi coup.

The federation had branches all over Iraq, and it is estimated that it had about two hundred thousand members in 1982 (Joseph 1991: 182). It was initially generously funded by the regime and organized in a strict hierarchical structure, similar to the Ba'th Party (Helms 1984: 99). Although the federation was a branch of the ruling party that lacked political independence, the government's initial policies of social inclusion and mobilization of labor did facilitate a climate in which the federation could play a positive role in promoting women's education, labor force participation, and health, as well as providing a presence in public life. The GFIW collaborated with state-run industries in training women, with trade unions in providing educational and service programs, and with peasant co-operatives in educating women (Joseph 1991: 182). It also participated in implementing the law that grew out of the literacy campaign in 1978, requiring all illiterate adults from the ages of fifteen to forty-five to participate for two years in one of the numerous literacy programs established by the regime (181).

Iraqi-born anthropologist Amal Rassam, who visited some rural GFIW centers in the 1980s, provides a nuanced analysis. During her visits some of the achievements were clearly evident: women were instructed in sewing and other domestic crafts (1992: 85), and, most importantly, were taught how to read and write. Rassam describes how many women would walk a long way after a day's work in the fields to reach one of the GFIW centers, where dedicated young teachers would eagerly wait for them (86).

It is obvious, however, that the literacy campaign of the Ba'th was not merely aimed at encouraging women's labor force participation; education was also perceived as a vehicle for their indoctrination. The creation of the "new Iraqi woman" and "new Iraqi man" required resocialization, which mainly happened at schools, in universities, in the media, and in the various workplaces. Adult education was one way to reach those men and women who were moving outside state institutions and channels of indoctrination (Al-Ali 2007: 137–38).

The more progressive women in the Ittihad (GFIW), many of whom had originally been members of the communist-led Iraqi Women's League, demanded more radical reform of the personal status code of 1959 and to reverse the amendments that had been made in the 1960s. Yet the regime was reluctant and consciously avoided being "revolutionary" with regard to patriarchal family structures and the role of religious authorities (see Farouk-Sluglett 1993; Joseph 1991; Rassam 1992). Many women of the federation advocated the secularization of the personal status laws (Joseph 1991: 184). More concretely, women activists, such as Nasrin Nuri, Budor Zaki, and Su'ad Khayri, asked the government for the following changes: banning polygyny, eliminating the ambiguity in the minimum age of marriage (stated as the age of "sanity and puberty" in Article 7 of the 1959 code), outlawing forced marriage and marriage by proxy, prohibiting divorce outside court, and guaranteeing women's right to divorce, prolonged custody rights for mothers, and women's equal right to inheritance (Efrati 2005).[6]

However, many women activists were disappointed when their demands for the secularization and more radical changes of the laws were not met. Instead, the regime combined more progressive aspects of Sunni and Shi'i interpretation of laws and modified them (Joseph 1991: 184). Being careful not to alienate a large part of the male population that was benefiting from the prevailing power structures within families as well as conservative religious establishments, the regime was far more ready to engage in land reform than in the reform of gender relations. In a speech at the Seventh Congress of the GFIW in 1976, Saddam Hussein was reacting to the criticism that the government's legal reforms with respect to women were lagging behind other more radical reforms: "But when the revolution tackles some legal matters related to women without taking a balance of attitudes to the question of equality and its historical perspective, it will certainly lose a large segment of the people" (quoted in Hussein 1981: 36–38). Hussein went on to carefully articulate a position that expressed commitment to changes in gender relations and greater women's rights but also a consideration of prevailing conservative norms and values. His strategy did not differ much from the modernist secular regimes in other Muslim countries, most notably the Egyptian regime under Nasser, which restricted its revolutionary policies and laws to the so-called public sphere and stopped short of revolution in the private sphere.

POLITICAL REPRESSION

One of the strategies of the Ba'th was to gain more broadly based support by trying to indoctrinate large segments of the population. Iraqis of all ethnic, religious, and social class background were first encouraged and later pressured to become party members. At some point, in the late 1970s, it became clear that certain career paths and professions were available only to people who had officially affirmed their loyalty to the party. Teachers and headmistresses were under particular pressure, since schools were seen as one of the main sites for indoctrination of the future generations.

Dalal M., who had also been an active member in the Iraqi Women's League since the mid-1950s, found herself under growing pressure at work: "When I was in the teacher's union, I was approached by a colleague who said that all teachers are required to attend a speech directly coming from the Ba'th Party every Thursday. All teachers should deliver the content of the speech to all their students even if they are not members of the Ba'th Party. I refused and went to the head of the teachers' union. He said: 'I might be able to accept your refusal now, but within one year all teachers should be Ba'thi'" (Al-Ali 2007: 119). Dalal and many of her comrades had to escape Iraq shortly after this incident in 1978, as the clampdown on communists and other political opponents to the Ba'th became increasingly brutal and dangerous. By 1979, most of the communist activists who had not been arrested or killed had fled the country.

Many women we talked to were not as lucky as Dalal, however, and experienced severe political repression, including arrest, torture, and rape. Several women gave sad accounts of their fathers, brothers, and husbands being killed by the regime. One of the most gruesome stories Nadje heard was from Zeinab M., an activist with the Islamist Da'wa Party,[7] mother of three children, now living in Dearborn, Michigan: "My husband was active with the Da'wa Party in the seventies. He was killed at Baghdad University in front of my eyes. They dissolved him in a chemical solution. I was one month pregnant with our second child. I was taken to prison as well and was tortured. When I was released I could not work anymore as a teacher." During the 1970s, the regime was also embroiled in a conflict with the Kurdish nationalist leadership. It began to move Arab families to the predominantly Kurdish city of Kirkuk in order to prevent the oil-rich city from coming under Kurdish control. Suspicion between the Kurdish leadership and Baghdad resulted in all-out war by 1974 (Tripp 2000: 199–214). The Kurdish fighters *(peshmerga)* received help from the Iranian government and the United States, although this was withdrawn following the Algiers Agreement of 1975.

It became obvious from our interviews that women had experienced the first decade of the Ba'th regime (1968–1979) rather differently depending on whether they or their families had been politically active or not. The state did not just rely on its coercive and repressive control mechanisms to rule the country. It also managed to silence dissent and even obtain people's approval by providing a prospering socioeconomic context in which many Iraqi families flourished. Many small businesses, companies, and small-scale industries benefited from the economic policies of the state and experienced instant capital accumulation and wealth (Farouk-Sluglett and Sluglett 2003: 232). Shi'i and Kurdish areas benefited from new infrastructure developments as the regime attempted to co-opt potential opponents through patronage (Tripp 2000: 204, 214). Many secular and apolitical middle-class Shi'i, Kurdish, and Christian women concurred in their perceptions of the achievements of the Ba'th with many of the middle-class Sunni women we interviewed. Even some women who had been imprisoned or had had to flee as political refugees during the 1970s or early 1980s acknowledged the positive impact of developmental modernist policies on women during that period. Iraq is not the only country in which a repressive dictatorship initially opened up certain social, economic, and professional spaces for women. Without doubt, those women who either suffered directly themselves or had relatives who suffered from the brutal state oppression did not share a sense of appreciation for the former regime's developmental policies. For most women we talked to, the atrocities of the Ba'th regime became more obvious with the start of the presidency of Saddam Hussein in 1979, which was associated with a series of wars.

THE IRAQ-IRAN WAR (1980–88)

In 1980, Saddam, with the support of the United States, launched a war against the newly created Islamic government in Iran. The war, according to various sources, killed between 150,000 and 340,000 Iraqi soldiers and between 450,000 and 730,000 Iranian soldiers. During the war with Iran, there was a shift in state rhetoric and government policies regarding women and gender relations. Maybe more than before, women were needed in the public sphere as thousands and thousands of Iraqi men were fighting and dying in a war that was meant to be quick and to present an easy victory. Instead, years of intense warfare negatively affected not only the Iraqi economy but the social fabric itself. Most families lost male relatives, friends, or neighbors to one of Saddam Hussein's many senseless wars. Women were carrying the burden of doing most of the work in the state bureaucracy and the public sector and being the main breadwinners and heads of households as well as caregivers and mothers. Amal G., an accountant and mother of three, remembers: "The Iran-Iraq War had a big effect on society. It showed the efficiency of women in a very clear way. Most of the men were fighting at the front. There was a great dependence on women. And women proved their strength and their resourcefulness. You could even see women at gas stations or women truck drivers. They not only took responsibility for work but also for the home and the children. Our women all became superwomen." The women who were living closer to the front in the south had generally much worse and difficult times during the war. Leila G., a young Shi'i who grew up in Basra and was a student during some years of the war, had to see her family home nearly destroyed and neighbors dying across the street during the numerous bombing raids on the city:

> Because we were so close to the battlefields, we were bombed many times during that war. We had to rebuild some walls and the roof of our house three times. But at least we were not hurt. One day, I saw our neighbors all torn to pieces and all lying dead after a bomb hit their house. Both of my brothers were fighting in the army, so we could never relax and always worried about them. My father was too old so he was working. We had a really difficult time. I volunteered in a local hospital to help with the injured and I still cannot forget the images of all these terrible injured men, some of them with missing limbs, some of them too shocked to say anything. (Al-Ali 2007: 152–53)

Leila, like many of her contemporaries, was helping with the war efforts by volunteering in a hospital. Other women with whom Nadje talked concurred with Leila's description of Iraqi women stretching themselves to respond to the changes wrought by war.

During this period the state moved away from images of men and women working side by side to develop a modern progressive nation to images of men protecting the land assaulted by the enemy—the land being represented as a woman whose honor had to be protected. These changes became particularly obvious in late stages of the war (1986–88), when morale was falling and the country faced economic difficulties. Even though women were needed to replace the male labor force in all sorts of areas, the Iraqi leadership clearly distanced itself from previous calls for women's rights, reforms, and equality. Society was becoming increasingly militarized, and certain types of masculinity—that of the fighter, the defender of his nation, and the martyr—were becoming glorified. Women were simultaneously encouraged to "produce" more Iraqi citizens and future soldiers. The glorification of a militarized masculinity coincided with the glorification of the Iraqi mother. During the last years of the war, the regime launched a fertility campaign asking every woman to bear at least five children. Initially the state attempted to address the demographic imbalance with Iran and to create a large generation of future soldiers. Later it had to appease an increasingly frustrated male population and prepare for the return of the troops to an economy and labor market in crisis. Within this context, Achim Rohde argues that the Iraqi regime traded its earlier commitment to gender equality for internal security: "For eight long years the regime was in constant need to mobilize the male population into the war effort at the front and to rally the unconditional support of the civilian population for the troops, including the acceptance of a superior social prestige awarded to soldiers as compared to women and other civilians" (2006a: 231). The regime's rhetoric shifted away from education and work toward procreation and motherhood (214).

Among the women Nadje interviewed, experiences of the Iran-Iraq War varied greatly. Overall, women stressed that despite the hardship and loss of life, life was still more bearable during this war than any of the subsequent wars (in 1991 and 2003). Especially middle-class families in cities far from the actual front in the south experienced minor disruptions in their everyday lives in comparison to the traumas related to later wars. However, for the tens of thousands of women who lost husbands, sons, fathers, and brothers during the Iran-Iraq War, life was never the same again.

TARGETING IRAQI SHIʻI

Despite some discontent with the regime and also some sectarianism as a result of discrimination before and during the Baʻth regime, there was no call for a merger with Iran or self-rule of Shiʻi in the south during the war with Iran. Instead, most Iraqi Shiʻi continued to stress their Arab identity and allegiance to the Iraqi nation, though not necessarily to the Iraqi regime. Saddam Hussein, on the other hand, continued to fear the disloyalty of the Shiʻi population and collectively punished hundreds of thousands by forcibly deporting them to Iran. During the late 1970s, about 250,000 Iraqis of "Persian descent" had already been deported and their property confiscated. The deportations were stepped up with the beginning of the Iran-Iraq War. During the first year alone about forty thousand Iraqi Shiʻi were forced to leave their homes, and over the eight years of the war, an estimated four hundred thousand Iraqis ended up in Iran (Abdullah 2003; Tripp 2000).

Many of the Iraqi Shiʻi refugee women Nadje talked to in Dearborn had vivid memories of *zamn al-tasfirat* (the time of deportations). Suad K., a lively and vivacious mother of three, followed her father and husband to Iran in the mid-1980s, fleeing the increasingly threatening security forces of the regime one night with two toddlers and an eight-month-old baby. She explained to Nadje how a tactic of draft evasion during the Ottoman Empire was used by Saddam Hussein against many people:

> In Ottoman times, they [the Ottoman administration] established a system of who is Ottoman and who is not. Those who did not want to fight in the army asked for an identity certificate *(tabaiya)* that would say "of Persian origin." Many Shiʻi managed to get out of the draft at the time by getting a *tabaiya* with "Persian origin" on it. But Saddam said that all Iraqis of Persian origins were traitors and could not be trusted. They were pulling people from their beds and putting them at the border to Iran. These poor people could not even take spare clothes, or money or anything. My father was deported to Iran in '79. My parents did not send me to school because they were afraid, because of the *tabaiya*. (Al-Ali 2007: 156)

Iraqi Shiʻi with Persian *tabaiyas* were especially vulnerable to Saddam's allegations of disloyalty and deception toward the Iraqi nation-state in the context of Saddam's Qadisiya campaign—a reappropriation of a historical battle in which Arab Muslims were victorious over Persians. History books, magazines, newspapers, articles, poems, and other cultural productions all stressed Iraqi and Arab cultural superiority, the evil intent of everyone Persian, and the corrupting influence of Persian culture on Arab Muslim civilization (Davis 2005: 183–90). In 1982, a law was passed offering financial rewards to men who would divorce their Iranian wives (Abdullah 2003: 189).

The harshest treatment, however, was saved for members or sympathizers of Islamist underground organizations, such as the Daʿwa Party, which are now part of the political alliance in government. In 1977, the Daʿwa Party and other Shiʿi Islamist organizations used the occasion of the demonstrations linked with the religious festival of Ashura to express their resentment against the secular government. Over thirty thousand people took the security forces by surprise as their prolonged demonstrations against the repression of religious authorities and the governments' networks of patronage ceased to be religious in nature (Tripp 2000: 216). Troops were dispatched to Najaf and Kerbala, and about two thousand people were arrested (Farouk-Sluglett and Sluglett 2003: 198). In the aftermath of the Islamic Revolution in Iran in 1979, the Daʿwa Party organized numerous antigovernment rallies and carried out a series of assassinations and assassination attempts of top Baʿth officials. A severe crackdown followed, with hundreds of arrests and a new law making membership in the Daʿwa Party punishable by death, since the Iraqi regime feared the spread of the Islamic Revolution to Iraq. According to Hamdiya H., a Dearborn resident who fled Iraq in the mid-1980s, membership in the underground organization became increasingly difficult: "I was a member of the Daʿwa Party and I was wearing a *hijab*. The culture was secular at the time. Wearing the *hijab* was a sign of resistance, a challenge to the regime. I was afraid of the regime, of neighbors, family, friends. If you were not a member of the Baʿth Party, you were in trouble. Back in the '60s and '70s, they were accusing you of being communist. Later on in the '80s, they were accusing people of being Islamists" (Al-Ali 2007: 160).

The Iraqi regime under the leadership of Saddam Hussein clearly targeted the Shiʿi population as part of his attempt to totally control and terrify the Iraqi population. However, experiences of the regime differed among Shiʿi. Indeed, many individuals who in post-Baʿth Iraq are identified or identify themselves as Shiʿi then thought of themselves as Iraqi and secular in orientation. They were part of the growing urban middle class that had benefited from the developmental policies of the 1970s. They had more in common with their Sunni, Christian, and Kurdish middle-class neighbors in mixed neighborhoods than with lower-class Shiʿi or members of Islamist political parties. Outright sectarianism hardly existed among non-Islamist Shiʿi prior to 2003 but was widespread among the Shi'i Islamist refugees residing in Dearborn and London whom Nadje interviewed. Fatima G. told Nadje in a meeting of several Shi'i women activists in Dearborn: "The Sunnis were all working with the regime. When I was imprisoned no Sunni was in the prison. It was only us. Now it is our time to have a say in Iraq." The members of Shi'i Islamist parties whom we interviewed hardly acknowledged the suffering of non-Shi'i Iraqis, such as political opponents of all backgrounds, including Sunni Iraqis, as well as Kurds. However, non-party-affiliated Shi'i women were less condemning of Iraqis of other religious and ethnic backgrounds and spoke about friendships and good neighborly relations with them; some even mentioned Sunnis who had resisted the regime.

WOMEN'S INVOLVEMENT IN THE KURDISH STRUGGLE

Although Kurdish society continued to be very conservative and tribal, many Kurdish women were involved in the struggle for independence: they not only supported their male relatives who were fighting by taking over responsibilities traditionally associated with men, providing logistical support, cooking for *peshmergas,* passing on secret messages, working as couriers, and transporting and distributing leaflets but also provided political leadership. Taavga A. recalls the anxiety and fear that her older sister's involvement in politics created for the family:

> My sister had become one of the leaders of the Kurdish freedom movement. And even my mother had been very active for the Kurdish cause. We were living in the city of Kirkuk, in one of the poorest neighborhoods. Al-Amn [the security apparatus of the Ba'th regime] started to find out about people involved in the Kurdish struggle. They went around with their big moustaches and sunglasses and arrested people. In 1974, Leila Qasim, a Kurdish student who was studying at Baghdad University, tried to assassinate Saddam Hussein. Her show trial was public and we watched it on TV every day. They had tortured her and finally executed her by hanging. We were all scared that this would happen to my sister as well. And then, one day, they came to our alley and caught a woman who was about my mother's age. They drugged her and shaved her hair. They took her from house to house and asked her to identify people involved in the Kurdish struggle. She identified my sister-in-law. We knew we had to leave immediately as we would be next in line. (Al-Ali 2007: 125)

Twelve-year-old Taavga fled her hometown of Kirkuk with her mother, a teenage sister, her politically active sister Nisreen, and a nine-month-old nephew in the middle of the night. They spent two weeks walking, riding donkeys, and wading through rivers.

More than one hundred thousand Kurds fled to Iran during the period when Taavga and her family fled their home. As it had become increasingly clear that the Ba'th regime was not ready to implement an agreement signed with the Kurdish leadership in 1970, Barzani and even some of his rival factions confronted the Iraqi government, and open war broke out by summer of 1974. The Kurdish *peshmerga* inflicted a heavy toll on the Iraqi army, increasingly relying on Iranian military support (Tripp 2000: 212). Despite the Iranian government's repression of its own Kurdish population, the shah was initially eager to help the Iraqi Kurds in order to destabilize what he perceived to be a hostile regime. Yet in what proved to be devastating to Barzani and the Kurdish resistance, secret negotiations between Baghdad and Tehran led to the Algiers Agreement in 1975. Without Iranian support, the Kurdish resistance collapsed and thousands of Kurds fled while many *peshmerga* and civilians were killed in reprisals by the Iraqi army, which destroyed about 1,500 villages (Yildiz 2004: 23). About six hundred thousand men, women, and children were deported to collective resettlement camps as the regime tried to create a security belt along the Iranian and Turkish borders (McDowall 2000: 339). Deported Kurds were threatened with death if they tried to return to their home villages, many of which had been razed to the ground and were uninhabitable (Tripp 2000: 214).

During the 1980s, the Iraqi government pursued its Arabization policies of the Kurdish region, forcefully moving thousands of Kurdish families and encouraging Egyptian and Iraqi Arab families to take their place.[8] Another strategy by the regime to attack and infiltrate Kurdish society was to offer Iraqi Arab men an equivalent of one thousand British pounds at the time to marry Kurdish women (Cobbet 1986: 132). The regime's heavy investment in Kurdish infrastructure and economy was part of its overall strategy to develop and modernize the country and buy people's loyalty. But it was also a means of dividing and conquering, as the state's system of patronage benefited some Kurds more than others. By the end of the 1970s, the KDP had managed to regroup, with Barzani's son Massoud taking over the leadership. Yet tensions with Talabani's rival Patriotic Union of Kurdistan (PUK), which was more popular among urban Kurds, led to internal feuds and even armed conflict. For years, this internal struggle continued, not only weakening Kurdish resistance against the regime but causing death and destruction among the Kurdish civilian population.

After initially focusing his attention on the war with Iran, Saddam Hussein became more concerned about the north after the KDP and PUK managed to end their feud and enter into an alliance in 1985, enabling more effective military operations against the Iraqi army. As Kurdish *peshmerga* had been receiving military and financial support from Iran, the Iraqi government retaliated brutally. The most known element of this systematic killing of Kurds was the 1987–88 Anfal campaign, nominally a counterinsurgency operation but in reality a carefully planned and executed program of ethnic cleansing in which fifty thousand to two hundred thousand people are estimated to have been killed, most of them men and adolescent boys.[9] Thousands of Kurdish villages were systematically destroyed, and over a million and a half of their inhabitants were deported to camps with no water, electricity, or sewage. Others were executed as they were leaving their villages.

Adalat Salih, who fled Iraq over the border to Iran during the 1975 war in Kurdistan and has spent her adult life researching the events and repercussions of the Anfal campaign, spoke to Nicola about the tragedy of the "Anfal widows"—that is, the women who lost their husbands during the Anfal campaign. In an interview in April 2007, in which she was soft-spoken but clearly passionate about her work, she discussed some of the findings of research she had conducted among a sample of 147 "Anfal widows": "Ninety-six percent of women didn't remarry, and of these, 72 percent of their children didn't marry. Eighty-three percent of these have housing problems. Until 2003, 92 percent expected that their relatives would come back, but after the mass graves were opened, they became hopeless. Ninety percent of these women are illiterate. Ninety-four percent have psychological problems. Thirty-three point four percent are responsible for supporting their families. This study is of 147 families. The problems are more widespread than this." The Anfal campaign has been particularly associated with the use of chemical weapons, such as mustard and nerve gas. One of the most notorious attacks took place in the city of Halabja on March 16, 1988. Approximately five thousand civilians died on that day alone, and thousands suffered horrendous injuries. Many people were covered with horrible skin eruptions; others went blind and suffered severe neurological damage. Long-term effects have included various forms of cancer, infertility, and congenital diseases. According to one of the women Nadje talked to, Kurdish men have been reluctant to marry women who originally came from Halabja, fearing infertility and genetic mutations.

Although Kurdish men were the primary target of the Anfal campaign, many Kurdish women and children also died as a result of the widespread and indiscriminate use of chemical weapons. In some regions, especially those in which Iraqi troops met armed resistance, large numbers of women and children were among those killed in mass executions. Tens of thousands of women, children, and elderly people were deported to camps and forced to live in conditions of extreme deprivation. Children suffered from malnutrition and diarrhea, and many died as a result of the harsh conditions in the camps.

According to various human rights reports, rape was one of the weapons used against Kurdish women during the Anfal campaign. Sexually abused women not only suffered through the actual crimes committed by Iraqi soldiers and security forces but also had to endure becoming the "shame" of the family and Kurdish community. Some women who might have survived the atrocities committed by the regime even became victims of honor killings by family members and fellow Kurds (Mojab 2000: 93). In addition, according to official records discovered after the fall of the Ba'th regime, 705 girls were sold to Gulf countries and 18 girls were sold to Egypt during the Anfal campaign. One was as young as twelve years old (Nader 2004).

In the accounts of the hardship and struggles endured by Kurdish women, we were struck by the apparent contradiction between the extreme conditions endured by families, forcing women and men to challenge traditional gender roles and relations and the survival of strong tribal and patriarchal norms and structures. Nadje discussed this issue with a group of Kurdish women in El Cajun. Runak M., who has been working for a Kurdish human rights center, shared the following experience:

> For us Kurds, a girl's or a woman's freedom very much depended on social class and particular family background. I was 11 when we fled to Turkey. My family never told me to cover up and wear the headscarf. If I had wanted to go to school, my family would have been ok with that. But because my brother was a *peshmerga*, we had to move to the mountains, so I did not get much formal education. But I knew many women who were very much restricted. Society was very conservative. Some women had to eat after their husbands ate. Some parents did not allow their daughters to go to school. Some parents forced their daughters to marry someone they did not even know. I heard of several stories of young women committing suicide by burning themselves. And we also had problems with honour killings. (Al-Ali 2007: 167)

Although the two major political parties, KDP and PUK, recruited women into their military and political ranks and established their own women's organizations, the feminist academic and activist Shahrzad Mojab argues that these organizations were mainly cosmetic and did not actually help the case of Kurdish women (1996: 72–73; 2000: 90). In contrast, the Women's Union of Kurdistan, established after the Anfal campaign (not to be confused with the KDP-related Kurdistan Women's Union established in 1957), did help vulnerable women deal with their trauma and also promoted women's rights (Mojab 2003: 24). Yet it has been obvious that in Kurdistan, just as in many other nationalist and separatist struggles, women's rights and women's equality have been sidelined in favor of the fight for independence. Hedi F., a member of the Women's Union of Kurdistan who fled Kurdistan in 1990 and returned in 2005 to help rebuild her country, told Nicola in the spring of 2007: "At the end of the eighties, Kurdish people fled to the mountains and to Iran. A group of us women thought, 'We can't just sit here, we have to be included in the Kurdish revolution.' So the Women's Union of Kurdistan was founded with two aims: to support the national struggle and to support women. We were under attack by the government. Men were fighting and women were sitting and crying. We thought, we could provide nursing and support, to show that we can do something. Women needed education, health, and political awareness. So we provided this."

The link between nationalism and patriarchy has been widely documented in different historical and cultural contexts around the world. With respect to Kurdish women, Shahrzad Mojab (1996, 2003, 2004) has provided compelling evidence that despite the nationalist struggle the patriarchal system has been extremely strong in Kurdistan. As she argues, "Although the nationalist movement depends on rallying the support of men and women, it discourages any manifestation of womanhood or political demands for gender equality" (Mojab 1996: 73). Patriarchy has manifested itself in diverse tribal, rural, and urban social formations (Mojab 2004: 111). While Kurdish women have been members of parliament since the 1990s, women are increasingly victims of so-called honor killings and are even punished for associating with or talking to men (111).

It comes as no surprise that the atrocities committed against the Kurdish population have fostered an anger and hatred that has also taken the shape of sectarianism against Arabs. When Nadje met with Runak S. at the Kurdish Human Rights Center in San Diego, Runak openly stated: "It made me hate everyone who is not Kurdish. I did not even hate the government only, but all people [non-Kurdish Iraqis]. I was never aware of the suffering of other Iraqis until I came here when I was sixteen years old. I never thought anyone else had been persecuted by the regime." Other Kurdish women we talked to continued to stress the particular suffering

of Iraqi Kurds in relation to other non-Kurdish Iraqis, thereby parallel-
ing some of the Shi'i Islamist women Nadje had talked to in Dearborn.
Whether among Iraqi Shi'a or Kurds, the stress on the uniqueness of suffering was not merely an attempt to get the truth acknowledged but also
part of a process of claiming political and economic rights. While many
Kurdish women politicians and activists we talked to denied any sectarian hatred, numerous interviews revealed Kurdish nationalist and sectarian sentiments that were sometimes expressed in terms of a suspicion or
mistrust of Arab politicians but occasionally extended to include Arab
populations more generally. Yet some Kurdish women politicians and activists we talked to clearly came out against sectarian trends and stressed
their affiliation to Iraq as well as the cause for women's rights.

IMPACT OF THE 1991 GULF WAR
AND ECONOMIC SANCTIONS

Only two years after the end of the war with Iran, Saddam Hussein invaded Kuwait (August 2, 1990) and the Second Gulf War began (January–
March 1991). Nobody knows exactly how many civilians died in the
war in 1991, but estimates for civilian deaths as a direct result of the war
range from one hundred thousand to two hundred thousand (BBC News
Online 2003). The air campaign destroyed almost the entire infrastructure of the country, including water supplies, electricity grids, factories,
and storage facilities. After one month of relentless bombings with about
116,000 sorties (Abdullah 2003: 195), the ground war started.

Although the Gulf War in 1991 led to the deaths of thousands of civilians and the destruction of the country's infrastructure, the thirteen years
of economic sanctions—the most comprehensive and devastating ever
to be imposed on a country—had a particularly detrimental impact on
women and gender relations.[10] Aside from the most obvious and devastating effects, related to dramatically increased child mortality rates, widespread malnutrition, deteriorating health care and general infrastructure,
unprecedented poverty, and an economic crisis, women were particularly
hit by a changing social climate. The breakdown of the welfare state had
a disproportionate effect on women, who had been its main beneficiaries. State discourse and policies as well as social attitudes and gender
ideologies shifted dramatically during the sanctions period.

Women were pushed back into their homes and into the traditional
roles of being mothers and housewives. Women's employment rate went
from being the highest in the region, estimated at above 23 percent prior

to 1991, to only 10 percent in 1997 (UN Development Programme [UNDP] 2000). Monthly salaries in the public sector, which, since the Iran-Iraq War, had increasingly been staffed by women, dropped dramatically and did not keep pace with high inflation rates and the cost of living. Many women reported that they simply could not afford to work anymore, since the state had to withdraw its free services, including child care and transportation (Al-Ali 2005: 747).

There was also a sharp decrease in access to all sectors of education for girls and young women because many families were not able to afford sending all children to school. Illiteracy, drastically reduced in the 1970s and 1980s, rose steadily after the Iran-Iraq War and grew between 1985 and 1995 from 8 percent to 45 percent. The dropout rate for girls in primary education reached 35 percent (UN Development Fund for Women [UNIFEM] 2004). In the late 1990s, 55 percent of women aged fifteen to forty-nine years were illiterate (UN Office for the Coordination of Human Affairs [UN-OCHA] 2006).

The nuclear family became more significant in an environment where people had to struggle for their everyday survival, since they were largely dependent on the monthly food rations of the government. In the context of an economic crisis, high rates of unemployment, and a demographic imbalance between men and women, marriage patterns were also affected in various ways. For many Iraqi women marriage became an unattainable dream. For others, arranged marriages to much older men, sometimes expatriates, or even polygamous marriages became a "way out" (Al-Ali 2007: 195–98). At the same time that marrying became more difficult, young women in particular felt pressured by a new cultural environment marked simultaneously by a decline in moral values like honesty, generosity, and sociability and an increased public religiosity and conservatism (Al-Ali and Hussein 2003).

The demographic cost of wars, political repression, and the forced economic migration of men triggered by the imposition of international sanctions accounted for the high number of widows and female-headed households. In 2003, the Human Relief Foundation estimated that there were approximately 250,000 widows in Iraq, although other estimates were higher (UNIFEM 2004). Not only widows found themselves without husbands but also women whose husbands went abroad to escape the bleak conditions and find ways to support their families. Other men just abandoned their wives and children, being unable to cope with their inability to live up to the social expectations of being the provider. During the 1990s, female-headed households, rural households, and poor households had the highest rates of infant and child mortality. While those whose husbands were killed in battle received a small government pension, those whose husbands were killed by the former regime for political reasons received no benefits and were left to fend for themselves (Al-Ali 2007: 200).

Economic hardships pushed more women into prostitution—a trend that created much anguish in a society where a woman's honor is perceived to reflect the family's honor. Prostitution was initially supported by the regime, which, alongside an emerging class of nouveau riche war and sanctions profiteers, presented itself as the main clientele. However, responding to a changing domestic social climate of a population increasingly drawn toward religion and social conservatism as well as the attempt to increase regional and international support among the Islamic *ummah,* Saddam Hussein opportunistically engaged in a religious campaign *(al-hamla imaniya).* The government condemned prostitution and engaged in violent campaigns to stop it. In a widely reported incident in Iraq in 2000, a group of young men linked to Saddam Hussein's son Uday singled out about three hundred alleged female "prostitutes" and "pimps" and beheaded them (Amnesty International 2000).

The imposition by the government of the *mahram* escort for women leaving Iraq failed to stop Iraqi women from engaging in prostitution across the border. This law did not allow Iraqi women to leave the country without being accompanied by a male first of kin unless they were over forty-five years old. It was enforced after the Jordanian government complained to the Iraqi government about widespread prostitution by Iraqi women in Amman.

On the level of government discourse as well as within society, Iraqi women became the bearers of the honor of the whole country: they had to be protected because they were vulnerable to temptation, gossip, a tarnished reputation, and potentially prostitution. Teenage girls especially complained about increasing social restrictions and difficulties of movement.[11] Yasmin Hussein Al Jawaheri interviewed a number of Iraqi teen - agers only a few years prior to the invasion in 2003. The interviews reveal that while the parents of the predominantly middle-class young women Al Jawaheri talked to had mingled relatively freely when they were the age of their children, young Iraqis in the nineties found it increasingly difficult to meet each other. Schools became segregated between sexes, but even in coeducational schools interaction between boys and girls became more limited. Girls became extremely worried about their reputation and often avoided situations in which they could find themselves alone with a boy (Al-Ali and Hussein 2003).

These fears may have been aggravated by the not uncommon occurrence of so-called honor killings (Al-Ali 2005: 752). Fathers and brothers of women who are known or often only suspected of having violated the accepted codes of behavior, especially with respect to keeping their virginity before marriage, may kill the women in order to restore the honor of the family. Before 2003 this phenomenon was mainly restricted to rural areas, but knowledge of its existence worked as a deterrent for many female teenagers. Others may have been less worried about the most dramatic consequences of "losing one's reputation." What educated middle-class women from urban areas feared was not so much death as diminished marriage prospects (Al-Ali and Hussein 2003: 54).

The young women Al Jawaheri interviewed frequently spoke about changes related to socializing, family ties, and relations between neighbors and friends. Often they quoted a parent or older relative as stating how things had been different in the past, when socializing had been a much bigger part of people's lives. Zeinab, a fifteen-year-old woman from Baghdad, spoke of the lack of trust between people and suggested the following as explanations for the change in dress code for women and the social restrictions she and her peers were experiencing:

> People have changed now because of the increasing economic and various other difficulties of life in Iraq. They have become very afraid of each other. I think because so many people have lost their jobs and businesses, they are having loads of time to speak about other people's lives, and they often interfere in each other's affairs. I also think that because so many families are so poor now that they cannot afford buying more than the daily basic food, it becomes so difficult for them to buy nice clothes and nice things and therefore, it is better to wear *hijab*. Most people are somewhat pressured to change their lives in order to protect themselves from the gossip of other people—especially talk about family honor. (Al-Ali and Hussein 2003: 46)

Thus our research showed that many economic, social, and political factors at the levels of state and society converged during the most comprehensive sanctions system ever imposed on a country. In addition to widespread poverty and the collapse of crucial infrastructures, including the previously excellent health and education systems, a shift toward greater social conservatism and more restrictive gender ideologies and relations became evident. Religious ideology started to gain greater significance as many Iraqis tried to find solace in faith and Saddam Hussein opportunistically tapped into religious sentiments. Yet the drastic economic crisis, which included widespread unemployment, underemployment, and nonpayment of employees' salaries, cannot be overstressed in terms of its impact on the call for women to return home and take up traditional roles of mothers and housewives.

WOMEN IN THE "SAFE HAVEN"

Semiautonomy in Iraqi Kurdistan allowed women to establish civil society associations and become involved in party politics. Women also increasingly became involved in the expanding labor market and in the attempt to rebuild a destroyed society. In the first years of the sanctions regime, poverty, malnutrition, and hunger were widespread among the population. However, a combination of factors led to an improvement in living conditions, even though the Kurdish region suffered from a "double embargo": that of the United Nations imposed on Iraq and that of the Iraqi government imposed over the Kurdish region. Significantly, in northern Iraq the oil-for-food money included a cash component, while the center and south, under the control of the Iraqi regime, did not receive any cash. A report by the UN Food and Agriculture Organisation (UNFAO) in September 2000 linked the different impact of sanctions on the north and the south/center to "greater resources in the North, the North has 9% of the land area of Iraq but nearly 50% of the productive arable land, and receives higher levels of assistance per person." In addition, the Kurdish region's geographic position bordering Turkey, Iran, and Syria allowed for lucrative smuggling on small and large scales.

Another important factor was the major presence of humanitarian agencies undertaking relief and development work: in 1999, there were thirty-four NGOs in the north, while in the rest of the country there were only eleven. According to Sarah Graham-Brown (1999: 303), "The collaboration between international agencies, local NGOs and villagers themselves in restoring rural life produced some remarkable results." Women became increasingly involved in the emerging civil society and the expanding economy. New organizations were created, networks were formed, and campaigns were launched. As Zana L., the founder of a women's center in Sulaymaniya, told Nicola: "In 1991, society was completely destroyed. Women didn't have any rights, which is why I joined the women's movement. In addition to the wars, the law was against women's rights. For example, honor crimes were allowed. Women in Kurdistan started to demonstrate to get this law repealed, and we succeeded. It still exists in the rest of Iraq. There have also been campaigns against female circumcision and raising awareness of female suicide, setting up women's shelters and centers for women's rights."

Independent women's initiatives and political participation were not always welcomed. Some conservative Kurdish male politicians were hostile to the idea of women's rights. Roxanne S., a legal expert and women's rights activist, told Nicola that she had been criticized when, in 1994, she opened a center for women in Erbil providing training, legal aid, sports facilities, and social services: "This was taboo at the time." Meanwhile, the two major Kurdish political parties were suspicious of activities not linked to their organizations. Some Kurdish women activists campaigning against widespread honor killings in the north have been subject to harassment, and a newly established women's shelter for victims of domestic violence had to close down because of political opposition. Zouzan H., a Kurdish women's rights activist based in London, told Nadje in an interview in the spring of 2005:

> I was one of the founding members of a new women's organization in 1991. We were campaigning against honor killings, which became very widespread in 1992 with PUK coming into power. We were a mass orga -
> nization and were very active. We had branches all over Kurdistan. In 1993, we founded the Independent Women's Organization, which was supported by the Workers' Communist Party. But both political parties, the PUK and the KDP, gave us a hard time. They really harassed us. There was even a small bomb attack in our office. Some of us decided to leave Kurdistan and to set up branches abroad. (Al-Ali 2007: 207)

Paradoxically, domestic violence against women appeared to increase dramatically after the establishment of the "safe haven" in 1991 and the creation of the autonomous Kurdistan Regional Government in 1992.[12] According to Shahrzad Mojab, who has done extensive research on what she calls "gendercide" of Kurdish women (2003: 25), a parliament "dominated by males and especially the conservative KDP, refused to initiate new legislation" that would protect women against so-called honor killings (Mojab 2007). While the more progressive PUK issued two resolutions that treated honor killings as punishable crimes, they were in no position to implement these (Mojab 2007). However, women activists galvanized to campaign against this violence and expose the conservative gender policies of the parties. In some cases, Kurdish politicians claimed that women's oppression, including honor killings, were part of Kurdish tribal and Islamic culture (Mojab 2004: 122). We also came across the "culture" argument during interviews with female Kurdish politicians and activists in 2007.

In the 1992 elections women and men were forced to line up separately to cast their votes, although Kurdish men and women had formerly socialized freely in rural areas. Only 5 of the 105 elected members of parliament were women (Mojab 2004: 119). Hasan M., a former *peshmerga* turned local politician, told Nicola candidly, "The problem is, men don't want to give up their power to women." The political leadership of both factions tried to incorporate patriarchal tribal leaders, using women as a bargaining chip much as Saddam Hussein had tried to co-opt tribal leaders in central and southern Iraq during the 1990s (129).

Peace between the two rival Kurdish parties faltered in May 1994, followed by a period of tensions and internal war. NGO activist Chiman A. recalls, "This was bad for people and for women's rights. Islamic groups increased. People became hopeless because of the war. They turned to religion, which fueled the growth of the Islamic parties. This had a negative effect on women's rights. After the KDP and PUK stopped fighting, things became better. But during the fighting, the Islamic parties had a chance to occupy Hawraman [an area of Iraqi Kurdistan], and they turned it into Afghanistan. They set up checkpoints. Women were made to cover up. Music was forbidden. Even pictures of women on the wrappings of products were removed." Women activists marched from Sulaymaniya to Erbil to protest this "fratricidal" or "suicidal" war (Mojab 2007). However, it took many years of a "destructive cycle of sporadic fighting interspersed with tenuous cease-fires" (Tripp 2000: 273), which led to the deaths of thousands of Kurds, before a cease-fire was finally signed in September 1998. The United States provided intensive mediation, since, in the context of the crisis over weapons inspections, they viewed a unified government for Iraqi Kurdistan as increasingly necessary (273).

WOMEN'S CHANGING LIVES

Throughout Iraq's modern history, women have played an active role in all aspects of society: the education system, the evolving labor market, intellectual and artistic productions, and politics and civil society. Changing economic and political conditions, rather than Islam, have affected women's lives and rights over the past decades. Certainly patriarchal and tribal culture has been responsible for many of the values, norms, and practices that have been oppressive and harmful to women. However, the influence of traditional culture over women has waxed and waned according to changing state policies and economic conditions. Facing a deteriorating economy and a weakening hold over the populace, the Iraqi state under Saddam Hussein opted to revitalize tribal leaders and conservative practices as a means of stabilizing state power;

those conservative practices were not an inherent feature of a predominantly Muslim country.

Despite a fierce and often brutal dictatorship, a series of bloody wars, and the deterioration of daily living conditions under economic sanctions, Iraqi women have not been passive victims but have been active in resisting these negative events within the social, political, and cultural spaces available. Iraqi women participated in the struggle for national independence in the 1940s and 1950s and were part of political parties and organizations that demanded greater social equality. The campaign for women's rights in education, the workforce, and politics has also been waged vigorously by Iraqi women's rights activists since the 1940s. However, it is also important to mention that some Iraqi women were themselves part of oppressive political and social structures, whether as Ba'th functionaries or as leading members of the GFIW.

The regime itself drastically changed its rhetoric and policies on women and gender between 1969 and 2003. An adherence to developmental modernist ideas about national progress, in conjunction with an economic boom in the early 1970s, initially led to a form of state feminism that enabled many Iraqi women to benefit from a growing education system at all levels including the university level, an expanding labor market that required skilled labor, and the attempted replacement of local religious and tribal authorities with centralized state power. Many women of the middle classes acknowledge having been co-opted by a state that ruled not merely through force but also through generous welfare programs and considerable socioeconomic rights.

But although many women of the urban middle classes benefited from rapid modernization under the Ba'th, simultaneously thousands of women and their families suffered the brutality of the regime. Wars and the devastating embargo contributed not only to the deterioration in infrastructures and everyday living conditions but also to the shift toward greater social conservatism, religiosity, and more restricted social spaces and mobility for women. In the later phase of the previous regime, the state lacked the financial means to support women in their double roles as mothers and workers and provide services related to education and health care. The state also withdrew its political support for women's equality and participation in public life, adopting a more conservative and restrictive gender ideology. The impact of thirteen years of economic sanctions was especially detrimental, as it worked on both the level of state policies and services and the level of social attitudes, values, and relations.

Contrary to popular views, sectarianism and religious extremism are relatively new phenomena in Iraq. The sense of being "Iraqi" grew with the development of the Iraqi state and the expansion of education and has historically prevailed over sectarian sentiments despite tensions at various historical moments. Most significantly, variables such as social class, urban versus rural identities, and even political orientation have historically cut across religious and ethnic groups. The eldest generation of Iraqi women to whom we talked describe a relatively harmonious multicultural and multifaith society in the years prior to the second Ba'th coup in 1968. However, Iraqi society at the time was divided along class lines, with the majority of the population living in extremely harsh conditions.

Ethnic and religious affiliations and communal identities started to gain ground as a result of Saddam Hussein's nepotism and brutal divide-and-conquer policies. Hundreds of thousands of Kurdish and Shi'i civilians were killed, imprisoned, and tortured as part of the Ba'th regime's uncompromising repression of the Kurdish nationalist and Shi'i Islamist movements, respectively. Yet other ethnic and religious groups, including Sunni Arabs, also suffered from wars, sanctions, and oppressive policies, particularly if they were involved in opposition politics. As the state began to disintegrate as a result of international sanctions, Saddam Hussein promoted the role of tribal leaders and manipulated growing religiosity to protect his regime's authority. Meanwhile, state-sponsored Islam and tribalism thrived as avenues for individual and family survival in the context of deteriorating social and economic circumstances.

The rise in religious extremism, sectarianism, and communal identities in the post-Ba'th period has to be understood partly as a continuation of the social trends rooted in the 1990s. In addition, many returning Iraqi political exiles in the diaspora imported outright sectarianism that was able to flourish in contexts where identity politics were promoted. This is not to argue that the violent sectarianism and communalism we witness today were inevitable. The occupation systematically eroded the structures and institutions that could have helped to contribute to national unity and instead fostered sectarian and communal sentiments. As we will show in the following chapters, Iraqi women have borne the brunt of the attempt by various social and political forces to symbolize a break with Ba'th rule and to replace centralized state power with tribal, religious, and communal leadership.

TWO

THE USE AND ABUSE OF IRAQI WOMEN

At the beginning of our research on the role of women in post-Saddam Iraq, we were presented with a paradox concerning the international community's relation to women in the new Iraq. All of the people to whom we spoke—in Iraq, the United States, the United Kingdom, and Jordan—agreed that the participation of women in postconflict reconstruction was important. Decision makers and program implementers in the U.S. and U.K. governments, international and multilateral organizations, and NGOs were all eager to tell us about the measures they were taking to include women in postconflict reconstruction and about examples of women's action to promote their rights and have a say at the decision-making table. But although we often heard people expressing their intention to "mainstream gender" into their policies and programs in Iraq, we found evidence that the situation of women was actually deteriorating as time went by.

This chapter outlines the policies and various measures implemented by the United States and other international agencies to empower Iraqi women after the invasion of 2003 and draws out some of the assumptions made with regard to Iraqi women. It also explains the gap between the rhetoric of women's empowerment and the reality of Iraqi women's lives and situates this within the overall strategy of U.S. foreign policy in the post-9/11 era.

WOMEN'S EMPOWERMENT ON THE AGENDA

The U.S. and U.K. governments have expressed concern over the situation of women in Iraq since it first became apparent that an invasion was on the cards. At a press conference two weeks before the U.S.-led invasion of Iraq, Paula Dobriansky, then undersecretary of state for global affairs, flanked by four members of a group called Women for a Free Iraq, declared: "We are at a critical point in dealing with Saddam Hussein. However this turns out, it is clear that the women of Iraq have a critical role to play in the future revival of their society" (Dobriansky et al. 2003). Women for a Free Iraq were a group of Iraqi women living in exile, formed in January 2003 to raise awareness of women's experiences of persecution under Saddam Hussein. The campaign received funding from the Washington-based Foundation for the Defense of Democracies. Though the foundation is nominally nonpartisan, its president, Clifford May, is a former Republican Party operative, and its board is stacked with prominent neoconservatives (see also Zangana 2006a).

High-ranking U.S. officials, including then–National Security Advisor Condoleezza Rice and Vice-President Dick Cheney, met with Women for a Free Iraq to hear their personal stories and to discuss the future of the country. The U.S. State Department publicized the abuses women had experienced at the hands of the Iraqi regime, including beheadings, rape, and torture (Office of International Women's Issues 2003). In the United Kingdom, Tony Blair met a delegation of Iraqi women in November 2002 (Russell 2002), and the Foreign and Commonwealth Office listed the regime's crimes against women as part of its dossier on human rights abuses in Iraq (Foreign and Commonwealth Office 2002).

The timing of this sudden interest in the plight of Iraqi women cannot be overemphasized. For decades, many Iraqi women activists in the United States and United Kingdom had tried to raise awareness about the systematic abuse of human and women's rights under Saddam Hussein, the atrocities linked to the Anfal campaign against the Kurds, and the impact of economic sanctions on women and families. But as London-based Amal K. told Nadje, "We wrote so many letters and we organized many events: talks, workshops, seminars, demonstrations. They did not want to know. They were just not interested. It was only in the run-up to the invasion that the governments started to care about the suffering of Iraqi women."

Official U.S. interest was not limited to the period leading up to the war against Iraq. Following the invasion, there were also a number of official speeches and statements about women's role in the reconstruction of Iraq and its transition to democracy.[1] On April 11, 2003, Paula J. Dobriansky (2003b), in a speech to the Heritage Foundation, a conservative think tank, proclaimed, "[We] believe that democracy and human rights are not just for some people but for all people. They are universal principles that every man, woman, and child is entitled to. We want to help Iraqis take back their country after decades of tyranny and build foundations of a democratic society." And in a July 2003 op-ed in the *Washington Post,* Dobriansky (2003a), responding to critics, defended the administration's record with regard to women in post-Ba'th Iraq, saying, "We are working to advance the interests of Iraqi women in every area, from human rights to political and economic participation to health care and education." Delegations of self-selected Iraqi women visited Washington regularly after the invasion, holding press conferences hosted by the State Department and meeting President Bush at the White House in November 2003 (White House Office of the Press Secretary 2003). When Nicola visited Washington, D.C., in March–April 2005, a number of officials were keen to stress the U.S. administration's concern to support women in Iraq and to see them play a role in the country's future. As one former member of the Coalition Provisional Authority (CPA) in Baghdad, Janet W., said, "From the time that I arrived at the CPA, [L. Paul] Bremer always talked about including women. He met with lots of women." Indeed, the CPA included an Office for Women's Affairs. Similarly, Leslie F., a senior State Department official, stated, "We are committed to women in Iraq and we've put our money where our mouth is."

FUNDING "WOMEN'S EMPOWERMENT"

The Bush administration allocated considerable sums of money to reconstruction in Iraq, including projects aimed at improving women's participation in political, civil, and economic life. The United States represents the largest single donor to Iraq. At the International Donors' Conference for Iraq in October 2003, the United States pledged approximately $18.6 billion for reconstruction in Iraq (approximately half the total amount pledged by the international community), in addition to $2.47 billion that had been initially allocated by Congress in April 2003. This money was directed at supporting economic development, training and education, health, water and sanitation, rebuilding of infrastructure, local governance, community participation, Iraqi oil sector repairs, and law enforcement (Special Inspector General for Iraq Reconstruction [SIGIR] 2007a: Appendix G). By the end of 2006, approximately 80 percent of this amount had, on paper at least, been spent (SIGIR 2007a: "Highlights"). It is difficult to find exact figures for the amount of money allocated to supporting Iraqi women. This is partly because funds are channeled through different government institutions: the U.S. Agency for International Development (USAID), the Department of State, the Department of Defense, the Department of Health and Human Services, and the Department of the Treasury (SIGIR 2007a: Appendix G). Also the vast majority of funding is not specified for either men or women but targets both. Indeed, most of the funds are allocated for the rehabilitation of infrastructure (water, electricity, oil industry, transport, and communications) and for security and law enforcement (in total, $15.2 billion, of which $11.86 billion had been spent by the beginning of 2007), which, in theory, should benefit all Iraqis, regardless of gender. The United States has spent money on the education sector ($1.15 billion) and the health sector ($530 million) in programs that mention women and girls specifically as beneficiaries of programs, such as accelerated learning programs for children out of school (USAID n.d.) and the rehabilitation of a maternity hospital in Baghdad (SIGIR 2007a: 96). However, as we discuss later in greater detail, one of the major problems in the postinvasion period has been the lack of actual improvement and reconstruction of severely debilitated basic services and infrastructure.

Despite the absence of disaggregated data with regard to the number of Iraqi women benefiting from U.S. reconstruction funds, we found plenty of evidence of Iraqi women being targeted through programs and projects in Iraq. The U.S. Institute for Peace (USIP) is a U.S.-based NGO that received money directly from Congress, in October 2003, to participate in rebuilding Iraq. The grant, worth $10 million, was allocated "for activities supporting peace enforcement, peacekeeping and post-conflict peacebuilding."[2] With this money, USIP has conducted programs for training senior Iraqi officials and has given $1.5 million in small grants for capacity building of NGOs in Iraq. Congress did not specify that any of the $10 million should be directed for the support of women. Nevertheless, Peter K. at USIP told Nicola: "We see women's inclusion as important. . . . Women are 60 percent of the population. They have a moderating impact on politics." USIP aims to include women as 40 percent of participants in its training programs and conflict resolution dialogues, but in Iraq this goal has not always been reached, largely because of security concerns and conservative norms about women's participation among certain sections of the Iraqi population. Sara J. at USIP told Nicola that a focus of the small grants scheme is to promote women's empowerment and that USIP has allocated six grants (out of a total of thirty-four), worth between $5,000 and $20,000, to women's organizations. According to Sara, "We don't impose criteria on the NGOs that we fund with regard to women's participation, but we do ask them whether there is a component of their work dedicated to women."

The United States has also funded some Iraqi women's organizations for their work on advocating women's rights in the constitution, raising awareness of women's rights, and educating women voters. USAID provided a $500,000 grant to the Rafadin Women's Coalition, "comprised of more than 30 [Iraqi] women's organizations[,] to launch conferences, leaflet distribution, media and television spots promoting women's rights in a constitutional democracy" (USAID n.d.). Meanwhile, the U.K. Department for International Development (DFID) has also funded some women's organizations through two of its grant programs—the Political Participation Fund (£7.5 million—i.e., approximately $14.25 million) and the Civil Society Fund (£5 million—i.e., approximately $9.5 million). These pots of money are administered by the British Council in Baghdad in the form of small grants to NGOs: for example, the Political Participation Fund has provided funding for a monthly magazine on women's issues, published by one Iraqi women's organization. Through the Civil Society Fund, international NGOs are working to strengthen the capacity of Iraqi NGOs: for example, Christian Aid has received money to support a women's shelter in Iraqi Kurdistan. However, promoting women's organizations is not the single priority of these programs.

Some projects have the stated aim of "empowering" women through bringing them together in conferences and workshops. In the first year following the fall of the Ba'th regime, Janet W., in the Women's Affairs Office of the CPA, helped to organize several conferences in different parts of Iraq, which were funded by the United States: "We assisted a group of women in organizing a small conference in Baghdad in July 2003. The women selected their own steering committee. The conference discussed all sorts of issues, such as constitutional reform, social welfare, education, the economy, etc. They presented these recommendations to the [Iraqi] Governing Council. Following this Baghdad meeting, regional meetings were held in the south, south-central, the north, etc. We provided the support that they requested. They had a lot of ideas about what they wanted." Women Waging Peace and the Woodrow Wilson School brought Iraqi women together in several workshops in the United States and in Beirut to discuss how to involve women in postconflict reconstruction and how to guarantee women's rights in the constitution. Hind S., working on the Middle East program at Woodrow Wilson, told Nicola: "Our role was to facilitate discussion and reach out to these women. The women were from different religious and ethnic backgrounds. Some were active at the grassroots level. They were well received by the U.S. administration—Bush, Wolfowitz, and others—they were very receptive to meeting the women. And money has been allocated for programs targeting women." Finally, several workshops were held by international NGOs throughout 2005 to bring Iraqi women together to discuss the future constitution, which was drafted over the summer of 2005, and to formulate recommendations to send to the drafting committee, which was made up of selected members of the Transitional National Assembly (TNA). Rouba F., one of several NGO workers based in Amman but working on Iraq, told Nicola in the spring of 2006: "We held two workshops and a conference in June 2005. For the conference, we invited members of the drafting committee and members of parliament. The workshop recommendations were fed into a committee to be considered in the drafting process. Workshop participants were concerned that their recommendations would not be considered. They were frustrated, but they were also determined."

The vast majority of funding in support of women appears to have been directed toward the training of women as participants in political, civil, and economic processes. This approach to women's empowerment is based on two assumptions. The first is that Iraqi women need training to bring them into the public sphere: "[Iraqi] women are capable and they need knowledge and skills," as Leslie at the State Department told Nicola. The second is that women, if equipped with appropriate skills, merely need encouragement to participate and flourish in public life. Such an approach does not consider the social and political context in which women operate and that undoubtedly affects their ability to participate. A key example is the twenty women's centers that the CPA and USAID funded throughout Iraq, including Baghdad. The first of the nine Baghdad centers, supported by a grant of $1.4 million, was opened on March 8, 2004 (International Women's Day) by CPA head L. Paul Bremer. The centers were meant to offer women training in vocational and business skills, computers, and the English language, as well as providing legal advice. However, both of us encountered several criticisms about their sustainability (which we will discuss below). Some of the types of support also demonstrate neoliberal assumptions about the significance of private entrepreneurship as a pillar of democracy. In addition to the centers, women's business associations have been supported. The Center for International Private Enterprise (CIPE), a U.S.-based NGO that receives funds via the National Endowment for Democracy, worked throughout 2005 with two women's organizations: the Iraqi Business Women's Association (IBWA), established in 2004, and the Iraqi Professional Women's Association (IPWA), established at the beginning of 2005. According to Fares J. of CIPE, who spoke to Nicola in Washington: "We are doing training and capacity building, raising awareness about economic reform. . . . We have provided start-up costs for furniture, et cetera. . . . We bring them to Amman for training in corporate governance."[3]

Save the Children USA is one of several NGOs that received money from USAID's Community Action Program in Iraq. The grant, worth $64 million, has been used to train community organizers to work with the community to identify and prioritize development needs and to fund some of the projects identified by members of the community. In particular, the program aims to include vulnerable groups, such as women, young people, and refugees. As part of this project, Save the Children has trained women and men as community organizers. According to Valerie G.:

> We had a problem with some male team leaders not allowing female members or not allowing women to participate. We tried to solve that by having more female team leaders. Some of them are very creative in their work. For example, there is a tribal area and two of the tribes are fighting each other in an area where one community development team was trying to work. The female team leader met with one of the tribal leaders to secure access for her team. She addressed the issue straight on, and he said they could come as his guests and would be escorted by his men.

Women have also been trained to take part in the political process as candidates, voters, and advocates of women's rights. The National Democratic Institute (NDI) is a U.S.-based nonprofit organization, originally established by the Democratic Party but nonpartisan in nature, that runs programs globally to promote democratization through training of political parties, election monitors, and civil society groups. Ruth G. at NDI told Nicola about some of NDI's work in Iraq in the run-up to the elections at the beginning of 2005:

> We trained women candidates around the country as part of the political party work. In Basra, we had a huge turnout for the women's candidate training. Women were very keen to participate and get training—although they were not keen to publicize their candidacy due to security reasons. [In accordance with the election system chosen, the electorate voted for lists rather than individual candidates, so it was not necessary to publicize

individual candidate names.] We trained thirty-five of the eighty-six women elected to the Transitional National Assembly [in January 2005]. We trained one hundred women altogether, but not all of them got elected.

Meanwhile, one Iraqi NGO that receives international funding for local community development was involved in training some "nonofficial" election monitors. Sitting in the lobby of the Ashti Hotel in Sulaymaniya, Chiman A., a committed worker for this NGO since 1997, told Nicola, "There were some women among the observers, and they were so happy. Just to vote was a good thing, but to be an observer was even better. The women were so proud to be observers. It was a big thing in their lives." Ruth also highlighted women's role in election monitoring. "We organized an election monitoring network of 142 organizations. The Election Information Network has a woman director, and half the staff is women. So women are participating and they are doing all the work."

WOMEN'S POLITICAL PARTICIPATION

Despite the existence of such programs, the U.S. State Department decided to pump extra funds into promoting women's political participation. This suggests that there may have been concerns about the marginalization of women from emerging governance structures and the threat to women's rights. In May 2003, soon after the toppling of Saddam, U.S. Deputy Secretary of State Richard Armitage told the BBC, "If there's an area where I feel thus far we've fallen short . . . it is in the representation of women. We need to have even higher levels of participation of women in this process [of establishing an interim administration]. We've realised that we haven't done as well thus far in that area and we're redoubling our efforts" (Westcott 2003). Indeed, the "big tent meetings" that brought representatives of Iraqi political parties, tribal leaders, and other public figures together to discuss the composition of an interim administration included only a handful of women delegates (Westcott 2003). The IGC, formed in July 2003, included only three women out of twenty-one members. Then, in December 2003, the IGC passed Decree 137 to abolish the relatively progressive unified personal status code (governing marriage, divorce, child custody, and inheritance, as discussed in the previous chapter) and to place personal status matters under the jurisdiction of religious leaders, thereby threatening women's rights. In response, several women's rights activists and members of civil society wrote to CPA head L. Paul Bremer and U.K. Ambassador Jeremy Greenstock to "call attention to the sex discrimination Iraqi women have suffered under the Coalition Provisional Authority and the councils created and appointed by the CPA" (Civil Society Groups and Concerned Citizens of Iraq 2003; see following chapters for further details).

However, it was not until March 8, 2004, that then–Secretary of State Colin Powell announced a new allocation of $10 million for the Iraqi Women's Democracy Initiative. According to Undersecretary of State for Global Affairs Paula Dobriansky, the initiative aimed "to help women become full and vibrant partners in Iraq's developing democracy" (Kaufman 2004). Richard T. at the U.S. State Department, who was charged with managing the allocation of grants, said: "We were under pressure for immediate results. Deputy Secretary of State Armitage said, 'No dilly-dallying. We need results.' There was a need to bring women into the political process immediately."

The money was allocated to seven organizations (out of thirty-three submitting proposals) that were based in the United States but working with organizations inside Iraq. Richard described the criteria for allocating the grants in order to facilitate a quick turnaround in disbursing the money. The grantees (i.e., the organizations receiving grants) would have to have a presence in Iraq already, and their projects would have to include a "training of trainers" component in order to increase the long-term impact. They were not allowed to spend more than 10 to 15 percent of their budget on security, and none of them were to be based in the Green Zone. The projects were chosen in June, and most of them were running by September 2004.

The grants were given to NGOs to carry out democracy education, leadership training, political training, NGO coalition building, organizational management, media training, and, that all-important pillar of U.S.-style democracy, "teaching entrepreneurship" (Office of the Senior Coordinator for International Women's Issues 2004). The Independent Women's Forum (IWF) used their portion of the grant to train 150 women in a "Women Leaders Program." The central activity of this training was a Women Leaders Conference held in Jordan in April 2005: "Over a period of a week, Kurds, Sunnis, Shiia, Christians and Jews worked side by side gaining not only a better understanding of the universal principles of democracy, but learning about each other's issues and building coalitions for a continuing dialogue on democracy and constitution-making. . . . Many of the participants in the program went on to become parliamentarians, members of local councils and key figures in Iraqi civil society" (IWF 2007). Another grant recipient, the Johns Hopkins School of Strategic and International Studies, worked with Iraqi NGOs to collect and translate national constitutions, international covenants, and other conventions on women's rights into Arabic to serve as a resource. The Kurdish Human Rights Watch worked with Iraqi women and other groups to mobilize households to vote in the 2005 elections.

Even though some people reported difficulties in initially meeting quotas for women's involvement in reconstruction and the political transition, everyone in the U.S. administration, U.K. government, NGOs, and other international organizations who spoke with Nicola stressed their continual insistence to get women involved. Sometimes this was to meet organizational commitments to quotas for women's participation in training sessions. In other cases, it was the outcome of a "clearly articulated principle of women's empowerment" despite the lack of clear mechanisms for implementing it, as Jennifer L., a U.S. diplomat who was sent to an Iraqi province from May 2003 until June 2004, told Nicola. Jennifer tried to ensure women's participation on the local council and council committees by asking "to speak to fifteen professional women, . . . [including] bank managers, headmistresses." When Nicola asked Janet W., formerly of the CPA's Women's Affairs Office, whether in retrospect she would have done anything differently with regard to getting women involved, she said, "No, not really. We did what we could do. We met with women in their homes. Some were tentative about getting involved. Some wanted to get involved. We listened to what they wanted to do. We accomplished a lot and we got women's inclusion recognized."

Yet although Nicola heard many stories about how women had been involved in political, economic, and civil processes, both of us also heard many stories about how women were becoming excluded from these processes. In Amman, in the spring of 2006, Nicola met with Rana J., a member of an international agency working in Iraq: "Now [Iraqi] women are more experienced and more confident. But after the invasion they were more hopeful and they wanted to work together to promote women's issues. Now women are more frustrated. Now they see women's issues dropping off the agenda. Some women have left the country because of their frustration and disillusionment. Then [after the invasion], women would do anything. Anything was possible. Now you ask whether they can do something and they say, 'Well, I don't know if it's possible.'"

MEETING WOMEN'S BASIC NEEDS

"Iraq is not a typical situation. It has been through three wars, decades under a repressive regime, sanctions, and occupation. You may find a country that has been through one of these, but it is very rare to find a country that has gone through all of these things." This is what Layla A., working for an international agency dealing with humanitarian assistance to Iraq, told Nicola in spring 2006. These exceptional conditions contributed to creating adverse social and economic conditions for Iraqi women on the eve of the U.S.-led invasion. As one activist told Nadje in 2005: "After all these years of sanctions, we were already in a terrible situation by the time the invasion happened. It was so difficult to find medicines, and hospitals could not provide adequate care anymore. Many people were barely surviving on the monthly food rations given out by the government. And you know our problem with electricity and water." Addressing a conference in Washington a couple of weeks after the fall of Saddam Hussein's regime, Nesreen Sadeek (2003), minister of Reconstruction and Development in the Kurdistan Regional Government, listed the priorities for Iraq as she saw them, including launching public works in basic services and infrastructure; restoring order and safeguarding the rule of law; promoting respect for human rights; restoring oil production; and arranging for the return and resettlement of internally displaced persons. A couple of months later, in July 2003, at the first women's conference held in Iraq after the fall of the Ba'th regime, women participants drew up a number of recommendations, including creating constitutional bodies to monitor and follow up conditions for women; eradicating illiteracy; improving maternal health care; promoting women's participation in the economy and economic decision making; and outlawing violence against women, including so-called honor crimes (Various 2003).

Indicators for Iraq before 2003 are sporadic, but those that exist portray a dire humanitarian situation. Following the Iran-Iraq War, the Gulf War of 1991, and over a decade of sanctions, health indicators worsened. By July 2003, health outcomes were considered the worst in the region. As the World Bank and UNDP reported (2003: 16), "Maternal and infant mortality and malnutrition are high, certain communicable diseases have reemerged to join non-communicable conditions in a double burden of disease. Malaria, cholera, and leishmaniasis are endemic in several parts of the country." These trends were largely due to a failing health system and to a deterioration in the water and sanitation systems (21). In addition, in 2000, the Iraqi Planning Commission found that the food ration was inadequate to meet the nutrition needs of the general population (Hamzeh 2004: 35). Meanwhile, increasing numbers of Iraqi women reported suffering from anxiety, sleeplessness, and fear (35). Education also suffered under the effect of sanctions. During the

1990s, education enrollment rates fell. Girls in rural areas made up a disproportionate amount of this trend, with up to 50 percent not attending school (World Bank and UNDP 2003: 14). By the end of the 1990s, illiteracy rates among women aged fifteen through forty-nine were a staggering 55 percent (Al-Ali 2007: 192).

DEVELOPING IRAQI INSTITUTIONAL CAPACITY FOR RECONSTRUCTION

Following the invasion, Iraq was in dire need of rebuilding and humanitarian assistance. As in other cases around the world, donors initially looked to work with NGOs to implement reconstruction programs and projects and to provide humanitarian aid, reflecting commonly held beliefs that NGOs are the most efficient and effective way of reaching the grassroots of society to implement development programs. However, as Ruth G. at NDI told Nicola, "It hasn't been easy to find groups to give money to on the ground. They need a lot of capacity building in order to receive money." After years of dictatorship, independent organizations had been stamped out or forced underground. Johann D., based in Amman with a European NGO, differentiated between the experiences of Iraqi Kurdistan, which was autonomous between 1992 and 2003, and the rest of the country in this respect: "You see that in the north, they have much more experience and less need for capacity building. They do perfect project proposals. But, in the south, the proposals are very basic. In the north, they have between six and eight years of NGO experience."

In addition, donors had difficulties identifying NGOs in Iraq. Amal W., a member of an international NGO that works with Iraqi NGOs, told us: "Many NGOs operating in Iraq are not NGOs. They are businesses or political groups." This obviously encourages an intense focus on a small number of Iraqi groups and individuals known to donors. As Fares J. of CIPE pointed out: "Iraqi women are now in high demand by international donors. They are traveling a lot to different conferences and training sessions. But their capacity is low. They are still looking for an identity for their groups. IBWA wants to do social services, antiviolence campaigns. . . . Grants [from international donors] are available for all these things. This leads to groups splitting and new groups forming. This is the result of them being thrust into the limelight."

Johann D., the member of the European-based NGO who had been evacuated from Iraq in April 2004, was feeling quite dispirited in Amman when Nicola spoke to him in the spring of 2006: "Sometimes I ask whether things will develop or whether we [the international community] have spoilt civil society [in Iraq] forever." Indeed, some women activists, particularly in the diaspora, have been critical of the way the priorities of Iraqi women's organizations have been shaped by U.S. funding rather than the needs of ordinary Iraqi women and the way that women's organizations have been incorporated into the "soft occupation" of Iraq (Zangana 2006a, 2006b) and are helping to sustain a global neoliberal economic order (El-Kassem 2007; Mojab n.d.). From our research, we would agree that the U.S. administration seeks to shape Iraqi civil society organizations in support of its foreign policy objectives and that foreign funding has sometimes undermined the building of sustainable Iraqi organizations. Nevertheless, we have also found that women activists possess a range of attitudes toward foreign funding and that the impact of foreign funding is often complex, as we discuss in more detail in chapter 5.

State institutions have not been in much better shape than NGOs with regard to their ability to absorb reconstruction funds. According to Walid M. at the World Bank, who spoke to Nicola in Amman in June 2006, "Iraqi ministries are newly formed and there is new staff. Therefore, they lack the capacity for implementation." The inexperience of staff is, in large part, due to decisions taken soon after the invasion. When Bremer arrived in Baghdad in May 2003, one of the first actions that he took was the "de-Ba'thification" of Iraqi society—CPA Order No. 1—which states that "individuals holding positions in the top three layers of management in every national government ministry, affiliated corporations and other government institutions (e.g., universities and hospitals) shall be interviewed for possible affiliation with the Ba'ath Party, and subject to investigation for criminal conduct and risk to security. Any such persons determined to be full members of the Ba'ath Party shall be removed from their employment. This includes those holding the more junior ranks of 'Udw (Member) or 'Udw 'Amil (Active Member), as well as those determined to be Senior Party Members."[4] In promulgating this order, Bremer sought to dispel any influence of the Ba'th Party that had ruled Iraq for most of its postindependence history, with bloody and repressive consequences. Meanwhile, U.S. allies among the members of the political opposition returning from exile, such as Ahmed Chalabi, saw the de-Ba'thification order as a means of removing any potential political competitors from power (International Crisis Group 2006b: 9–10). However, this decision did much to undermine the rebuilding of state institutions after the fall of the Ba'th regime. The U.S. administration had not considered that Ba'th Party membership was almost compulsory for public sector workers, particularly at the management level, much as Communist Party membership had been compulsory in the former Soviet bloc. Overnight, the Iraqi public sector, already debilitated by years of sanctions and postinvasion looting chaos, lost almost all of its managerial cadres. This had negative consequences for the ability to rebuild basic services and infrastructure—such as the health care and education systems, water and electricity, and general security for Iraqi citizens (Herring and Rangwala 2006: 66–81).

The rebuilding of the Iraqi state, which should have been a priority in the immediate postinvasion period, was further undermined by the political process. At the national level, the first few years after the downfall of Saddam were punctuated by changes of personnel as Iraq shifted from one interim government to another. Silvia T., working in an international agency dedicated to child health in Iraq, told Nicola in the spring of 2006: "There is no sustainability because governments keep on changing. People are paralyzed and are not taking decisions because they know that there will be changes with the new government. The best people for the job are not taking up positions because they are waiting to see what positions they get offered in the new government. The time lines that have been imposed have encouraged short-termism. We asked ourselves whether we wanted to invest resources in the previous government because we knew that they wouldn't be there for long. However, we decided to go ahead anyway." In addition, in many cases, the political parties dominating national politics have used state institutions as a way of building up networks of patronage and nepotism rather than hiring the most competent people to implement much-needed reconstruction. Ann B., working for an international humanitarian agency, complained to Nicola in the spring of 2006: "One of the ministers doesn't have a clue. She is a political appointee. She is there because she is a member of a certain political party. She's hired her husband and her niece. This sort of cronyism is embedded within political institutions." Shereen W., an Iraqi diplomat, similarly told Nicola that "for women to get ahead in the Ministry of Foreign Affairs, they must be supported by a political party, even if they are very qualified. . . . All the current appointments are political. It shouldn't be like that, but it is."

THE BIGGEST CORRUPTION SCANDAL IN HISTORY

One of the concerns of donors is not only that state institutions lack the experience or resources to implement reconstruction but that there is a significant problem of corruption. Walid M. told Nicola that the World Bank in Iraq was "helping to build the capacity of national institutions, in particular, with respect to fiduciary aspects." Here *fiduciary aspects* refers to the mechanisms for accounting for government expenditures in a transparent way. A report by the international watchdog Transparency International, issued in 2005, claimed that Iraq could "become the biggest corruption scandal in history" (2005: 87). The corruption ranges from petty bribery of civil servants to the misuse of millions of dollars of reconstruction funds. Shereen W. told Nicola, "There was a lot of corruption under Saddam because salaries were very low. This encouraged corruption. Now there is a different type of corruption." Siham R., a women's rights activist in southern Iraq, concurred that corruption seems to have gotten worse since the invasion: "There was a black market under Saddam, but now it has gotten bigger because government officials are corrupt. They came from outside Iraq, and they want to make the maximum amount of money and then leave. They have no local links. Their families are not here. They are like migrant workers." Indeed, on a visit to Iraqi Kurdistan, the black market in oil seemed ubiquitous, with illegal stalls lining the main roads around towns and almost everyone reporting that they bought their gasoline on the black market rather than queuing for hours at gas stations. Nobody believed that this level of corruption could happen without official support.

Giving a testimony to the House Committee on the Judiciary on "war profiteering and other contractor crimes overseas," Stuart W. Bowen Jr., the U.S. Special Inspector General for Iraq Reconstruction, noted that the Commissioner of Public Integrity, an Iraqi office created by the CPA to increase accountability for public corruption in Iraq, had told him that he was investigating two thousand cases involving $5 billion in alleged corruption (U.S. House 2007: 2). While the loss of U.S. money to Iraq through fraud constitutes a small part of total U.S. funding, SIGIR still estimated it to be tens of millions of dollars. SIGIR auditors uncovered the "Bloom-Stein conspiracy" in al-Hilla, a city in central Iraq, engineered by Philip Bloom, the contractor, and Robert Stein, the CPA comptroller for that region; it involved kickbacks and bribery worth over $10 million in reconstruction funds. At the time of this writing, SIGIR had opened over three hundred cases and was pursuing over seventy investigations, while thirty-two cases were under prosecution at the Department of Justice (U.S. House 2007: 3–4).

One of the biggest scandals involving Iraqi reconstruction funds relates to the spending of the Development Fund for Iraq (DFI). The DFI was set up according to UN Security Council Resolution 1483, on May 22, 2003, to administer proceeds from the export sales of Iraq's oil, as well as funds remaining from the UN Oil-for-Food Programme and other assets seized from the defunct regime, in order to meet the humanitarian needs of the people of Iraq. The DFI was placed under the control of the CPA until the handover of power in June 2004. A report by the accountancy firm KPMG, which had been assigned to monitor the spending of DFI funds, found, among other irregularities, a number of discrepancies in the reporting of disbursements and evidence of contracts with no public tender. They were prevented from accessing the accounts of the Kurdistan Regional Government, which had received $1.4 billion of DFI funds in cash in April 2004 (KPMG Bahrain 2004). A SIGIR report found that "the CPA provided less than adequate controls for approximately $8.8 billion in DFI funds provided to Iraqi ministries. . . . Consequently, there was no assurance the funds were used for the purposes mandated by Resolution 1483" (SIGIR 2005: i).

There has also been criticism of the use of large U.S. contracting companies to undertake projects in the rehabilitation of essential services and infrastructure. Maysoon H., who worked in a hospital in Baghdad, angrily told Nadje: "Our engineers and architects could have helped to rebuild the hospital. They could have rebuilt bridges and get back the electricity in no time. We have done it before, after the Gulf War. Instead they brought these foreign contractors who don't know what they are doing, and they just put money in their pockets. The hospital I am working in was supposed to be renovated. We have not seen any improvements yet." In particular, a spotlight has been shone on Halliburton and Bechtel, both of whom were awarded multi-billion-dollar contracts to build schools and hospitals and repair essential services, such as water and electricity, and whose CEOs have close links to the U.S. administration (Chatterjee 2004).

Many people with whom we spoke believed that contractors wasted money. Valerie G., talking about reconstruction in Basra, told Nicola: "USAID relied on contractors and not NGOs for infrastructure rebuilding. The contractors typically have high-level security and live with the military. Therefore, they are outsiders to the community and not trusted, making them easy targets for violence. Iraqis link the contractors to the occupation. There is a lot of money spent on security." Jennifer L. didn't mince her words when discussing the work of one large contractor, responsible for building local governance capacity and ensuring women's participation, in the small town where she was posted: "I think they [the contractor employees] were appallingly bad. They caused problems. . . . They bought the most expensive real estate and behaved badly—drinking and getting prostitutes. They were getting high salaries. There were people working there who had no previous experience of working in the Middle East. They were naive. There was no oversight from Baghdad. Everyone complained about them. They were not implementing anything."

The use of "cost-plus" contracts, in which U.S. corporations have been reimbursed for all costs with an additional percentage added as profit, has provided an incentive for contractors to waste money rather than spend it efficiently (Chatterjee 2004: 34). Also, some contractors are known to have subcontracted to smaller companies, who charged less money for the job while the contracting company kept the difference (Transparency International 2005: 85–86).

Not only have significant amounts of reconstruction funds been "lost" or misused, but the CPA has been shockingly slow in administering funds. As mentioned above, the United States pledged more than $18 billion to Iraq in November 2003. Given that the joint World Bank and UNDP report at the end of the summer of 2003 had clearly indicated funding priorities, the United States should have been able to target reconstruction funds to meet urgent needs. But although the report identified a necessary $17.5 billion just to restore services and infrastructure to prewar levels, the United States only managed, as of September 30, 2004, to spend $5.2 billion (Office of the Inspector General, CPA 2004: 4). The record for the rest of the international community was no better, partly because of the security situation and partly because of lack of coordination (International Crisis Group 2004b: 24–26).

THE FAILURE OF RECONSTRUCTION

The slow pace of reconstruction has affected the provision of essential services. Lack of adequate electricity and water has been a burden to Iraqis, particularly women, who are generally responsible for the day-to-day survival of their families. When we visited Iraqi Kurdistan in spring 2007, four years after the fall of the regime, electricity was a major topic of conversation for women that we met. It is time-consuming and exhausting to negotiate the erratic electricity supply. At the time, Iraqis could expect about four to five hours of electricity a day through the national grid.[5] The remaining demand was met by a combination of neighborhood and private generators. This involved obtaining jerry cans of diesel to power private generators and/or negotiating with local entrepreneurs to hook up to a neighborhood generator. Sitting one evening in the garden of Jamelia R., a journalist and women's rights activist based in Kurdistan, Nicola remarked that the oil-burning lights were pretty. However, the pleasant ambience was quickly destroyed when Jamelia was forced to power up the rather noisy generator so she could recharge her mobile phone. The lack of electricity prevented many of the people we met in Iraq from carrying out activities that we otherwise take for granted. Jamelia complained to Nicola that she felt very frustrated. In the evenings, once the sun had gone down, she couldn't read a book or write an article. It was difficult to go out unaccompanied because the streets were so dark and she feared for her personal safety. And even if she could go out, there were practically no places for women to socialize in Kurdish towns.

Another obvious failure has been the rehabilitation of the health care system. Despite the dire need to rebuild the system after the war, as detailed in the World Bank and UNDP joint assessment (2003), less than $1 billion of U.S. funds has been allocated to the health sector. Moreover, by April 2007, fewer than half of the planned projects had been completed. In particular, progress has been slow in building primary health care centers, which are crucial for rural communities and especially for women. Indeed, the establishment of a primary health care system throughout neighboring Iran since the 1980s has managed to bridge the gap between the health of urban and rural residents in a cost-effective way (Mehryar et al. 2005). In Iraq, where maternal mortality rates have been increasing since the early 1990s, primary health care facilities could be effective in helping to protect mothers and prevent deaths. Yet of the 142 primary health care centers planned by USAID, only 15 had been built by April 2007 (SIGIR 2007b: 61–62). A similar story of failure is heard with regard to drinking water supplies and sewage disposal services (Herring and Rangwala 2006: 66–67). Before the invasion, 12.9 million Iraqis had access to drinking water. Three years after the war, only 9.7 million Iraqis enjoyed this basic right (O'Hanlon and Campbell 2007: 47).

Reconstruction has also failed to generate employment. It is extremely difficult to know exact figures, but the World Bank's most recent data put the figure of economic participation among the working age population as 49 percent (World Bank 2005). The Brookings Institute estimates unemployment figures falling from an initial rate of 50–60 percent in June 2003 to 25–40 percent in 2007 (O'Hanlon and Campbell 2007: 40), although anecdotal evidence would suggest that unemployment remains higher than this. The majority of the unemployed are women. This is often because men are hired over women in the competition for scarce jobs. In some cases, women are leaving their jobs because of the lack of security on the streets. However, in many cases women cannot afford the luxury of not working. Even professional women are taking jobs for which they are overqualified in order to earn much-needed income.

"In most cases, they seek work as housekeepers," says Mayada Zuhair, vice president of the Women's Rights Association of Iraq. "But you can also find doctors working as hairdressers, dentists working as chefs and engineers working in laundromats. They're desperate, and with poverty increasing, the situation could get much worse" (UN-OCHA 2006a). Some women are turning to sex work, a trend that was already apparent under sanctions but has not been reversed by the fall of the Ba'th regime. Najwa F. told Nadje during a visit to Amman in 2006: "It is so sad, but whether you are in Iraq itself or in neighboring Amman or Damascus, Iraqi women are now associated with prostitution. What kind of humiliation do we have to face just to be able to survive?"

Despite many recommendations to get Iraqis into work, employment creation was not a CPA priority (Center for Strategic and International Studies [CSIS] 2004: 46, 49)—unlike promoting a shift to a market-based economy and entrepreneurship. Unemployment in postinvasion Iraq was exacerbated by de-Ba'thification and the dissolution of the military, which, it is estimated, put 430,000 individuals out of work (Herring and Rangwala 2006: 73). The CPA's plans to privatize Iraqi public enterprises also threatened to greatly increase unemployment, since the public sector workforce would have been downsized to make companies more attractive to private buyers. In the face of opposition, Bremer backtracked on his initial privatization plans. Yet the specter of public sector job losses continues to loom, with specific repercussions for women. Mohammad F., an Iraqi doctor working for an NGO based in Amman, told Nicola in 2006:

> In Iraq, we have many women schoolteachers and many women working
> in government offices. Under the sanctions, the number of women in gov-
> ernment offices increased because men left to work in the private sector
> to make extra money. Women can take one year fully paid maternity leave,
> so it was easy for women to go to work. These laws are still in place, but
> the government says that it hasn't got the money to pay for these measures.
> They have taken soft loans from donors whose conditions include reform
> of the civil service and decrease in public spending. They are changing the
> pension laws to facilitate early retirement, and they are reducing paid mater-

nity leave. This will encourage women to leave the workplace. They think that they might as well take early retirement because of the risky security situation.

High unemployment and poverty in Iraq mean that families have to be inventive in securing their livelihoods. These coping strategies take different forms. As noted above, some people are forced to take jobs for which they are overqualified or jobs that are stigmatized by society. In other cases, children are taken out of schools and put to work in order to earn extra income for their families. Or young girls are married off at an early age to relieve their families of the financial burden of looking after them. Alia H. encountered such a fate and told Nadje sadly in June 2005, while drinking tea in her modest living room in a low-income neighborhood in Amman: "My parents agreed to my marriage when I was sixteen. I did not even know my husband. I did not like him when he came to visit to ask for my hand in marriage. But my parents were struggling to feed us all at home. I have five brothers and sisters. They wanted to make sure I have something to eat and somewhere to live."

Certainly women are working hard to make ends meet. Yet the opportunities available for supplementing low incomes, such as selling small items or homemade goods, are more and more rare because of the violence on the streets of most Iraqi towns and cities. Indeed, the majority (84.3 percent) of women in a sample interviewed in 2004 reported that they did not receive any financial compensation for their work (Women for Women International 2005: 17). With a significant number of women widowed, divorced, or abandoned because of wars, ongoing violence, and previous political repression, women-headed households made up 11 percent of all Iraqi households in 2004 (UNDP 2004). A UN World Food Programme survey ([UNWFP] 2004: 27) found that 27.8 percent of female-headed households were "extremely poor" compared to 13.4 percent of male-headed households.

Lack of employment opportunities has contributed to increasing support for religious groups and political parties at the expense of building trust in the newly emerging Iraqi state institutions. In the same 2004 survey that identified women's financial insecurity, 12.7 percent said that religious institutions had "done something in the past year to improve their lives," compared to only 5.5 percent of women who thought that the government had done so. Indeed, 16 percent of women said that "the government [had] done something to make their lives much worse over the past year," while only 8.4 percent of women "blamed worsened conditions on religious institutions" (Women for Women International 2005: 18). The high level of unemployment provides possibilities for new types of nepotism, as the political elite have become important gate-keepers for access to jobs via recommendation letters from political parties in power (Rangwala 2005: 174–75).

"The humanitarian situation is at the core of the problems in Iraq," Shirouk Alabyachi, a women's rights activist based in Baghdad, told a meeting in the British city of Norwich. High unemployment and poor basic services since the toppling of the Saddam regime have meant that the United States and its allies have had a hard time winning the "hearts and minds" of Iraqi men and women. Aysha J., working for an international agency concerned with child welfare in Iraq, told Nicola in the spring of 2006: "People are shifting their opinions toward the U.S. In the beginning, they were very happy that the U.S. got rid of Saddam. But now they do not see any benefits from this. Things are not improving."

Several women complained to us that the United States had made "too many mistakes" in Iraq. These mistakes were not only costing the Americans support among ordinary Iraqis but also helping to fuel the violence. A 2004 report by the International Crisis Group argues (2004b: i), "Economic hardship and violence (political and criminal) feed on each other: heightened popular dissatisfaction and unemployment swell insurgent ranks and the growing insurgency further hampers development." Deprived of conventional pathways for becoming the family breadwinner, some men with limited employment prospects have turned to militias, insurgent groups, or criminal gangs as a means of earning money and also restoring their dignity in the face of the humiliations suffered under occupation. The poor neighborhood of Sadr City, where unemployment is particularly high, is a stronghold of Muqtada al-Sadr, whose militant anti-U.S. views mobilize many young men to join the Mahdi Army.

DETERIORATING SECURITY

While the slow pace of reconstruction is having a negative effect on the humanitarian situation, the deteriorating security situation is similarly having a negative impact on reconstruction. Because of the security situation, many contractors have pulled out of work in Iraq and many funds originally earmarked for infrastructure building have been shifted to security (Richter 2004). Angela M., a diplomat shuttling between Amman and the Green Zone, told Nicola:

Well, one particular donor allocates 30 percent of project costs to security. However, many Iraqis say that in practice, when you read carefully, this ends up being 50 percent of funds being spent on security. You have to weigh up the costs of being based in Amman and bringing people from Iraq here or being based in Iraq and the security costs that that entails. For example, even to have one person in Baghdad overseeing the disbursement of grants is very expensive. The Brits charge $30,000 per month to stay in the British compound in the IZ [International, or Green, Zone]. Most internationals get extra financial incentives to be in Iraq. So that's an added cost too.

By early spring of 2005, almost all international agencies and organizations reported difficulties working inside Iraq because of the terrible security situation. Almost all international agencies evacuated their international staff from Iraq after April 2004, when the United States and its allies were facing attacks from the Mahdi Army in the south and from the insurgency around Baghdad and in the so-called Sunni Triangle. However, the problem was not only the growing violence against the occupation troops but also the high level of criminality, such as kidnappings and killings. Most foreign personnel relocated to Amman were implementing "remote management" of continuing programs inside Iraq. These programs were mostly staffed by Iraqis. A few international organizations had relocated to Iraqi Kurdistan. In Iraq, unlike other countries, foreign and international organizations did not identify themselves publicly by putting their logos on their vehicles, on their literature, or outside their offices. Meanwhile, Iraqi staff in these organizations were obliged to keep their employment secret by not taking anything work related home. Fatima Z., remotely managing programs from an office in Amman, told Nicola: "In the last workshop we held in Amman, two people didn't come because one of them, his brother was killed, and the other person, a relative was seriously injured. This is affecting people on a personal level. It is not just something on the news. The head of one of our partner NGOs is in hiding, and the family of the head of another of them has been displaced. Things are worse than before. The employees of one of our NGOs have not been able to leave the house for fifteen days."

The dire security situation has not only hampered the work of international agencies. More significantly, it has had a tragic effect on the Iraqi population, resulting in high numbers of dead, injured, and traumatized men, women, and children. Reliable figures are difficult to find since no one body is responsible for keeping count. Conservative estimates at the end of August 2007 were between 70,749 and 77,272 Iraqis dead as a result of military, paramilitary, and criminal actions since the invasion

(Iraq Body Count 2007), more than double the number estimated in December 2005.[6] Other statistics are much higher and range in the hundreds of thousands. (See, e.g., the Burnham et al. 2006 *Lancet* report, which estimated that 655,000 Iraqis had died since 2003.) Reporting in spring 2006, the Iraqi Ministry of Health declared that one child in ten suffers from chronic disease or illness and that 50 percent of children are malnourished. A survey by the Association of Psychologists of Iraq that year found that 92 percent of children had learning impediments, largely as a result of the insecurity and fear in which they were living (cited in Reif 2006). One gynecologist in a Baghdad maternity hospital reckoned that "for at least two women in every 12 who seek emergency delivery assistance here, either the mother or her child dies," largely because of the difficulties of accessing hospitals or midwifery services (UN-OCHA 2007).

While men constitute the majority of victims of violence, the lack of security affects women in particular ways. Layla A., working with an international agency providing humanitarian assistance to Iraq, told Nicola in the spring of 2006:

> Women are afraid of raising their voices because of fear. Because of the security situation, women are prevented from leaving the home to get educated or go out to work. Women are targeted through abductions, and there are cases of women being sold into sex trafficking. Women are threatened in universities for not wearing the headscarf. You see slogans on the walls telling women to wear the *hijab*. Women are being attacked and killed. Domestic violence has increased and honor killing has increased because it is easier to get away with it now. Death is an everyday occurrence, so it is easy to hide honor killings. Early marriages have increased. Women detainees are tortured and subject to sexual abuse. . . . Families are afraid, and as a result society has become more conservative. Women's mobility is constrained. If they leave the house, they must wear the veil.[7]

One illustration of how violence has prevented women's participation in the rebuilding of Iraq is the fate of the women's centers, funded by the United States as places where women could get the training and information they needed to become economically active. Alia T., based in Baghdad until March 2006 with an international NGO working on women in conflict zones, told Nicola: "We got a building from the CPA for a woman's center. It was burnt out and we did it up. Then the Ministry of Finance took it off us. I don't blame them. After that, we didn't go through with the women's center idea. This was because of the security situation and also because of the experience of women's centers in the south. There was no budget for maintenance or training. It was just the building and hardware. So it wasn't sustainable. These were just what I call 'Kodak moments.'" Ziba H., sent to Iraq by the U.K. government between September 2003 and April 2004, was also critical of the women's centers: "There was no ownership over these centers in the local communities. They would be suspicious of the centers—What are they for? What are our women doing there? There was a flawed consultation process. After Fern Holland [an American woman, working with the CPA, who had been involved in opening women's centers in the south-central region of Iraq] was assassinated, people were scared to go to the centers and they failed. I strongly advised DFID not to support the centers."[8]

VIOLENCE AGAINST WOMEN

Yet although violence was keeping many women from being full participants in the rebuilding of Iraq, dealing with the causes of violence against women was not a priority. In the early days after the fall of the Saddam regime, the United States and its allies failed to act quickly to provide adequate security, even though the Geneva Conventions hold occupying powers responsible for the security of the country they occupy. At a seminar organized by USIP on April 16, 2003, to discuss immediate postinvasion needs, experts stated that public security was an immediate priority (USIP 2003). Prewar planning was inadequate for establishing the sort of mechanisms necessary for ensuring security, since the U.S. administration had assumed that Iraqi institutions would remain more or less intact following regime change (Rand Corporation 2005: 11). As lawlessness broke out, images were broadcast of U.S. soldiers standing by as people looted public buildings. Salwa H., a medical doctor to whom Nadje talked in 2006, was in tears as she recalled the following incident:

> I saw soldiers laughing and encouraging a group of young men who looted a hospital. They were just standing there and grinning, making jokes about Ali Baba. It was so humiliating. I shouted at the soldiers asking them to help. I told them that under international law they must keep things under control. But they said they had orders not to intervene. I was so angry and cried when I saw the thieves going off with hospital beds. That afternoon, two U.S. soldiers could have easily prevented this happening. But they did not care. They only protected the Ministry of Oil and the Ministry of Interior. (Al-Ali 2007: 223)

The lack of security was exacerbated by the dissolution of the police force and the military. Recruitment and training for a new police force have been slow (Cordesman 2004) and beset with difficulties of sectarianism. In this context, Layla A. told Nicola, "Some people are saying that it was better under Saddam because there was greater safety and security. You knew you would be okay so long as you didn't oppose Saddam. Now you have a hundred Saddams. . . . There is extreme lawlessness."

When Nicola questioned a U.S. official about the responsibility of the United States for preventing violence against women, she was told: "Iraqi families dealt with violence against women in their own way—by keeping their women at home. This was the best way for them to deal with it. What could we do? Send an armed guard to escort every woman? This is not possible. Our responsibility was for general security of the whole population and not toward specific groups. Anyway, I don't think women were more targeted than any other group within Iraq. Violence against women increased in proportion to the violence in general. There is no evidence that they were specifically targeted." But a few blocks away from the White House, Nicola heard a different story from Valerie G., who described the situation for her colleagues in Basra: "The Mahdi Army monitors women's behavior and harasses them. The mosques are calling for women to cover up. Our women staff are furious. The Mahdi Army is policing public behavior, and people are not happy. Female staff are being threatened. . . . Nobody is dealing with the violence on the street of the Mahdi Army." Siham R., located in a southern Iraqi town that has experienced significant fighting between different Islamist factions, also told Nicola: "The coalition forces have not bothered to arrest or monitor these people. Even when we told them the names of people who are terrorists, they did nothing." Valerie G. and Siham R.'s comments suggest a continuum of violence between the verbal harassment of women in public places and physical violence against women. The attitude of U.S. officials has been to ignore this continuum of violence and to focus only on the violence directed against the coalition troops—that is, for the most part, the insurgency. Alia T. told Nicola that the violence against women "was dismissed as 'women's affairs' and no one wanted to talk about it."

Contrary to the apparent attitudes of U.S. officials, however, the violence against women reported in the early days of the occupation was both an early warning sign and an integral part of the increasing violence and criminality that were flourishing in the lawlessness of post–Saddam Hussein Iraq. Iraqi police testified that "some gangs specialize in kidnapping girls, they sell them to Gulf countries" (Rosen 2006). As the feminist international relations scholar Spike Peterson argues (2007: 26–27), the trafficking of women is integral to the political economy of war zones. It "simultaneously 'satisfies' male desire for access to women's bodies in the combat economy (occupying forces as well as Iraqis) and provides illicit profits for pimps and traffickers in the criminal economy."

Meanwhile, the targeting of women also plays an important role in transforming predominant notions about women's roles in society and relations between men and women. The harassment of women on the streets, death threats against professional women, the enforcement of the *hijab* upon female employees—in other words, the monitoring and regulation of women's dress and behavior—are all integral to the construction of new notions about women and gender relations. In addition, this sort of targeting of women is an important way in which Islamist groups attempt to enforce their authority in particular locations. In effect, women are symbolic markers of the break from the nominally secular Saddam Hussein regime and a means of differentiating Iraqi society from the "foreign culture" of the United States and its allies. The violence against women is essential in enforcing this new gender ideology, which is also propagated by politicians and mosque imams. Sheikh Salah Muzidin, an imam at a mosque in Baghdad, was reported as saying, "These incidents of abuse just prove what we have been saying for so long. That it is the Islamic duty of women to stay in their homes, looking after their children and husbands rather than searching for work" (Rosen 2006).

NEOCONSERVATISM, WOMEN'S EMPOWERMENT, AND GENDER MAINSTREAMING

For the U.S. officials to whom we spoke, Iraqi women were simultaneously the victims of the Saddam regime who needed to be saved, the heroines who would "give birth" to the new Iraq, and the objects of U.S.-funded training to fulfill their assumed new roles. Ironically, rather than bringing Iraqi women into the reconstruction process, U.S. policies have forced the majority of women back into the home and have increased their daily burden of ensuring their family's day-to-day survival. For people working in international agencies and NGOs, Iraqi women represent the moderating influences in the reconstruction process—an idea that in some ways reiterates long-standing assumptions about women's nature. For political forces inside Iraq, women are the symbols of post-Ba'th Iraq and its "Islamic" nature.

These different perceptions of women and their roles in the new Iraq have put women center stage, but this has not resulted in an improvement in their welfare or the welfare of their families. Despite talking about Iraqi women, the United States, its allies, and the international community in general failed to allocate sufficient resources and expertise in the immediate aftermath of the fall of the Saddam Hussein regime in order to address women's needs. Denise W., who was sent to Baghdad soon after the invasion, told Nicola, "I think the CPA was actually very quick off the mark to *consider* gender issues. The problem was it was very slow and bureaucratic about supporting gender issues materially." Rachel F., working for a development agency, told Nicola, "I was employed in August 2004 [i.e., sixteen months after the fall of the Ba'th regime] . . . to develop a [gender] strategy. But when I started working, I realized it was too late for a strategy because there was already work being implemented. Instead, I looked at the current programs and tweaked them to make them more gender-sensitive." There also seems to have been some confusion over how to translate the apparent official commitment to Iraqi women into practice on the ground. Jennifer L., a well-established U.S. diplomat with several years of Middle East experience who was sent to an Iraqi province from May 2003 until June 2004, found that "it was not self-evident how to go about promoting women's participation." Shelley B., who worked in Iraq throughout 2004 with USAID, the CPA, and then the U.S. Embassy, told Nicola, "There was no guidance from Washington on the policy for women. My old boss feels that women's issues get short shrift." Meanwhile, Ziba H. was quite cynical about the seriousness of her U.S. counterparts with regard to empowering women. "My U.S. colleagues had no experience of gender or development. All they were doing was to bring a handful of 'Westernized' Iraqi women to meet Bremer on a regular basis. . . . At these meetings, nothing was ever discussed. The women would make small speeches about what was happening and praise Bremer. Bremer would listen and leave."

If women's needs had been effectively addressed in the early days of the occupation, not only women but men too would have benefited. Attention to the basic needs of Iraqi women would have prioritized the rapid rehabilitation of education, health care, water and electricity, the generation of employment, and, most significantly, the effective maintenance of law and order. In other words, what's good for women is also good for men.

The failure to invest in reconstruction and effective general security at an early stage helped to create the conditions for the reconstruction of a "hyperpatriarchy." While Saddam Hussein was no champion of women's rights (or of anybody's rights), despite his early policies of inclusion in the context of economic expansion in the 1970s, the post-invasion situation has created new and even more devastating forms of oppression for women by a range of social and political actors. The deterioration in the provision of basic services and infrastructure has not only increased women's burden with regard to domestic duties but helped to fuel the violence and criminality that is preventing women from participating in public life. Simultaneously, the negative situation for women is being rationalized in the form of new conservative social attitudes propagated by Islamist parties. The Islamists have made political gains because of the situation on the ground. Alia T. told Nicola, "People are turning to the Islamists because they don't have other options. The international community failed to provide other options."

The problem is not only the failure to ensure that resources were deployed sufficiently early or one of poor planning and decision making. The problem is also the way in which the notion of women's empowerment is being promoted. The political discourses of neoconservatives and of political actors within Iraq, as well as the spread of new international norms about women's empowerment, are intersecting in ways that help to reconstruct patriarchy in post–Saddam Hussein Iraq.

As we have argued elsewhere (Al-Ali and Pratt 2008), by speaking publicly about the abuse of Iraqi women under Saddam Hussein, U.S. officials implicitly provided a justification for U.S. military intervention in Iraq. The use of women to justify foreign interventions is not new. From Algeria to India, European colonial administrations saw fit to ban or openly criticize a number of practices that they regarded as harmful to women, from the wearing of the veil to widow burning (or suttee). The postcolonial critic Gayatri Spivak has described this process as "white men saving brown women from brown men" (1988: 93). More recently, many commentators and writers have noted how the Bush administration focused on the abuse of Afghan women under the Taliban regime to implicitly justify the invasion of that country in 2001 (Raha 2004: 177–80; Charlesworth and Chinkin 2002: 600–605).

However, this focus on saving women in non-Western countries from the barbaric practices of "their" men employs two long-standing tropes in the history of colonial/imperial domination: the protection scenario and Orientalism (Stabile and Kumar 2005: 769). The "protection scenario" refers to men rescuing women from danger. This is a common trope in various genres of Western popular culture—from fairy tales to romantic novels to action films—and is often invoked in attempts to persuade men to go to war. Meanwhile, Orientalist scholarship, as Edward Said (1978) argued, portrays men in colonized countries as despotic, barbaric, morally degenerate, and oversexed, and women as oppressed and passive victims. This helps to justify the need for colonial rule.

"White men saving brown women from brown men" is not necessarily rooted in concerns about women living in oppressive conditions. It is about white men's masculinity and the need to assert that masculinity over other men. In the wake of the devastating attacks of 9/11, commentators observed how the United States (its news media, popular culture, and political discourse) became concerned with projecting images of U.S. masculinity at home (e.g., portrayals of brave male firefighters) (Sturken 2002). These images were intertwined with official discourse that paved the way for the attacks on Afghanistan and Iraq as a means of "remasculinizing" U.S. international identity (Shepherd 2006; Wadley 2006). By highlighting the plight of female victims in faraway lands, U.S. officials not only provided a pretext for military invasion but also restored the image of the United States as the strong hero rather than the victim of terrorist attacks. This was an important message to send to its enemies as well as its allies.

Simultaneously, U.S. administration efforts to "save women" in Iraq (and, previously, in Afghanistan) also appear to reflect emerging international norms surrounding women's role in peace and security. In 2000, the UN Security Council passed Resolution 1325, which recognized not only women's particular needs as victims of conflict but also their role in the prevention and resolution of conflicts. The resolution was passed largely as a result of the efforts of transnational women's networks, led primarily by the Women's International League for Peace and Freedom, as well as a growing body of scholarship identifying the particular ways in which women are affected by war.

The call by activists to recognize women not only as victims but also as active participants in peace building has been appropriated by the U.S. administration. The U.S. military invasion of Iraq not only purported to "save" Iraqi women, who had been long-suffering victims of the Saddam Hussein regime, but transformed them from victims to heroines. Following the invasion, Paul Wolfowitz, then U.S. deputy secretary of defense, wrote that Iraqi women were "helping give birth to freedom" in the post-Saddam order (Wolfowitz 2004). The image of the heroic Iraqi woman appeared with regularity in the media (e.g., holding a purple-colored finger during the coverage of the first elections) to embody the U.S. administration's attempts to build a new Iraq. In the 2005 State of the Union address, Safia al-Suhail, an Iraqi woman activist, stood in the gallery with Laura Bush as the president honored her for being one of Iraq's "leading democracy and human rights advocates" (Bush 2005). For supporters of the administration, Safia al-Suhail represented "the courage and determination of Middle Easterners, and in particular Middle Eastern women, to build free and just societies" (Gordan 2005).

It is not only in relation to Iraq that the U.S. administration appears to be championing women. According to the director of the Office for International Women's Affairs, "Secretary [Condoleezza] Rice believes in the empowerment agenda—not seeing women as victims but as agents of change." This commitment to women's empowerment is also represented in the U.S. administration by Undersecretary of State Paula Dobriansky, who was a signatory to the neoconservative Project for the New American Century. This (neo)conservative "feminism" is also embodied in the IWF, one of the recipients of the Women's Democracy Initiative grant. The IWF is a nonpartisan, nonprofit, U.S. NGO that "fosters greater respect for limited government, equality under the law, property rights, free markets, strong families, and a powerful and effective national defense and foreign policy" (IWF 2006). In other words, for (neo)conservatives, the prowoman rhetoric represents the restructuring of gender relations in support of their other policy goals—neoliberal economies and the protection of U.S. national security interests. Ironically, the neoconservative "feminists" recognize what liberals have chosen to ignore but (socialist) feminists (on the basis of the writings of Friedrich Engels) have long argued: that the family is essential for the functioning of capitalism and the existence of a strong state (Engels 1972). Yet while the vast majority of feminists have argued that the role played by the institution of the family in maintaining capitalism and strong states contributes to unequal gender relations, the neoconservative feminists argue that women's role in the reproduction of the status quo empowers them and that consequently this role should be embraced. Despite the apparent contradictions—from a feminist point of view—between women's empowerment, free markets, strong families, and strong national defense, this ideology has strong appeal for those seeking greater participation for women because of its refusal to see women as victims.[9]

On the ground in Iraq, however, the Bush administration's "empowerment agenda" has done little to empower women. The rhetoric of women's empowerment is instrumentalized by the administration for its own foreign policy ends. The apparent acknowledgment of Iraqi women's active role has been restricted to that of symbols of a new post–Saddam Hussein order that is congruent with U.S. foreign policy interests.

Feminist scholar Cynthia Enloe (2001) instructs us to always ask, "Where are the women?" in international politics. In examining the impact of the policies of the United States and other international actors in terms of reconstructing Iraq, we found lots of talk about women. The United States partly justified its invasion of Iraq by calling attention to the abuse of women by the Saddam regime. International agencies and NGOs received money (mostly from the United States) to train women to enable their participation in peace building, reconstruction, and the transition to democracy.

But while the rhetoric of the United States and others within the international community hailed women as the heroines of the new Iraq, the reality on the ground is that women's needs have not been met. There has been a failure to allocate money and expertise sufficiently early to rehabilitate basic services, generate much-needed jobs, and guarantee security. The reconstruction process has undermined capacity building within Iraqi institutions and has enabled the spread of corruption. Meanwhile, the failure of the reconstruction process has fueled violence, the spread of conservative social agendas, and the rise of Islamist parties— all with negative consequences for women.

The gap between rhetoric and reality undermines the notion that the United States is committed to empowering Iraqi women. Indeed, our analysis suggests that the rhetoric was not really about empowering Iraqi women. Instead, Iraqi women represented the objects of a U.S. mission to restore its seriously tarnished superpower identity in the wake of 9/11. The postinvasion reconstruction process has been framed by the trope of "white men saving brown women from brown men," and this rhetoric has shaped the decisions that have shaped the reality of women's lives in Iraq. Given that the priority of the invasion was U.S. national security, it is unsurprising that the security of ordinary Iraqis was an afterthought. The prioritization of U.S. security concerns has undermined not only the reconstruction process but also the political process, as the next chapter explores.

THREE

ENGENDERING THE NEW IRAQI STATE

"Women entered a lot of professions under Saddam. However, they did not hold key positions. Under the sanctions, laws were introduced that were against women. With the fall of Saddam, women can now occupy high positions. However, the violence against women is a problem," Mishkat Moumin, one of five women ministers in the outgoing government of Iyad Allawi, told Nicola in February 2005. Despite the ever-increasing violence, the first free elections of the new Iraq had been held a couple of weeks before this conversation, on January 30, 2005. They represented an important milestone for millions of Iraqis, as well as for the U.S. and U.K. governments, in the transition from brutal dictatorship to supposed freedom and democracy. Although there are no gender-disaggregated data, many people told us that women turned out in huge numbers to vote, while women candidates won 31 percent of seats in the TNA—a level of participation in a national legislature for which women in the United States and United Kingdom still strive.[1]

The significant presence of women in the political process and newly emerging political structures appeared to vindicate the efforts of the United States and other international actors to ensure women's participation in the political transition, as well as the hard work of the new Iraqi women's movement to put women's political participation on the agenda. It also represented a significant reversal of fortunes for Iraqi women, who had been practically absent in the official political arena in the first year following the invasion. Yet despite the substantial numbers of women elected to the TNA and later the Council of Representatives, this chapter demonstrates how women have become largely marginalized within emerging political institutions and how women's rights have been eroded. This has taken place as a result of the rise of sectarian and ethnic-based political parties on the national level, together with the often violent fragmentation of political authority throughout Iraq, both of which trends have resulted from the U.S.-led occupation.

GOVERNING IRAQ AFTER SADDAM HUSSEIN

Mary E., who was sent to work with the Office for Reconstruction and Humanitarian Assistance (ORHA) in February 2003, recalled: "I spent the war in Kuwait City. I drove to Baghdad with the military and arrived on April 14. I was the first civilian to arrive with the U.S. . . . People came onto the streets to see us arriving. They looked stunned. The first thing we did was to find the ministries and find people to work with. We set up a humanitarian assistance center." ORHA was established by the United States in the run-up to the invasion to manage an expected postwar humanitarian crisis and was led by a retired army general, Jay Garner. Mary E. went on to tell Nicola, "In May, Jay suddenly left and Bremer arrived. It was a shock. Jay had wanted to get an Iraqi government in place. Bremer started by introducing de-Ba'thification. He disbanded the army and delayed forming a government. It was very different from what had been planned."

The replacement of Garner with Bremer reflected a growing recognition by the U.S. administration that installing a new government in Baghdad would prove to be more politically complex than originally anticipated. The United States was seeking to gain control over an increasingly anarchic postinvasion situation. Iraqi state institutions, which were already extremely weak following years of sanctions, were in complete disarray because of looting and insecurity. Meanwhile, various political, religious, and tribal groupings, as well as local militias, were independently taking control of towns throughout Iraq (J. Cole 2003).

Attempts by Jay Garner to establish a legitimate Iraqi government to replace the Ba'th regime proved to be difficult. Only eighty delegates, many of whom had only recently returned from exile (Dodge 2005: 32), attended a conference organized by the United States in the southern Iraqi town of Nasiriyya, on April 15, 2003. Meanwhile, allegedly thousands, led by the Shi'i Islamist Da'wa Party, protested outside the conference, claiming that the conference participants did not represent them (J. Cole

2003). The Nasiriyya conference was followed by another meeting in Baghdad in early May. While this one attracted greater Iraqi attendance, it still failed to meet the expectations of the coalition with regard to forming a government (Steele 2003).

From reports it was clear that the previously exiled parties brought into Iraq by the United States were far from popular with large sectors of the Iraqi population (Salbi 2003; Melia and Katulis 2003). All these parties were united in their opposition to the Ba'th regime of Saddam Hussein, but they differed in their religious or ethnic bases. They were the secular-oriented Iraqi National Congress (INC), led by Ahmed Chalabi; the secular-oriented Iraqi National Accord (NA), founded by the CIA in 1992, composed predominantly of ex-Ba'thists and military offi - cers and headed by Iyad Allawi; the two Kurdish nationalist (and secular) parties—the KDP and the PUK—that had been running the Kurdistan area in northern Iraq since 1992; and the Supreme Council for the Islamic Revolution in Iraq (SCIRI), an Islamist Shi'i party founded in 1982 during the Iran-Iraq War and funded by Iran. Another important opposition party that quickly gained influence in post-Ba'th Iraq was the Da'wa Party, an Islamist Shi'i party that had been founded in the late 1950s.

As the United States attempted to install some form of Iraqi government, it was clear that ensuring women's participation in it was not a major consideration for the U.S. occupation. The Da'wa Party and its supporters were not the only ones to protest about the big tent meeting in Nasiriyya. Many women were also frustrated that they were not adequately represented at the meeting. Reports suggest that between one and six women were invited.[2] Shatha Besarani, a founding member of Iraqi Women for Peace and Democracy, expressed her deep frustration about the lack of transparency surrounding the organization of the meeting: "This is a very undemocratic meeting in Nasiriyya. It is called by the Americans and [Ahmed] Chalabi. Who are the women attending this meeting? Is this the good democracy that they are promising us?" (Abdela et al. 2003).[3]

Specialists in gender and postconflict reconstruction emphasize the need to include women in decision-making arenas from the beginning of the postconflict phase in order to ensure their inclusion over the long term (see, e.g., Anderlini 2000). UN Security Council Resolution 1325 on Women, Peace, and Security, which was passed in 2000 following extensive lobbying by women's movements internationally, states that the international community is responsible for increasing women's participation in decision-making bodies for peace-building processes. Joan Ruddock, a U.K. member of parliament who lobbied to ensure women's participation in postconflict reconstruction in Afghanistan, told Nicola, "In postconflict, the focus is always on men who have carried arms, and these are the ones that grab power. You cannot build a peaceful and sustainable society without the involvement of women. . . . Women's voices need to be heard in peace negotiations. You have to build institutions to ensure women's access." As we discussed in chapter 1, we do not agree that women are inherent peace builders. Nevertheless, it is a matter of equity that women (who are, after all, half the population) should have access to national institutions shaping the future of their country.

Iraqi women were not only excluded from postconflict political processes by the occupation authorities but disadvantaged by the lack of independent women's organizations inside Iraq before the invasion, which could have played a role in pressuring for women's inclusion in the big tent meetings in April and May. In the diaspora, Iraqi women and men have organized, as we discuss in the next chapter, but within the exiled groups and parties that supported the war, women were marginalized, as Nadia S., a women's rights activist who had been part of the Kurdish opposition in exile, explained to Nicola: "Before the war, I became involved in establishing Women for a Free Iraq. This was primarily a media campaign highlighting human rights abuses under Saddam Hussein. We were a multiethnic and multireligious group. We felt that women's voices were lacking in the discussions about Iraq before the war. We wanted our voices to be heard. . . . The Iraqi opposition didn't take us seriously. They thought our campaign was useful for their objectives. But they didn't give us any real support. Our campaign was not a priority for them." Similarly, at a conference of the Iraqi opposition in exile, held in London in 2002 to unite in preparation for a political takeover in Baghdad (P. Cockburn 2002a, 2002b), apparently only five women (out of three hundred delegates) were invited and only three out of sixty-five were members of the follow-up committee.

For many women activists it was shocking that U.S. and U.K. officials, despite their rhetoric before the war about supporting women's rights and their apparent concern to listen to the voices of women like Nadia, were now failing to include women in the political process. Given women's marginalization within the opposition in exile and the absence of independent women's organizations inside Iraq before the fall of the Ba'th regime, it was especially crucial to try to include women in emerging political structures from the start.

Instead, the U.S.-appointed head of the CPA, Paul Bremer, was concerned about governing Iraq by maintaining a balance of power between the United States and the Iraqi political parties to keep any one particular party—particularly one of the Islamist parties—from taking control (Herring and Rangwala 2006: 13–19). This meant putting a brake on the process started by Jay Garner to establish an Iraqi government, much to the frustration of the Iraqi political parties. Nevertheless, in the end, Bremer was persuaded by the UN special representative for Iraq, Sergio Vieira de Mello—before his death, along with twenty-one of his colleagues, in the bombing of the UN Baghdad headquarters in August 2003—to establish a governing council of Iraqis (Dodge 2005: 33).

THE IRAQI GOVERNING COUNCIL:
JULY 2003–JUNE 2004

In July 2003, the IGC was formed as an advisory body to the CPA following intense negotiations between Bremer and the principal Iraqi political parties (Tyler 2003). The twenty-five-member council was largely selected from members of the opposition in exile and was dominated by the two Shi'i Islamist parties (Da'wa and SCIRI), the two Kurdish nationalist parties (PUK and KDP), and the two secular-oriented U.S. allies (the INC and the INA). The United States hoped that these political leaders would provide the occupation with greater legitimacy, while providing time for U.S.-favored (secular) politicians to gain greater currency with the Iraqi population. The representative character of the council was deemed to lie in its sectarian balance, supposedly reflecting the balance of different religious and ethnic groupings inside Iraq (Dodge 2005: 33). The council was made up of twelve Shi'i, five Sunnis, five Kurds, a Turkmen, and a Christian. At the time, observers criticized the "external sectarian and ethnic-based engineering of Iraq's first post-war governing structure" and argued that Bremer had "started Iraq on the road to Lebanonization" (Alkadiri and Toensing 2003)—referring to the way sectarian quotas are institutionalized throughout Lebanon's political system, thereby dominating political interactions. In retrospect, the creation of the IGC did indeed start Iraq upon a path of de facto Lebanonization. In addition, it empowered the sectarian and ethnic-based political parties in national politics, with particularly negative consequences for women's inclusion in the political process as well as the safeguarding of their rights.

Despite the introduction of ethnic and sectarian quotas for the IGC, Bremer refused to introduce a gender quota for the council. Jessica K., a former minister of state in the U.K. government, told Nicola, "After the main fighting ended, the thoughts were to bring women into the political process. Patricia Hewitt [U.K. secretary of state for trade and industry and minister for women, 2001-5] was responsible for this. But the U.S. was skeptical about it. They thought it was a nice idea, but it wasn't a priority for them." Ziba H., a U.K.-based gender consultant who had arrived in Iraq in September 2003, told Nicola: "By then, the IGC had already been selected. It was very disappointing. Despite all the lobbying by the U.K. government, Iraqi women, and even Judy Van Rest [the CPA women's affairs officer], there were only three women appointed to the IGC, and only one of them really had any experience of governance." Negotiations to create the IGC were conducted behind closed doors between the CPA, the major Iraqi political actors, and the United Nations. The United States was keen to include the major political allies at all costs, and this meant giving them a veto over the overall composition of the council (Tyler 2003). Another principle was that the council would include "the broadest possible representation of ethnic and religious social categories" (International Crisis Group 2003: 12). According to Ziba:

> The U.S. asked all known tribal and political leaders to suggest people. . . . When the nominations came in, there were no women nominated, not even from amongst the Kurds. The CPA tried to find some women, but they did a botched job of it. . . . They couldn't find suitable women despite the fact that seventy women had attended the July conference ["The Voice of Women of Iraq"]! They found three women. One had experience, and she was soon assassinated. One was a gynecologist and one an engineer. The latter two had no experience. . . . They said that they weren't even briefed as to what they would be doing.[4]

Nadra B., who had fled Saddam's gas attacks on her village at the end of the 1980s and had eventually ended up in Washington, where she was involved in advocating Iraqi women's rights, was also critical of the women appointed to the IGC: "They were not qualified. There are rumors that Bremer appointed them because they were 'yes' women."

It is perhaps indicative of the difficulties that women face in political participation that these women were so criticized and discredited—even by other women. After all, what made them any less "qualified" than their male counterparts on the council? At least they had been living in Iraq throughout the previous decades and were familiar with the problems faced by people there. More telling than their lack of experience or qualifications is perhaps the fact that the women chosen lacked links to political parties or other resources that could have been converted into "political capital" (Enloe 2004: 291–92). Without political backing or experience, these women were vulnerable and isolated: one of them, Aqila al-Hashimi, was assassinated only two months into the job. They struggled to make their voices heard within the IGC. Female IGC member Raja al-Khuzai complained, "It's hard. They don't respect women. They don't listen to women" (Daragahi 2003). She said that she had almost resigned.

The sectarian and ethnic quotas devised by Bremer clearly operated to exclude women in selecting the IGC members. Suzan R., an Iraqi-Kurdish women's rights activist who had returned to Iraq in May 2003 and was part of the organizing committee for the first postinvasion women's conference in July 2003, told Nicola: "The CPA was trying to put us [women] in the picture. But the Iraqi male leaders were not ready to have us in the picture. They thought that there was no place for women in the transition because this was a difficult period. The CPA wanted me to be part of the IGC as a Kurd, but the Kurdish leadership would not agree because they only had five places and they did not want to give one to a woman." The women who were chosen to sit on the IGC were selected for their religious and ethnic identity (Shi'i-Arab), suggesting a possible deal in which SCIRI "gave up" some of its sectarian quota for the appointment of women in exchange for vetoing the inclusion of Muqtada al-Sadr on the IGC (International Crisis Group 2003: 12).

Meanwhile, the IGC was regarded at best as irrelevant and at worst as illegitimate by a large proportion of the Iraqi population. They were suspicious that the body was dominated by people who had only recently returned to Iraq after years of exile; that it failed to include representatives of a number of governorates (where, not coincidentally, insurgent groups later took root) (Herring and Rangwala 2006: 107); that it excluded Muqtada al-Sadr (who, not coincidentally, was highly critical of the occupation and would lead armed resistance to the coalition troops); that it was divorced physically from society—walled up in the Green Zone and dependent upon protection from the coalition troops; and that its members were selected according to ethnic and sectarian quotas rather than their technical abilities (Dodge 2005: 33). After several months, it became clear that the IGC was ineffective and incapable of reaching important decisions.

Overwhelmingly discredited, even by the CPA officials who had appointed it, the IGC struggled to find a justification for its existence. It is no accident that, in attempting to assert its authority in the context of sharp criticism, some members of the IGC decided to pass a resolution aimed at transforming gender relations within Iraq. Women and gender relations are almost universally employed as both a symbolic and a strategic mechanism in national, ethnic, religious, and state-building processes (Yuval-Davis 1997). In times of upheaval, gender relations and gender identities become contested terrains as different political and social forces attempt to shape the future identity of the polity. Moreover, an important way for political leaders to demonstrate their authority is through their control over the women of "their communities."

Decree 137, passed under "Any Other Business" at the session of December 29, 2003, under the rotating chair of Abdul Aziz al-Hakim, head of the SCIRI, stated that the relatively progressive and unified personal status law that had existed, more or less, since 1959 (discussed in chapter 1) should be replaced by shari'a administered by religious clerics, depending upon the sect to which the relevant parties belonged.[5] Overturning the relatively progressive code that had been created in the postrevolutionary era in 1959 and had continued during the Saddam Hussein era represented a symbolic break from the past, as well as from the U.S. occupation, which had also claimed women as a symbol of the new Iraq. Simultaneously, replacing the code with more conservative interpretations of Islam served to reshape gender relations in postinvasion Iraq as a foundation of the new state and to reflect the conservative religious identity of the Shi'i Islamist parties. In the summer of 2005, the issue of overturning the unified personal status code would return to center stage as a new constitution was being drafted.

The passing of Decree 137 was shrouded in some mystery and was not leaked to the press until January 13, 2004. Leslie F. in the State Department told Nicola: "When I got an e-mail about [Decree] 137, I spoke with the National Security Council, Capitol Hill, and my counterparts. It's like a chess game. Bremer was maneuvering his way through difficult discussions in order to get the resolution rescinded. He couldn't go in strong. A lot of coalitions had to be built in order to overturn it. However, credit is due to the Iraqi women. They really did all the work." Indeed, the announcement of the decree quickly resulted in the mobilization of women to oppose it. As we will reveal in greater detail in the following chapter, women activists inside and outside Iraq issued press releases outlining the implications of the decree, which were distributed widely by e-mail. In Baghdad and the Kurdish region, thousands of women protested, calling for the decree to be repealed. In the end, Bremer did not sign the decree into force (thereby making it void).

Rachel F., a gender consultant working on Iraq but based in Washington, D.C., found the "137" episode very confusing: "How come it took ten weeks to repeal 137? Wasn't the U.S. running the show? There was nothing forthcoming from the U.S. officially to oppose 137. Not even some sort of tepid statement. I know that you can't come down with a hammer because this will alienate people. This is a sensitive issue. You have to engage your enemies. But what would the U.S. have said if the IGC had passed a law making commercial law governed by shari'a?" Rachel's comments appeared particularly pertinent to us in light of the fact that the CPA, under Bremer, had imposed a number of decrees determining the shape of the Iraqi economy, which, by admission of the CPA, would have "far-reaching social implications" (quoted in Herring and Rangwala 2006: 228). While Bremer was concerned not to trample over the (limited) sovereignty of Iraqi politicians with regard to women's rights, he was not so concerned to respect the sovereignty of Iraq with regard to the future of its economy. This meant that women's rights and gender relations became one of the only areas over which Iraqi political leaders could assert their sovereignty against the occupying powers, thereby setting the context for later struggles over women's rights.

THE TRANSITIONAL ADMINISTRATIVE LAW

The blueprint for the political transition was contained in the Transitional Administrative Law (TAL), introduced on March 8, 2004.[6] The TAL was drafted by a select number of individuals from the IGC—among them no women—largely behind closed doors. It reflected quite arduous political bargaining between the different Iraqi parties on the IGC on the one hand and the United States on the other. To get an agreement, a number of difficult issues were glossed over, such as the future boundaries of the Kurdistan region, the distribution of oil revenues, the role of Islam in legislation, and the legal status of the foreign troops. Nevertheless, the document laid out a clear, and very ambitious, timetable for the political transition: the creation of a sovereign interim government by June 30, 2004; elections for a transitional national assembly by January 31, 2005; the drafting of a permanent constitution by August 15, 2005; a popular referendum on the constitution by October 15; and elections for a permanent government to be held by December 15, 2005.

The TAL, with all its weaknesses, constituted the guiding document for Iraq until a permanent constitution could be drafted. Yet it was not mentioned in the UN Security Council resolution that sanctioned the political transition process and the status of coalition troops (Resolution 1446). This was because of objections by the revered Shi'i cleric Ayatollah Sistani (see J. Cole 2004d). By dropping any mention of the TAL in the UN resolution, the United States hoped to show the Shi'i Islamist leaders, who were unhappy that the TAL constituted a check on their majoritarian power, "that its balancing process [between different factions of the IGC] would sometimes tilt in their direction too" (Herring and Rangwala 2006: 84).

U.S. appeasement of the religious Shi'i parties was interpreted by some activists as ultimately a compromise on human rights and women's rights (Tinsley 2004). The TAL contained articles that guaranteed equality among citizens, rights to freedom of speech and assembly, prohibition of torture, and a target of 25 percent of elected officials as women.[7] Nevertheless, the TAL did not completely protect women's rights, since it made no explicit guarantee for women's rights in personal status matters (UN High Commissioner for Human Rights [UNHCHR] 2004: para. 86), although these had been threatened earlier by Decree 137. For Ziba H., this omission was clearly problematic. "The U.S. overlooked the significance of the 137 event," she told Nicola. "It was a warning by the Shi'i political forces."

Other observers also concurred that the TAL, despite its inclusion of several liberal articles, was highly problematic for women's rights. Article 7 stated that Islam was "a source of legislation" and that no law enacted during the transitional period might contradict "the universally agreed tenets of Islam." In the view of one observer, this article lent "symbolic support to those who call for a greater measure of Islamic legal influence" (Brown 2004: 5). Meanwhile, others argued, "The prominence of Islam need not undercut women's rights, but if the Fundamental Law [i.e., the TAL] is interpreted in a fundamentalist or patriarchal way, women could be harmed" (S. Cole and Cole 2004).[8]

In many ways, the TAL set the stage for the constitution drafting in 2005, for what it stipulated as much as for what it did not clarify. The document had been negotiated, behind closed doors, by avoiding discussion of highly contested issues, including the future of women's rights, the role of Islam, the borders of the Kurdistan autonomous region, and the functioning of federalism. Iraqi political leaders had reached a tenuous compromise over the TAL on the basis that the real negotiations over interests would take place during the constitution drafting in the summer of 2005. This made it even more important for the various political parties to consolidate their power in the transitional political structures, and they did so at the expense of creating an open and inclusive political system as well as effective state institutions.

THE IRAQI INTERIM GOVERNMENT:
JULY 2004–MAY 2005

In June 2004, the IGC was abolished and replaced by the Iraqi Interim Government (IIG). This marked the handover of power from the CPA to Iraqis. George Bush described the handover as "a day of great hope" for Iraqis and proclaimed, "Fifteen months after the liberation of Iraq, and two days ahead of schedule, the world witnessed the arrival of a full sovereign and free Iraq" (Staff and Agencies 2004). Politicians in Washington and London as well as Iraq celebrated the creation of a sovereign government for Iraq as a means to stem the rapidly growing insurgency. The IIG was tasked with preparing Iraq for elections to the TNA, which would draft a constitution for the new Iraq, thereby supporting the next stage in Iraq's political transition.

Although the IIG would have "full sovereignty" and responsibility for governing Iraq, its decision-making powers were limited. It could not pass laws or take any actions that would "affect Iraq's destiny beyond the limited interim period until an elected Transitional Government of Iraq assumes office" (UN Security Council Resolution 1546, 2004, no. 1). Moreover, coalition troops on Iraqi soil would remain under U.S. command (nos. 9, 10). While the IIG was given the seal of approval by a UN resolution, its composition was largely decided by the political groups that had dominated the IGC in negotiation with the United States (J. Cole 2004b). The United Nations had envisaged that the interim government would be a nonpolitical, technocratic body to avoid the problems that had dogged the IGC. However, in line with U.S. and IGC wishes, a political body was formed, reflecting the political, sectarian, and ethnic makeup of the IGC (Herring and Rangwala 2006: 31–32).

Iyad Allawi, former IGC member and head of the INA, was chosen as prime minister. Ghazi Mashal Ajil al-Yawar, a former IGC member and a Sunni Arab who had spent fifteen years in exile as a businessman in Saudi Arabia and who claimed tribal leadership, was chosen as president. Ibrahim al-Ja'fari of the Da'wa and Rowsch Shaways of the KDP were selected as deputy presidents, and Barham Salih of the PUK was chosen as deputy prime minister, in an ethnic/sectarian balancing act that also extended to other government posts. This would have repercussions for the effectiveness of the new body in terms of addressing Iraq's escalating problems. The renowned Iraqi female blogger Riverbend wrote, scathingly, on June 18, 2004: "At a point when we need secure borders and a strong army, our new Defense Minister was given the job because he . . . what? Played with toy soldiers as a child?" (2005: 273–74). Other commentators of the Iraqi political scene were equally uncomplimentary about the new cabinet (see, e.g., J. Cole 2004c; Dodge 2005: 36). Instead of fixing the problems with the IGC, the interim government merely reproduced those problems, including the tensions between ensuring ethnic/sectarian balance on the one hand and women's representation and rights on the other. Many women activists were disheartened that the new cabinet included only five woman ministers and six deputy ministers out of a total of thirty-one ministers and deputy ministers. Leyla Mohammed of the Iraq Women's Association said, "This will not be good for women. . . . This government will not pay attention to women in Iraq" (UN-OCHA 2004). KDP member Nesreen Mustafa Berwari, who had been the only woman minister in the previous provisional cabinet, was kept on as minister for public works. Pascal Esho Warda, a member of the Assyrian Democratic Movement, was appointed minister of immigration and refugees. Leila Abdul-Latif became minister of labor and social affairs, and Mishkat Moumin, former Baghdad University professor and part of the organizing committee for the conference "The Voice of Women of Iraq," was appointed minister of the environment. Nermin Othman, a PUK member and a former minister in the Kurdistan Regional Government, was appointed minister of state for women's affairs.

THE SECURITY SITUATION
AND THE POLITICAL PROCESS

What was supposed to be an auspicious step toward sovereignty and democracy in June 2004 was marred by the ever-increasing violence in Iraq. April 2004 witnessed a notable upsurge in violence against the United States. Ongoing tensions between the antioccupation Muqtada al-Sadr's Mahdi Army and U.S. forces came to a head at the end of March after Bremer closed Sadr's newspaper, *al-Hawza*. Throughout April, the coalition forces battled with the Mahdi Army in Najaf and other locations. Meanwhile, in April, the United States decided to take on the insurgency in the city of Fallujah, northwest of Baghdad, following the killing and dismemberment, live on TV, of four U.S. private security personnel. The ensuing military standoff resulted in the deaths of at least six hundred Iraqis and the displacement of thousands more (Herring and Rangwala 2006: 30).

For the new interim government, defeating the insurgency and stemming the violence became a number one priority. Mishkat Moumin, a member of Iyad Allawi's cabinet, told Nicola in February 2005: "The major issue for reconstruction is the security problem. At the weekly cabinet meetings, the major issue we discuss is security." Defining Iraq's mounting problems, such as rehabilitating electricity and water supplies, in terms of national security helped to shift power to those who controlled the security forces. This posed further dangers to the openness of the political system and the ability of women politicians to participate in it. Allawi introduced new emergency powers to deal with the insurgency. An Iraqi National Guard was created to enforce order, while the United States designed a new strategy to defeat the insurgency ahead of the January 2005 elections (Herring and Rangwala 2006: 33).

Yet several people argued that the growing violence was a consequence of the problems within the political process, thereby suggesting that the security strategies of the new Iraqi government and coalition forces were inadequate to address the problem. Writing at the end of April 2004, the International Crisis Group argued that there was an "urgent need for a credible, transparent and inclusive political process. . . . As long as basic grievances are not addressed and a wider spectrum of Iraqis is not included in the political process, violence will increase rather than diminish" (2004a: 29). In particular, Sunni politicians argued that their political marginalization was fanning the flames of the insurgency (Hashim 2006: 73). In addition, the large numbers of former exiles in the cabinet of Allawi, the continuing presence of U.S. forces exempt from Iraqi command, and U.S. interference in the political process boosted the popularity of the antioccupation, Iraqi nationalist ideology of insurgent groups and Islamist militias, such as that of Muqtada al-Sadr (Dodge 2005: 16–17).

Other factors besides the failures of the political process helped to fuel the conflict. The heavy-handed counterinsurgency measures of the U.S. forces further alienated ordinary Iraqis and increased sympathy for those perpetrating the violence. The year 2004 featured the killing of civilians and the creation of a humanitarian crisis in Fallujah and other towns and cities in the so-called Sunni Triangle; attacks on the holy city of Najaf, where Sadr was based; shocking revelations of the abuse of Iraqi prisoners by U.S. guards in the Abu Ghraib prison; and anger and frustration over the impunity and lack of accountability of coalition actions

(Herring and Rangwala 2006: 179–94; Hashim 2006: 101). The attacks and abuse overwhelmingly targeted Iraqi men, in what Adam Jones calls the "gender-selective victimization of Iraqi males that lies at the heart of U.S. occupation policies," thereby fueling feelings of humiliation and rage among Iraqi men (2004: 71).

While men were and continue to be disproportionately victimized in the vicious cycle of violence and counterviolence caused by the U.S.-led occupation, women have been targeted too and suffer in specific ways, as discussed in the last chapter, that have implications for their ability to participate in the political process. The specific targeting of women in public positions by armed groups has helped to drive some women out of politics. Shereen W., a senior member of Allawi's executive office in the interim government, was forced to leave her job and flee Iraq after receiving a death threat from Tawhid wa Jihad, an insurgent group linked to al-Qaeda. From her office in exile, she told Nicola, "I was so into my job. I lived outside the Green Zone. I had no security. I didn't realize the danger until I got the death threat. At least they used to send you a letter first. Now they just execute you." Further, women like Shereen have been criticized from some quarters for their failure to oppose the violence of the occupation: "The silence of the 'feminists' of Allawi's regime is deafening. The suffering of their sisters in cities showered with napalm, phosphorous and cluster bombs by US jet fighters, the death of about 100,000 Iraqi civilians, half of them women and children, is met with rhetoric about training for democracy" (Zangana 2004). While the United States and the rest of the international community have declared their efforts to support a political transition in Iraq, the U.S.-led occupation has been delegimitizing the political process and women's participation in it.

THE ELECTIONS OF JANUARY 2005

Because of the escalating violence against the occupation and the growing specter of sectarian and ethnic unrest (Blanford 2004), the United States was keen to push ahead with the political process and called in the United Nations to help mediate a plan that would be acceptable to the major Iraqi political parties. Paul W., working on electoral assistance to Iraq, visited Iraq in January 2004 as part of a UN mission to address the issue of the political process: "We met with a wide range of actors. We also held town hall meetings. The agenda included discussion of women's representation, type of political system, type of electoral commission, party development, population distribution, administrative infrastructure for elections, electoral law. . . . All these issues were addressed systematically in all meetings." According to the International Institute for Democracy and Electoral Assistance (International IDEA), a widely respected think tank focusing on democracy promotion, "One important variable influencing the likelihood of women being elected to the (national) legislature is the electoral system used in a country" (Larserud and Taphorn 2007: 4). Research shows that women are almost twice as likely to be elected under proportional representation (PR) systems as under majoritarian electoral systems (Larserud and Taphorn 2007; Norris 2004: 2). Under party-list proportional systems, parties receive seats in parliament that correspond, more or less, to the proportion of votes received. Women's representation is made easier because each party presents the voters in a constituency with a list of candidates rather than a single candidate. Moreover, the larger the number of representatives per district, the more likely it is that a woman from a particular list will be elected (Larserud and Taphorn 2007; Norris 2004).

Women's representation was definitely a consideration for the United Nations in designing an electoral system for Iraq, since the TAL had mandated a goal of having "women constitute no less than one-quarter of the members of the National Assembly" (Article 30c). As Paul indicated to Nicola: "The U.S. doesn't like quotas. So it isn't a quota. A quota would mean stipulating that 25 percent of seats in the assembly are reserved for women. In order to implement the 25 percent goal, we created the electoral law so that every third candidate put forward on a party list has to be a woman."[9] In addition, the particular system was chosen to be inclusive and practical, in line with TAL requirements that there be a fair representation of minorities and that elections be held by the deadline of January 31, 2005 (United Nations 2005). Elections expert Paul W. told Nicola that, following discussions with the IGC: "We established a list system with . . . proportional representation and a low threshold. . . . If you have a high threshold, this keeps out minority parties and encourages large national parties. A high threshold in Iraq would lead to Shi'i dominance. However, we set the threshold very low. You only needed five hundred signatures to stand. Therefore, you can have independent candidates or locally based parties." In other words, the proposal put forward by the United Nations was meant to ensure women's presence within parliament. In addition, other experts argued that the low threshold would "entic[e] former combatants and violent rivals to participate in elections," while the single-constituency system would "encourage alliances and coalitions among such groups" (Fischer 2004). Paul concurred with this assessment. Speaking a few weeks after the elections of January 2005, as the different political parties were negotiating over the composition of the cabinet, he told Nicola: "I think that the current situation is good because politicians are being made to talk to one another and the public is now pressuring them to come to a compromise to form a government. People were intractable in their positions before. Now they are forced to compromise. This is a good lesson to learn in preparation for drafting the constitution. This makes constitution drafting easier." The choice of this particular electoral system also had another important advantage: it was easy to implement given the little time available. Determining Iraq as a single constituency, rather than allocating national assembly seats to distinct electoral districts in Iraq, meant that the authorities could avoid the politically sensitive process of designing constituency borders, as Mary E., an expert in electoral assistance who had been sent to Iraq immediately after the invasion, pointed out. She felt that with more time more could have been done to prepare for the elections, but "you can't wait for perfection." Ayatollah Sistani and his supporters certainly did not want to wait.

Nevertheless, some observers criticized the chosen system as a recipe for increasing conflict in Iraq rather than encouraging cooperation and consensus. The main problem, as they saw it, was the designation of Iraq as a single constituency. This meant that those elected would not be representing particular districts, thereby making them less accountable to the electorate and more accountable to their political parties, and that some areas of the country, where voter turnout was low, could end up without any elected representation (M. Rubin 2004). Larry Diamond, a former senior adviser to the CPA and a senior fellow of the Hoover Institute at Stanford University, predicted that "the biggest winners will be the best-armed and most-organized forces—the Kurds in the far north and the Iranian-backed Islamist parties in the Shiite south. The American occupation could wind up paving the way for the 'election' of an Iranian-linked Islamist government in Baghdad" (2004).

For some women activists, the issue was not what type of electoral system would be inclusive and legitimate but whether holding elections in the prevailing security climate would guarantee women's representation. In a meeting in Baghdad with UN envoy Lakhdar Brahimi, one woman in the audience stood up and told him: "I want to talk about a basic issue concerning the voice of women. Iraqi women today have difficulty even meeting. The security situation fills us with fear. If Iraqi women can't move around freely, can't express their opinions freely and can't protect themselves and their organizations, then how can proper elections be held?" (Pachachi 2004).

Despite these concerns and criticisms, no brake would be placed on the juggernaut of political transition. Voter registration began on November 1, 2004. This consisted of voters checking information on the UN "Oil for Food" lists compiled in the 1990s—which, although not entirely accurate, enabled the elections to go ahead within the designated timetable. Iraqis living abroad (estimated at four million before the invasion in 2003) were also eligible to vote. Despite grave concerns about the security situation, a large number of women's groups around Iraq were involved in campaigns to educate potential voters about the democratic process and to "get out the vote," particularly among women. Simultaneously, women candidates attended training on how to campaign successfully, while hundreds of organizations registered as election monitors and a network of monitors was formed, in which women played a leading role. Despite the setbacks that women had faced since the invasion of 2003, many women activists were enthusiastic for democracy (Iraqi al-Amal Association 2004).

Registering of parties and individuals seeking election occurred between November and December. On paper, the electoral law appeared to encourage broad-based coalitions. Yet in reality the two main coalitions were associated with either the Kurdish national parties or the Shi'i religious parties. The United Iraqi Alliance (UIA) was brokered by Ayatollah Sistani and dominated by the two major Shi'i parties—SCIRI and Da'wa. Other smaller Shi'i religious parties, including supporters of Muqtada al-Sadr and the Fadila Party, also joined the 228-candidate list. Some non-Islamist Shi'i—including Ahmed Chalabi—and thirty Sunni candidates were also included. The Kurdistan Alliance was dominated by the KDP and the PUK, who put aside historic rivalries to join on the same list, but also included the Kurdistan Communist Party, the Assyrian National Party, the Chaldean Democratic Union Party, the Kurdistan Islamic Union, and other smaller parties based in the Kurdish region.

A few lists tried to cut across ethnic and religious lines and to present a secular agenda. Notably, these were the "Iraqi List" of Iyad Allawi, which was led by his INA Party but also included the Movement of Democratic Iraqis. This list included former IGC member Raja al-Khuzai and Safia al-Suhail, one of the few women who was visible in the former exiled opposition and who, following the elections, was invited to Washington for President Bush's State of the Union Address. "Al-'Iraqiyyun" (the Iraqis) was led by former interim president Ghazi al-Yawar and included tribal leaders and some small parties. Former IGC member Adnan Pachachi headed a list called "the Independent Iraqi Democrats," while the ICP, once a powerful force in Iraqi politics, fielded candidates under the name of "People's Union."

The Association of Muslim Scholars, the largest and most coherent organization of Sunni Islamists, called for a boycott of the elections on the grounds that they would be illegitimate under occupation. The Sunni Iraqi Islamic Party, which originally had decided to enter the elections, pulled out following the November assault on Fallujah. Several other parties and groups also supported a boycott, while other prominent politicians, including Ghazi al-Yawar of al-ʿIraqiyyun and Adnan Pachachi of the Independent Iraqi Democrats, called for postponing the elections because of the adverse security situation.

The two major electoral lists formed in preparation for the January 2005 elections vied for power not on the basis of ideological distinctions or political platforms but on the basis of sectarian/communal affiliations. Election campaigning began on December 15. The UIA list, which was not only brokered by Sistani but also endorsed by him, explicitly promoted its religious Shiʿi credentials through posters depicting Ayatollah Sistani. The Kurdistan Alliance campaigned for a federal Iraq and protection for Kurdish autonomy. The Iraqi List campaign centered on the personality of Iyad Allawi and was meant to represent the secular, nonsectarian voter. His campaign had high visibility, given his privileged access to the media as the interim prime minister. His campaign slogan was "Vote for the Iraqi List, for the sake of strong leadership and a secure country."

The security situation meant that many candidates were afraid to publicize their names and campaigning was kept to a minimum, so that voters did not know the names of who they were voting for. This was obviously an obstacle for campaigning, particularly for independent candidates or those of smaller parties without the resources or militias to protect them. Hanaa Edwar, founder of the Iraqi al-Amal NGO and a prominent women's rights activist, stood on a small, independent list called Watani ("My Homeland"). She said: "You have to do small meetings at homes or in schools, or in some other institutions, and contact the media and through the media maybe we can make our announcements to the people or speak about our programs, or we have to make [our publicity] through publications, through posters or calendars, or stickers and so on. Personally, I don't feel this is really satisfactory or exactly how we were expecting to participate in elections" (Recknagel 2005). The need to guard one's anonymity from the voting public was highlighted when several candidates were either threatened or assassinated before the elections. Women candidates in particular felt vulnerable to the threats of violence. Salma al-Khafaji, a former member of the IGC and a conservative Shi'i candidate, survived an assassination attempt for the second time at the beginning of January 2005. Wijdan al-Khuzai, a candidate standing on a secular platform, was found tortured to death on December 24, 2004. The sons of two women candidates were killed as punishment for their mothers' electoral ambitions (Eltahawy 2005). Several male candidates were also killed or threatened.

Despite the ongoing violence and the calls for boycott, the elections went ahead on January 31. Official turnout was 58 percent of registered voters across Iraq—although there were great variations. Turnout was 89 percent in the Kurdish region but as little as 2 percent in al-Anbar province (in the so-called Sunni Triangle). Forty-four people were killed in attacks that day. For the United States, the elections were heralded as a great triumph. Pictures of smiling Iraqis holding up purple-stained fingers were beamed across the world. The opportunity to vote in the first elections following the fall of Saddam Hussein created an almost festive atmosphere, despite the obvious dangers. Zeina, a candidate for the National Democratic Party, wrote, "Everyone is so excited. We heard many bombs this morning but we didn't care because we have to use our right to vote. . . . I am so happy, so glad. Later this afternoon we will meet up with our friends for a celebration. We will have a meal, drink tea and eat cake. Then we will have to head back home because of the 7 pm curfew" (BBC News Online 2005b). Women's rights activist Shirouk Alabyachi, on a visit to the United Kingdom, told Nicola: "Despite the violence and the threats, so many women went out to vote. They did not vote for this party or for that party, but for a better future and for democracy." The Independent Electoral Commission of Iraq deemed the elections to have taken place without any major disruption. The International Mission for Iraqi Elections (IMIE 2006), which monitored the elections from Amman (because of security risks), also found that the elections "generally met recognized standards."

Yet despite the overwhelmingly positive portrayal of the elections, some women to whom we talked experienced them differently. Leila G., a teacher from Baghdad, while visiting Amman in the summer of 2005, told Nadje: "There was lots of intimidation prior to the elections. We had people with guns visit us a few weeks before the elections who told us we should vote for the Da'wa Party as they will make sure to finally give the Shiʻi of Iraq the rights and privileges they deserve. I did not want to vote for a sectarian party, but many of my family members voted for them out of fear." Women's rights activist Siham R., who stood for elections in her hometown in southern Iraq, where the Sadrists are strong, told Nicola: "They [the militias] wrote a list of people whom they want to kill. My name was on that list. . . . In the elections, I stood as an independent candidate and I got more than one thousand votes. I got more votes than some of the party lists, so they see me as a threat. . . . I was afraid to contest the election results because I would be targeted. I could have been given a seat because of the quota. However, instead, they gave the seat to a woman from their closed list."

We also heard about irregularities in polling stations established for the out-of-country voting. Meanwhile, many people did not or were not able to vote. The violence and intimidation kept them away from polling stations, even where they wanted to vote. Others felt that there were no candidates for whom they wanted to vote. Houzan Mahmoud (2005), an activist from the Organization for Women's Freedom in Iraq (OWFI), said, "If Iraqi women take part in the elections, who are they to vote for? Women's rights are ignored by most of the candidates. The U.S. government appears happy to have Iraq governed by reactionary religious and ethnocentric elites." The U.S.-based Human Rights Watch (2005) questioned the possibility of holding "free and fair" elections in a context in which violence and intimidation prevented candidates from campaigning freely, many Iraqis from voting, and election workers from preparing adequately for voting day.

The elections proved a cause for concern in other ways. The single-constituency system of the elections produced large winnings for the predominantly Shiʻi UIA (140 seats) and Kurdistan Alliance (75 seats). Meanwhile, the low voter turnout in those provinces that are predominantly Sunni meant that they were left without representation. Therefore, the elections further marginalized the Sunni community from the political process and entrenched sectarian and ethnic difference within newly emerging political institutions. The Iraqi List and al-ʻIraqiyyun, both of which had attempted to appeal across sectarian and ethnic lines, took only 40 seats and 5 seats, respectively, while the Independent Democrats failed to win any seats.

Many secular, nonsectarian Iraqis of all religious stripes felt alarmed by the prospect of a parliament dominated by Islamists. In particular, secular women activists feared for the future of women's rights, given that the Islamist-dominated parliament would be responsible for drafting the future constitution of Iraq. As Naba al-Barrak of New Hope for Women, an Iraqi NGO, said, "The results are disturbing indeed" (Prothero 2005). Despite the advantages of the electoral system selected in terms of its potential to ensure women's representation, in fact the worst fears of critics of the system had been realized. The elections had helped to consolidate a de facto confessional political system. This was partly due to the way Iraq was treated as a single constituency but also due to the security situation's impact upon the ability of small parties to campaign publicly. The makeup of parliament would have implications for women's participation in the drafting of the constitution and the guarantee of women's rights within the constitution.

WOMEN IN THE TRANSITIONAL NATIONAL ASSEMBLY

Finally, several months after the elections, on April 5, the presidency council was announced. The president was the leader of the PUK, Jalal Talabani; the vice presidents were Adel Abdul Mehdi of SCIRI and Ghazi al-Yawar of the 'Iraqiyyun. A few weeks and some more intense negotiations later, the prime minister was appointed as Ibrahim al-Ja'fari of the Da'wa Party. The remaining posts were shared out among the major political groupings that had dominated the postinvasion political scene and according to ethnic and sectarian quotas. Yet again it appeared that attempts at a sectarian/ethnic balancing act operated to limit the number of cabinet posts allocated to women to only six out of thirty-two ministers. Nesreen Berwari (of the KDP) and Narmin Othman (of the PUK) were reappointed as minister of public works and minister of the environment (as well as acting human rights minister) respectively. Basimah Yusuf Butrus, of the Assyrian Democratic Movement, was appointed minister of science and technology; Jwan Maasum, a member of the PUK, was appointed minister of communications; Suhayla Abd-Jaafar, a lawyer and human rights activist, was appointed minister of displacement and migration; and Azhar Abdel Karim al-Shaikhli, a women's rights activist and former member of the Independent Electoral Commission for Iraq, was appointed minister of state for women's affairs.

Despite their limited representation within the cabinet, women appeared to score a significant victory with regard to the composition of the TNA—particularly when compared to other legislatures in the Middle East and even the rest of the world. Because of the way the electoral system was designed, over 30 percent of seats in the new parliament were occupied by women. For many observers of political developments inside Iraq, as well as for Iraqi women themselves, the 25 percent quota has been one of the major achievements of the Iraqi women's movement. Nevertheless, the selection of women candidates on party lists would present an obstacle to promoting women's rights and women's voices within parliament. We discuss this issue in greater detail in the next chapter.

Despite their large numbers in the legislature, women were still under threat from the violence engulfing most of the country. When the Iraqi parliament opened on April 28, 2005, one fewer woman was there than should have been. Lame'a Abed Khadawi, elected on the UIA list, had been shot dead in the garden of her home in Baghdad the day before parliament was to meet. It was a chilling reminder to women in political life that the first MP of the new assembly to be killed was a woman (Steele 2005).

THE KURDISTAN REGIONAL GOVERNMENT
AND KURDISTAN NATIONAL ASSEMBLY

The elections that took place in January 2005 were not only for a national assembly in Baghdad but also for provincial councils around Iraq and for the Kurdistan National Assembly in Erbil (or Hawler, as it is called in Kurdish). As a result of the elections in Iraqi Kurdistan, the PUK and KDP each won forty-one seats. The other twenty-six seats went to a number of smaller parties (for full details, see Kurdistan Regional Government 2006). The domination of the KDP and PUK in the 2005 elections represented a continuation of the balance of power that had existed since the Kurdistan National Assembly was established in 1992 under the auspices of the international no-fly zone.

The experience of the Kurdistan region has been held up as a model of democracy for the rest of Iraq. Moreover, since 2003, the Kurdistan provinces of Erbil, Sulaymaniya, and Dohuk have not witnessed the terrible violence that has unfolded in the rest of Iraq. This is largely because the region was already politically and militarily autonomous and therefore did not suffer the consequences of a power vacuum opening up after the fall of the regime in Baghdad. However, the absence of violence does not mean that the region is enjoying a state of peace. The conflict in Iraq affects Kurdistan in various ways, with particular implications for the situation of women. Moreover, the case of Kurdistan illustrates how ethnically based politics underpins violations of women's rights and antidemocratic practices.

The violence beyond the borders of Kurdistan restricts the rehabilitation of basic infrastructure for the region. Electricity supply is limited in urban areas and practically nonexistent in rural areas. Clean water is also limited. This is a particular burden for rural women in Kurdistan. Meanwhile, violence in the rest of Iraq has created new "criminal economies" in which Kurdistan plays an integral part, such as receiving women and children trafficked from the rest of Iraq for prostitution.

However, the most shocking statistics relate to incidents of violence against women. Between January and March 2007 alone, the UN Assistance Mission for Iraq (UNAMI) received information on forty cases of "honor crimes" in which women had been murdered for suspected "sexual impropriety," while local NGOs recorded a worrying increase in female suicides through self-immolation, which could be a cover-up for honor crimes or an indication of the hopelessness felt by some women. At the time of writing, this violence has not been investigated by the Kurdistan authorities (UNAMI 2007a: 16–17). The failure of the authorities to address the question of violence against women could be seen as due to the desires of Kurdish national leaders not to upset their more socially conservative constituency and undermine their political influence within the region. In addition, as we discussed in chapter 1, there is a link between the Kurdish national struggle and the neglect of women's rights (with violence representing the most extreme form of maintaining women's oppression).

The construction of a de facto confessional political system in Iraq after 2003 has helped to perpetuate the political dynamics that work against women's rights (as we discuss in more detail in the next chapter), as well as human rights and democracy more generally. The Baghdad government has become another sphere in which the Kurdish national parties can consolidate their authority. The allocation of positions in the cabinet among the major political parties along sectarian and ethnic lines enables the Kurdish national leadership to retain their political supremacy within Kurdistan. The result of the almost unchallenged political domination of the Kurdish national parties was described to Nicola by Walid K., a human rights activist in Sulaymaniya: "Here parliament, government, parties are mixed together. There is no separation of powers. The PUK and KDP are controlling everything. It is like in the Soviet system! The budget goes to the parties and then they distribute it to government. They don't tell us the details of the budget. Party members are employed in invisible jobs such as 'manager of a directorate.'" This lack of transparency has affected economic development within Kurdistan, making it difficult to address ongoing problems of poverty. For example, a 2002 survey (in Kurdish) sponsored by Norwegian People's Aid found that 37 percent of women are illiterate and that almost 50 percent of women do not have adequate access to knowledge about women's health (Mojab n.d.). However, limitations on the freedom of the press prevent issues of corruption from being discussed openly, and several journalists have been harassed or even detained following articles that they wrote about corruption involving Kurdistan officials. Public opposition to corruption has also been suppressed. A series of peaceful demonstrations involving thousands of people broke out in July 2006 in a number of Kurdish towns, protesting government corruption and the lack of basic goods and services, such as fuel and water. Several hundred people were arrested, while two people were killed by police who fired on the demonstrators (U.S. Bureau of Democracy 2007). Meanwhile, ethnic minorities, which include Turkmen, Chaldeans, Assyrians, Shabak, and Armenians, have reported discrimination or harassment by Kurdish officials. There are incentives to "Kurdify" mixed provinces in the north in order to gain greater resources within a national political system that rewards groups on the basis of their ethnic or religious identity.

The treatment of prisoners in Kurdistan is also a problem, as highlighted by a human rights report in July 2007. There is widespread detention of individuals without charges and widespread use of torture, and one NGO activist in Erbil told Nicola about "private prisons" belonging to each of the parties and operating beyond the jurisdiction of the Ministry of the Interior (Human Rights Watch 2007a). On a visit to the Kurdistan National Assembly in April 2007, Nicola witnessed a group of about twenty women protesting that their male relatives were being held without charges, allegedly under the banner of fighting terrorism. The women were eager to tell their story and publicize what had happened. One woman recounted: "My husband is a political prisoner. He has been in prison for seven and a half years, and I haven't seen him for one and half years. He didn't do anything. He was just practicing Islam. They tortured him to confess. Solicitors are working on the case, but they don't succeed." The harsh security measures are opposed by many activists. Yet as Ali A., a civil society activist in Sulaymaniya, told Nicola: "With the current situation in Iraq, this gives Kurdistan to the 'parties.' People want to change the situation, but they are afraid that change may bring the same problems as the rest of Iraq." The tensions between Kurdish desires to protect their autonomy within Iraq, to extend Kurdish sovereignty to the province of Kirkuk, to retain the largely secular nature of the region, and to ensure women's rights were all manifested during the drafting of the permanent Iraqi constitution in May–September 2005.

THE DRAFTING OF THE
PERMANENT IRAQI CONSTITUTION

The major task of the TNA was to draft a permanent constitution for Iraq, which would enable the election of a new national assembly (or council of representatives). The TAL provided a deadline of August 15, 2005, for finalizing the constitution, after which it would be put to national referendum by October 15, 2005. As in the run-up to the elections, in which the United States and other international donors sought to support women's political participation through training and support for awareness-raising, international funding was marshaled to support women's participation in the constitution-drafting process. When Nicola visited Washington in the spring of 2005, the issue of the constitution was uppermost in the minds of many of those to whom she spoke, including those within the U.S. administration.

The constitution was considered to be important for women because this document would determine the future of women's rights in the new Iraq. It was also significant for the different Iraqi political players because it would define future access to power and resources. For the United States, the constitution would represent an important step toward establishing a supposedly democratic and stable Iraq.

As we discuss in greater detail in the next chapter, given the significance of the document, many Iraqi women's groups lobbied for at least a 25 percent share of seats for women on the constitution-drafting committee (to reflect their representation in the TNA). Yet only nine out of fifty-five committee members announced in early May were women: six from the UIA, two from the Kurdish Alliance, and one from Iyad Allawi's party, former IGC member Raja al-Khuzai. Moreover, none of these women were appointed as heads to the subcommittees in charge of drafting different parts of the constitution. Faiza Babakhan, a lawyer and former consultant for the Women Affairs Ministry, explained the limited presence of women on the drafting committee by saying, "The parceling out of these positions is determined not by merit but by complex calculations to achieve ethnic, sectarian and regional balances" (quoted in Goetz 2005).

Some women, however, regarded the drafting of a constitution under U.S. occupation as irrelevant to the protection of women's rights and the human rights of Iraqis. Haifa Zangana, a London-based activist who had fled from political persecution under Saddam Hussein, wrote in August 2005: "This process is designed not to represent the Iraqi people's need for a constitution but to comply with an imposed timetable aimed at legitimising the occupation. . . . Under Saddam Hussein, we had a constitution described as 'progressive and secular.' It did not stop him violating human rights, women's included. The same is happening now. The militias of the parties heading the interim government are involved in daily violations of Iraqis' human rights, women's in particular, with the US-led occupation's blessing. Will the new constitution put an end to this violence?" Certainly the process was not designed in a way that encour - aged openness and inclusivity. By international standards, three months was breakneck speed for drafting a constitution, and many "sticking points" had not been resolved in the TAL—among them, the organization of federalism, the status of Kirkuk, the distribution of oil income, the role of Islam in public affairs, and the nature of women's rights (Brown 2005; International Crisis Group 2005; BBC News Online 2005a; Kubba et al. 2005; Al-Marashi 2005). The short time period and the number of deeply contested political issues operated to limit public consultation. Given the small numbers of women on the drafting committee, public participation in the drafting process would be essential to ensure that women's voices would be heard. Alia T., who had helped to organize a workshop on guaranteeing women's rights in the Iraqi constitution, complained to Nicola: "You can't do a constitution in such a short period of time. . . . When we held our workshop on the constitution, all the parliamentarians wanted a delay, but the outside pressure was too strong. . . . Also, the political leadership wanted the constitution finished."

By the time that Sunni politicians were brought into the committee in June, the Shi'i and Kurdish parties had "already tailored the draft constitution to their liking" (Meijer 2005). The Islamist Shi'i parties wanted to guarantee that the numerical dominance of the Shi'i would translate into future political dominance, thereby reversing their historical marginalization from Iraqi nation-building processes. This meant writing a constitution that would give the national legislature (where Islamist Shi'i parties would probably be in the majority) significant leeway to shape the future of the political system. Connected to this, the Islamist Shi'i parties sought to reshape the identity of the new Iraq to reflect their majority status by promoting their political Islamist ideology through the law-making process.

The Kurdish political leaders wanted to guarantee the continuation of their de facto political control of Iraqi Kurdistan through the establishment of a federal political system and, relatedly, to fix the borders of the Kurdistan region, to decide the status of the oil-rich province of Kirkuk, which they claimed as part of the Kurdish region, and to ensure a claim to oil revenues. The Sunni politicians, representing Islamist and secular parties, sought to protect the Arab character and integral nature of the state and were hostile to federalism and the majoritarian power of the Shi'i parties. They also sought to prevent further de-Ba'thification (which they considered to be a cover for the exclusion of Sunnis from government) and to ensure that oil revenues would be centrally distributed (thereby guaranteeing oil revenues for the Sunni-majority areas with no oil reserves).

The considerable number of issues related to the constitution-drafting process meant that women's rights and representation were "in competition with so many other issues," elections expert Paul W. told Nicola. Nevertheless, women's rights were discussed by one of the subcommittees and would become an important source of contention. The first draft of the constitutional committee was released in the final week of July 2005. Mariam al-Rayyes, one of the six woman members from the UIA list on the drafting committee, stated, "Islam would be a 'main source' for legislation in the new constitution and the state religion. It gives women all rights and freedoms as long as they don't contradict our values. Concerning marriage, inheritance and divorce, this is civil status laws; that should not contradict our religious values" (quoted in Sengupta 2005). However, many women activists clearly feared that making Islam "the major source of legislation" would threaten to overturn Iraq's uni - fied personal status code and revive Decree 137. Linda Rashid of the constitution drafting committee said, "We are not worried about implementation of this [Islamic] law, but the arbitrary interpretations for it can cause the total loss of our rights in the country" (quoted in UN-OCHA 2005).

In addition to reframing the personal status laws, the committee had discussed removing the 25 percent quota for women's representation in decision-making bodies (Voice of America 2005; MacDonald and Rasan 2005; Sengupta 2005). Raja al-Khuzai (who was on Iyad Allawi's list) complained that fellow female parliamentarians had failed to back her demand for the retention of the 25 percent goal in the permanent constitution (Institute for War and Peace Reporting 2005). In response to these developments, as we discuss in the next chapter, secular Iraqi women activists mobilized publicly to promote women's rights in the constitution.

From experiences across the Muslim world, it was obvious that the role of Islam in the constitution and the designation of which authorities would have responsibility for interpreting Islam would affect women's rights, particularly with regard to the personal status code. However, less attention was given to the impact of federalism on women's rights in the new Iraq. While federalism appeared to present a solution to the Kurdish question, guaranteeing autonomy and protection of Kurdish rights as an ethnic minority, it also presented the possibility of imposing different rights for women of different regions, thereby undermining universal citizenship for Iraqi women. The danger of parceling out family law to the level of regions within a federal system was not lost on some women's rights activists. A federal system not only would enable the Kurds to protect their autonomy but could give greater autonomy to the Islamist Shi'i parties dominating the south of Iraq. "We're against federalism because we are against sharia," claimed Ghareba Ghareb of the Iraqi Women's Association (Carroll 2005). However, women members of the Kurdish political parties clearly saw protection of federalism as necessary not only for protection of Kurdish rights but also for guaranteeing women's rights against the Islamist-dominated central government.

The committee failed to meet the August 15 deadline (thereby contravening the TAL), as issues over federalism, the role of Islam, the status of Kirkuk, and women's rights continued to be debated by the different political groupings on the committee. The United States pressed the major sectarian and ethnic parties to come to a compromise. Within this context, women's rights became subordinated to other sectarian and ethnic interests.

After much wrangling, a "final" document was sent to parliament on August 28, 2005, and was put forward for referendum. This was greeted with great approval from the U.S. and U.K. governments, who ignored numerous problems with the document. The U.K. government stated, "It offers significant protection for women's rights," pointing to provisions that guaranteed equal opportunities for all Iraqis and required at least 25 percent female representation in parliament.[10]

However, almost all observers decried the fact that the drafting process had managed to further exclude Sunni politicians and that much of the language of the constitution was vague and left many issues to be decided by a future parliament—which was very likely to be dominated by Islamist Shi'i parties. Moreover, public "buy-in" to the document was almost nonexistent, as civil society groups had been given little opportunity to feed into the process. The major decisions about the constitution had been taken between the major political parties, behind closed doors (International Crisis Group 2005; Brown 2005). With an extremely short period remaining until a popular referendum (less than one month), there was practically no time for public discussion of the document, and many people complained that they did not know what the contents of the constitution were.

The referendum was approved through popular vote—although, as Joost Hiltermann (2005), an analyst for the International Crisis Group, commented, "This fact should not be interpreted as a public embrace of this document, but rather as a willingness to follow the call of political and religious leaders to go to the polling stations and vote in its favor." In Iraqi Kurdistan and the south of Iraq, the document was approved by between 63 and 99 percent of voters. In the three majority Sunni provinces, it was largely rejected—although not by the two-thirds necessary to veto the passage of the constitution (Independent Electoral Commission of Iraq 2005). Some women's rights activists either boycotted the referendum or voted against the constitution. Chiman B., a Kurdish-Iraqi activist, told Nicola: "The Kurdish leaders encouraged people to vote for the constitution because it was positive for Kurdish rights. I went to vote and voted 'no.' My brother tried to change my mind. Most women activists were angry with the constitution. But some women were influenced by the political campaigns, and they changed their minds. Some boycotted the referendum, but staying away was really like a yes vote." Many women activists were angry with the constitution because it effectively bargained away their rights in the attempt to reach a compromise between the sectarian and ethnic political leaders. As we have argued elsewhere (Al-Ali and Pratt 2006), the lynchpin of this compromise was Article 41, which stated, "Iraqis are free in their adherence to their personal status according to their own religion, sect, belief and choice, and that will be organized by law." This realized the worst fears of many women's rights activists in that it opened the way for a Lebanese-type system, where family law is governed according to religious sect, thereby legalizing discriminatory practices with regard to marriage, divorce, child custody, and inheritance. The system of federalism spelled out in Article 119 devolved authority to the regions to specify family law, thereby allowing regional differences in family law.[11]

Family law became an important arena of contestation over the future identity of the Iraqi nation-state, a mechanism for consolidating a multiethnic and multireligious state (Al-Ali and Pratt 2006). The new constitution sought to replace centralized state authority over women (codified in the existing personal status laws) with the authority of Iraq's communal leaders—that is, Shi'i, Sunni, and Kurdish political leaders—thereby encouraging their loyalty to the state. A similar process occurred in India and Israel, where personal status laws were "communalized" as part of "a project of state building to accommodate religious and social differences, and encourage loyalty to—or dependency on—the state by religious authorities" (Hajjar 2004: 20). Such a constitutional arrangement enables political leaders to consolidate their authority over different communities—whether defined in religious, ethnic, or regional terms. This is because it accommodates supposed ethnic and religious differences while at the same time constructing these differences. Moreover, the power that leaders assert over their "communities" is often demonstrated by control of "their" women—both symbolically and practically. In the process of creating a post-Ba'th Iraq, family law became part of a "social contract" that traded communal autonomy for women's rights. In this way, the constitution weakened women's citizenship rights while strengthening the significance of ethnic and sectarian "communities" within the political-legal system.

THE ELECTIONS OF DECEMBER 2005

Though it was clear that the political process was problematic and that a significant proportion of the population (i.e., women) was becoming excluded from that process because of the increasing violence and the domination of ethnic and sectarian-based parties, the elections for a national assembly that would rule Iraq for the following four years went ahead as planned in December 2005. While male politicians vied for power, many ordinary people were focusing on day-to-day survival. Economic recession, unemployment, lack of basic services, and, most importantly, lack of security were dominating people's thoughts—when they weren't watching the trial of Saddam Hussein. In light of the poor performance of the Islamist Shi'i UIA in government, there had been some hopes that the election results would give more seats to secular parties. In addition, the electoral system was revised to allocate seats in the national assembly in proportion to the number of registered voters in each province rather than to treat Iraq as a single constituency.

Nevertheless, voting patterns further entrenched sectarian and ethnic-based politics. All parties lost some seats to the Sunni Islamist coalition, which participated in the elections for the first time. However, the greatest loss was for the secular/nonsectarian candidates. The UIA (which by that time everyone was calling the "Shiʻi" list) won the most seats (128), although not the majority; the Kurdish Alliance won 53 seats; the Iraqi Accord Front (mainly Sunni Islamists) won 44 seats; the Iraqi National List (Iyad Allawi's list) won only 25 seats; the Iraqi Front for National Dialogue (a secular-oriented Sunni list) won 11 seats; the Kurdistan Islamic Union won 5 seats; and the remaining smaller parties took 9 seats. One commentator observed, "The break up of Iraq has been brought closer by the election. The great majority of people who went to the polls voted as Shia, Sunni or Kurds and not as Iraqis" (P. Cockburn 2005).

While voting along communal lines increased, the percentage of women elected to the parliament was reduced to 19 percent. This was a considerable decrease from before and was a result of the revised electoral system, meant to increase Sunni representation, that reduced the overall number of seats contested through direct elections (from 275 to 230). To meet the 25 percent "quota," women were allocated compensatory seats according to how many votes their lists had garnered at the national level.[12] At the cabinet level, the number of posts was increased to accommodate the newly elected Sunni parties who demanded a piece of the (ethnically and sectarianly divided) pie. This corresponded with a decrease in the number of female ministers, particularly those without party affiliation. Narmin Othman (of the PUK) remained as minister of environment; Wijdan Mikhael (of the Iraqi National List) was appointed minister of human rights; Bayan Diza'i (of the KDP) was appointed minister of housing and construction; and Fatin Rahman Mahmud (of the Iraqi Accord Front) was appointed minister of state for women's affairs.

In addition, some felt angry that women MPs had been excluded from the back-room haggling—which took almost five months—over leadership positions in government. Despite women's 25 percent presence in parliament, Safia al-Suhail said, "We have not managed to get women in roles where they have real power, where they will be taken seriously, and where they will be considered equal to men" (quoted in H. Ahmed 2006). She was referring to the fact that women had not achieved leadership positions within their parties and that they headed only two parliamentary committees ("Civil Society" and "Women, Family and Childhood"). In addition, many women's rights activists have complained that the Ministry for Women's Affairs cannot be considered a "real" government ministry. It has received practically no budget from the Iraqi government, relying instead on funds from international development agencies, such as UNIFEM.

Throughout 2006 and 2007, some women MPs attempted to establish a cross-party women's caucus in parliament to strengthen women's voice. After much effort, this was finally announced in September 2007 (UNIFEM 2007). The PUK member of parliament Suzan R. told Nicola in April 2007 about the difficulties in establishing the caucus: "We tried to talk with women in each bloc to get a unified caucus. But some women are under pressure from their political leadership. They are afraid. The male leaders are afraid that their women will be used by the West to undermine their political decisions. Also, some men still don't believe in women's rights. These are mostly Shi'i men, but also there are some Sunni men that think this." The establishment of a caucus despite the objections of party leaders represents a significant achievement for Iraqi women parliamentarians. But much must still be changed to give women more freedom to raise their voices in parliament. Most significantly, the domination of the political system by sectarian and ethnic-based party blocs will continue to divide women's voices on many important issues, including the future of women's rights in the constitution.

THE CONSTITUTIONAL REVIEW COMMITTEE

As noted above, a last-minute amendment to the constitution was made to entice Sunni politicians to support it. The inserted article stated that a Constitutional Review Committee would be formed and would report to parliament within four months on suggested recommendations to the constitution. The areas for discussion included the organization of federalism, the distribution of oil revenues, the status of Kirkuk, de-Ba'thification, and women's rights.

When the committee was formed, in September 2006, it included only two women out of twenty-seven members. Speaking at a closed meeting in London the following month, Rawan H., a deputy minister and women's rights activist, discussed the lobbying of the committee: "We aim to cancel Article 41 [regarding the personal status code], and we could succeed. The Kurds, Sunnis, and anti-SCIRI Shi'i parties say they will support a cancellation. But we fear that they may trade this for something else. For example, the Kurds will sacrifice this for Kirkuk. Therefore, we have also been working on drafting [alternative] legislation regarding personal status." At the time of this writing, the review committee has yet to produce its final recommendations. However, Rawan has become increasingly pessimistic. She told Nadje in August 2007:

> There was a huge pressure by women activists to abolish Article 41, but we feel that we have reached an impasse. We have had to compromise by offering amendments to 41, but they still refuse. There is not enough support from the UN, international NGOs, and the media. . . . We have managed to change the position of some political parties, including Fadila. We are working on the Sadrists. The most hard-core are SCIRI and Daʿwa. . . . Abbas al-Bayati [of the UIA] has said that he would rather abolish the whole constitution than Article 41. . . . He and others argue that Article 41 is about personal freedom and that it is the most democratic article in the constitution. Most of the Islamist Shiʿi women are for the article and against the unified personal status code.

SECTARIANISM AND THE MARGINALIZATION OF WOMEN

In effect, the construction of a political system based on ethnic and sectarian quotas not only undermined the idea of universal citizenship but also helped to establish religion and ethnicity as the primary sources of identification within the new Iraq and to encourage people to see the competition for political power and resources as a zero-sum game between different ethnic and sectarian "communities." This, coupled with the fragmentation of authority and widespread existence of armed groups, has provided a permissive environment for the outbreak of sectarian violence.

In February 2006, the bombing of the al-Askari shrine in Samarra—one of the holiest sites for the Shiʿi—began a cycle of vicious bloodletting along sectarian lines in central and southern Iraq (P. Cockburn 2006). Since then, hundreds of bodies have been dumped in the streets or in irrigation canals, usually tortured to death (Abdul-Ahad 2006). Whole neighborhoods of Baghdad have been "cleansed" by militia groups to create homogeneous areas by sect, causing thousands to flee their homes. This has added to the numbers of people displaced, injured, or killed as a result of military actions by the U.S.-led coalition (Samra 2007). According to the UN High Commissioner for Refugees (UNHCR 2007a), estimates from the summer of 2007 are that "more than 4.2 million Iraqis have left their homes. Of these, some 2.2 million Iraqis are displaced internally, while more than 2.2 million have fled to neighbouring states, particularly Syria and Jordan." As one women's rights activist based in Baghdad, Shirouk Alabyachi, told us: "Behind these numbers, there is real suffering. There are families living in tents in the desert without any basic services. There is no agency, no government looking after them. Children are traumatized by the violence. They are suffering from illnesses, such as diabetes, that they shouldn't be suffering from at this early age. How can we build a future when our children are like this?"

The United States and United Kingdom claimed that they would bring democracy to Iraq. Many women embraced the ideals of democracy as a means of rebuilding their country and their lives, after decades of war and sanctions. Women were at the forefront of getting out the vote, despite the terrible security conditions. However, a combination of U.S. security concerns and the political agendas of the parties that the United States empowered following the invasion are depriving all Iraqis of a better future.

From the point of view of the U.S. administration, the occupation of Iraq necessitated a number of compromises with its chosen Iraqi political players. This included pushing forward the political process at the expense of engaging ordinary Iraqis and to the detriment of the reconstruction process (and consequently the welfare of Iraqi people). The staging of elections in 2005 enabled George Bush to claim that democracy was taking root in Iraq and therefore that the U.S. mission in Iraq had been successful. The major Iraqi political parties supported the U.S. timetable because it would hand over greater powers to them.

Although women have participated in elections, in parliament, and, to a limited degree, in various cabinets, their room for maneuver is curtailed. De facto sectarian and ethnic quotas in government have operated to marginalize independent voices, particularly those of women. Indeed, women's participation in formal political institutions has decreased as communally based politics has increased in significance. Attempts at balancing power between the major parties have meant that political interests have been brokered, not via the democratically elected representatives in the national assembly, but through back-room negotiations between the leaders of the major groupings. Parliamentarians—men and women—follow the decisions of their political leaders, hindering cross-party alliances of women that could strengthen their voice. Simultaneously, women's rights have become a bargaining chip in constitutional negotiations between political groupings based on ethnicity and sect.

However, we concur with other observers of the Iraqi political scene that the emergence of political divisions based on communal identities has not been an inevitable consequence of Iraq's religious and ethnic makeup (e.g., Herring and Rangwala 2006; Dodge 2007). This chapter has demonstrated how the political decisions taken by the United States during the occupation have empowered ethnic and sectarian-based parties, helping to construct a de facto confessional political system and ultimately fueling the growth of sectarian identifications among ordinary Iraqis and provoking sectarian conflict.

Meanwhile, the poor security situation and fear of death threats and assassination have limited women's ability to participate openly in politics. To some degree, the political process has contributed to the violence by empowering some groups (namely, the Da'wa, SCIRI, and the Kurdish national parties) over others, thereby creating a situation where opposition politics may be more successfully conducted through bullets than through ballots. In addition, the failure of the political process to reconstruct effective central state institutions has enabled local groups to take the law into their own hands to assert their political authority. Their militias have fought against one another for political preeminence in places like Diwaniya, Amara, Basra, and other towns in southern Iraq and have attempted to impose political authority on local populations by policing public morality. Women as well as ethnic and religious minorities have been particular targets of these efforts.

Democracy has not brought Iraqi women the benefits for which they hoped when they bravely voted in January 2005. U.S. support for the rights of Iraqi women and their families has not stretched much further than the rhetoric, as we argued in the last chapter, and many Iraqi women activists quickly grasped this. In the next chapter, we discuss the ways in which women activists have attempted to identify and to pursue their own aspirations and goals—although, significantly, not in a context of their choosing. We would wholeheartedly agree with Alia T., who worked in Iraq during the first three years of the occupation to empower women in Iraq. "A lot of talk in U.S. government circles is that 'we gave Iraqi women a platform. What the Iraqi women do with it is up to them.' Actually, what the U.S. did is dig a grave for Iraqi women and now they have to lie in it." But while the grave may be dug, Iraqi women activists have not taken the challenge lying down.

OPEN SHUTTERS IRAQ

Open Shutters, which provided the photographs shown on the following pages, has trained women from all over Iraq to share their experience of the war and occupation using photographs and writing. Before choosing their stories, the women prepared and presented intimate life maps. All the content of the project was created and edited by the women themselves.

As the war in Iraq intensified and militias targeted more and more journalists, windows onto the normal, everyday lives of Iraqis closed. During her work in Syria, Eugenie Dolberg, director of Open Shutters, met many exiled Iraqis who spoke of the enduring courage of women in Iraq. She decided to create an opportunity for them to tell their side of the story in their own voices: the human reality of war, behind the collective headlines.

It was impossibly dangerous to do the work in Iraq itself, but Syria was a feasible alternative. There, women could come from Iraq to learn photography and share their experiences before returning home to shoot their stories. The Iraqi project manager, Irada al Jibbouri, a professor at the University of Baghdad and novelist, took leave from her work to undertake the difficult task of finding six women journalists who would, in turn, find six women outside the public forum to partner and support for the duration of the program. It was very important that the women came from diverse backgrounds; so, carrying a wide range of IDs and disguises, Irada traveled across Iraq to find participants and convince their families to take part in the project.

Everybody lived and worked together in a large, traditional house in the old city of Damascus. Over three weeks they sat around a big table in the courtyard and bore witness to one another's lives. Although most of the women had always lived in Iraq, this was the first time they could share their stories or listen to others from such a range of social, religious, and political backgrounds.

The work was intense and intimate. The thread of contemporary Iraqi history emerged through their tales of war, sanctions, broken marriages, grief, love, happiness, times of resistance, achievements, and small triumphs. No one had escaped unspeakable loss and trauma, and the unending destruction in Iraq has allowed no time for recovery. The women listened to one another with patience and compassion. Despite their differences, they shared an extraordinary determination and humanity.

Every day they studied different elements of photography, went on outshoots in the old city, and reviewed their photos in slide shows. By the time they returned to Iraq, they had all chosen and storyboarded a subject to shoot.

On the project's logistics form, the women were asked how they would protect themselves and minimize risk. Several wrote the same answer: "I will leave it to the will of God." This caused a lot of laughter at the time; it wasn't quite what had been expected, but their point was crystal-clear. When the world around you is falling apart, whatever precautions you take or preparations you make, in the end it is completely out of your hands.

During the six weeks of shooting in Iraq, the Iraqi project manager bravely overcame obstacles including death threats (unrelated to the project), militia kidnappings, bombings, curfews, and border closures, not to speak of the daily power cuts, road closures, petrol queues, lack of water, and blocked telephone networks that have become part of daily Iraqi life. Despite all of this, when the time came for editing, each group arrived in Damascus with huge amounts of shot material, which they edited and wrote about in a five-day workshop. Their stories bear unique, earth-shattering witness to the human crisis that is hidden behind news reports, in which people become mere numbers. They are a testimony to the bravery of a group of women living through the unthinkable horror this war has become.

This project was made possible by dedicated support from Index on Censorship and funded by the UNDP.

What's next: The work will be shown in exhibitions throughout the

Middle East, Europe, and America, and a book of the women's work and film by Maysoon Pachachi will be available in 2008.

In May 2007 one of the participants, Um Mohammad, discovered she had breast cancer. Um Mohammad is a forty-two-year-old from Basra, an area heavily affected by depleted uranium. She is a journalist, activist, and mother of three. There is no longer proper medical treatment in Iraq, and Open Shutters has relocated Um Mohammad to Lebanon, where she has begun treatment.

Please contact Open Shutters if you want to know more about or support the program or wish to help us with Um Mohammad's ongoing medical and living expenses. Contact Eugenie Dolberg at eugeniedolberg@gmail.com, or visit www.openshutters.org.

Antoinette. At home in Mosul.

"*I sit drinking my morning coffee and I get distracted. I think about my daughter. She says to me, 'We're trapped in the house and the terror in our streets is never-ending—I'm just afraid that my future will end before all this does . . . and I feel torn and deeply sad. . . . I can try to find her work in Erbil, but I'd collapse if she left my side. I'd be terrified constantly that she would get hurt.*"

Antoinette. At home in Mosul.

*"Tamara is standing, watching the street. She was ready to go to college
when she heard gunfire. She stands waiting till the noise stops. Maybe she'll
manage to get to college in time to take her exams."*

Dima. At home in Baghdad.

"Nour and Farah in the carport of our house. They've come to play with me."

© DIMA/INDEX ON CENSORSHIP/OPEN SHUTTERS

Lu'lu'a. At home in Kirkuk.

"*Fear has invaded my life, and guns have conquered every detail of my house. How I have tried to keep my home attractive . . . beautiful . . . but my eyes are forced to look at guns everywhere.*"

© LU'LU'A/INDEX ON CENSORSHIP/OPEN SHUTTERS

Lujane. At a secondary school in Baghdad.

"At a time when Iraqi women are being forced to wear hijab or abayas, *this rooster can walk proudly down the street without constraint, without concrete barriers, without being searched."*

Lujane. A street in Baghdad.

"*The curfew in Baghdad officially starts at 8 PM. However, life practically stops altogether in the afternoon. Our weddings and nights of pleasure begin at 10 AM. Plays are performed at noon, and with all the traffic jams, we have to start for home at 2 PM.*"

Lujane. Al-Alawe area in Baghdad.

Jalal Talabani, the president of the Iraqi Republic, keeps a watchful eye on American troops.

Raya. Baghdad.

"*Electricity, oh, electricity. . . . Her Majesty has announced her arrival in our house—
the bell we installed especially for that purpose just rang. My mother runs to turn
on the washing machine and then the vacuum cleaner so she can Hoover up our
dreams scattered on carpets all over the house, with the ash of our cigarettes and
of our spirit. My father switches on the iron, hoping he can finish pressing his shirt,
which hides in its fabric the story of a life frayed by war, shock, and the separation
from loved ones. My sister, with her Sumerian eyes, turns on the radio—maybe she
can unblock her ears deafened by the sound of car bombs; maybe she can hear
Fairouz singing, 'Beirut enjoys the glory of its ashes.' My son turns on the television;
on the screen, the 'dwarves' [politicians] who have twisted our days out of shape
and wrecked our dreams. He switches over to the satellite stations to watch cartoon
children. . . . Before anyone manages to do what they want, our national electricity
is cut—as crooked and unreliable as all the Arab governments. My young son,
Bashar, writes: 'Electricity, electricity, are you the dark, or a power cut, or are you
hot weather and boredom?'*"

Raya. Al-Mutanabi Street, Baghdad.

"*The Tigris mourned Baghdad when the Mongol leader Hülagü invaded the city and threw all the books and manuscripts into the river—the water turned the color of ink. Now Baghdad mourns its Tigris, which has become a hostage to barbed wire. Neighborhoods have emptied—their residents forced to flee for their lives. And the sky has turned gray and black. We are lost—between the grieving mothers—in streets where once we loved each other like brothers.*"

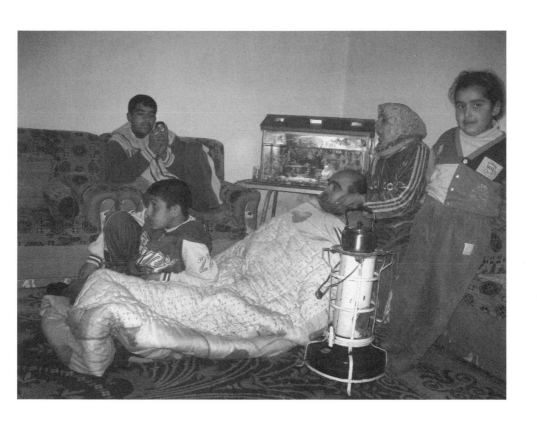

Sarab. At home, Baghdad.

> *"Even if it's midnight and even if we're busy doing something, the minute they give us an hour of electricity, we leave whatever we're doing and gather in front of the TV."*

Shamous.

> "A group of my colleagues at the university, Bab Al Mu'adham, Baghdad. A month
> after the beginning of the occupation, I went to my college . . . and I cried . . .
> everything had been damaged . . . finished . . . they'd burned everything they weren't
> able to carry away . . . they talked and they talked about the billions that were being
> earmarked for the rebuilding of Iraq. . . . I don't know whether it is corruption or
> fear that's the reason, but to date nothing has been fixed."

Um Mohammad. The old city, Basra.

> "*This is old Basra . . . now. . . . I remember how I loved its houses and its* shanashil
> *[balconies] . . . its river with the boats plying up and down . . . nothing is left of it but
> ruin and destruction, broken bricks, collapsing houses. Every day the river shrinks—
> it's full of garbage.*"

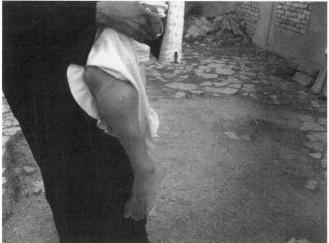

Um Mohammad.

> *"Bush, the father, called it 'Desert Storm' and Saddam Hussein, the 'Mother of All Battles,' but we just called it Purgatory. They filled my city with depleted uranium. This child suffers like hundreds of others from the cancers that it causes. Seeing her made me wonder whether my daughter, my daughter's daughter, or my daughter's grandchild will suffer in the same way. When I saw this young girl, I felt a terrible depression and a searing rage in my heart. There is nothing we can do to escape this pain."*

FOUR

THE IRAQI WOMEN'S MOVEMENT

In the summer of 2006, a London-based women's organization called Act Together: Women's Action for Iraq invited one of the leading women's rights activists from Iraq to help raise consciousness about the deteriorating situation of women under occupation.[1] Aside from talking about the general difficulties related to the increasing violence, chaos, lawlessness, and collapsed infrastructure, Sundus Abass and other Iraqi women activists inside Iraq wanted help in their campaign against an article of the Iraqi constitution that threatened women's rights in relation to family affairs. As we discussed in the previous chapter, Article 41 of the new constitution abolished the relatively progressive personal status law that had been in place since 1959. Iraqi women activists also had other concerns related to the constitution, which remained ambiguous about the role of Islamic law and did not explicitly state adherence to international conventions and laws pertaining to human and women's rights.

Act Together organized several public meetings, met with various NGOs at the Amnesty International headquarters in London, and lobbied relevant governmental and nongovernmental bodies, such as the U.K. Human Rights Bar, the National Commission for Women, and the All Party Gender Equality Group, as well as some individual MPs. Throughout the various meetings, it became clear that even within relevant nongovernmental and governmental circles the extent of the chaos, violence, and sheer horror facing the Iraqi population in general and women in particular had not been fully grasped. As Abass spoke passionately, often with tears in her eyes, about the plight of women, the difficulties of everyday life, the atrocities committed by the occupying forces, and the increasing encroachment of conservative militant Islamist forces, embarrassed silence was the prevailing response.

The London-based group had initially hesitated to get involved in the campaign around the constitution given that the constitutional and political processes were taking place in the context of an illegal occupation. The women of Act Together, like other Iraqis, were faced with the question of whether they would compromise their antioccupation stance by getting involved in the political process. This very question had deeply divided Iraqi activists and organizations in the diaspora, which had already been polarized prior to the invasion in 2003. Inside Iraq, however, political realities and the harsh conditions of everyday lives forced women to take a far more pragmatic approach, focusing on obtaining welfare, humanitarian assistance, and services and on gaining a voice, rather than being marginalized, in the political processes and institution building that were happening anyway.

In this chapter, we demonstrate how Iraqi women activists have negotiated the realities of war and occupation and map out the diverse scene of Iraqi women's activism. We describe and analyze their demands and activities, discuss the tensions and political rifts, and shed light on the obstacles and challenges facing women activists since 2003. We also attend to the relationships and tensions between Iraqi diaspora women's organizations and Iraqi women activists who never left Iraq.

WOMEN ADDRESSING PRACTICAL NEEDS

Women were at the forefront of efforts to cope with the humanitarian crisis and improve the exceedingly difficult living conditions that prevailed after the downfall of the previous regime. In 2003 and 2004, locally based women's initiatives and groups proliferated to address practical issues related to widespread poverty and supplement the inadequate state provision of health care, housing, and other social services. Women also pooled their resources to provide women's and girls' education and training, such as literacy and computer classes, as well as income-generating projects. Many of the initiatives have been created by political parties and religiously motivated organizations and groups. However, independent nonpartisan professional women have also mobilized to help.

In the early days after the invasion, initiatives were mainly directed toward people's most immediate needs. Ameena R. and other women in her social circle and Baghdad neighborhood organized themselves to feed patients left in a local hospital with no care after the violence and looting had scared away most doctors and nurses: "We started to get organized after the invasion. We went to a hospital where there were 50 people and no one was taking care of them. We took turns to cook for the patients. We organized the clean-up of our local schools. When I went with a group of women to clean up a school in our neighbourhood, there was an American soldier and he tried to prevent us, but we managed to clean the school anyway. We were still afraid to send our children to school, though" (Al-Ali 2007: 250). Despite the difficulties related to the chaos, lawlessness, and looting of this period, many women we interviewed said they had felt a general sense of opportunities, opening of doors, and optimism. As in most places, it was mainly educated, urban middle-class women who first came together to start women's projects and organizations, which later on merged to become a more self-identified women's movement.

Crucially, as many foreign observers have noted during visits to Iraq in the early phase after the invasion and as the people we interviewed reconfirmed, it was mostly Iraqi women who, in the words of Leila G., "came together to do something to help. We just felt it was our duty to help as so many people were struggling to make ends meet." And as one international NGO worker who had been in Baghdad in the immediate aftermath of the fall of Saddam told Nicola, "Iraqi women's organizations got themselves organized much faster than anyone else." Rabea K., who had returned to Iraq in 2003 after almost twenty-five years, was full of admiration and praise: "Women were so energetic and so ready to help, to get involved. They appeared to be more flexible and practical than many of the men I met. They were interested not only in their own personal lives but in the whole social situation."

Dr. Hala G., an educated and devoutly religious woman in the medical profession, told Nadje how she and a number of her friends and colleagues started a charity for extremely poor women, widows, and orphans in Baghdad:

> Bremer started to speak about civil society being open to all people. At that moment, we decided to start something, to start an organization. In the beginning, we wanted to help women. It was difficult for women to get outside their houses. We gathered women in our neighborhood and told them about our idea. We started with the project in May 2003. By July everything was settled. We knew what we wanted to do. We looked for a place. We wanted to help poor women in different ways: help them to learn something, to be

skilful, help those who lost their husbands, help women to get some work. We rented a big house for three years. The owner was a doctor living outside Iraq. We used the money from our own savings and individual contributions. We only had money for two computers. Some people helped with their own means. We opened a small clinic and a small computer centre. We brought some young women who were educated in computers and they started computer classes for girls. The centre is in the middle of a residential area. We recognized those who were extremely poor. We asked women to show us their documents to prove that they are widows. (Al-Ali 2007: 251)

The privileged status of highly educated professional and middle-class women has often meant that their projects are rooted in paternalistic ideas of welfare and charity. Yet many of the locally conceived projects run by professional Iraqi women who are rooted in particular communities have proved to be far more successful and sustainable than some of the programs initiated by foreign organizations, including the CPA and also some returnees.

The charity of Dr. Hala G.'s organization, like that of many groups that have emerged over the past years, is a desperate attempt to fill the gap left by the lack of government provisions and welfare. Not accepting money from either political parties or the occupying forces, the organization managed to raise some funds among friends and colleagues before receiving some charitable donations from nonpolitical individuals and organizations abroad:

After some time an organization of Iraqis based in the U.S. heard about us. They are called "Life for Relief and Development." They visited us and they asked what we need. Their Iraqi representative asked if we needed more computers, maybe a bigger refrigerator. They helped us. They sent us computers and an industrial sewing machine. After that we could accept ten girls for computer classes. The girls were without hope in the beginning. When the families knew that the women working in the charity were from good families and that they were religious, they let the girls come. Even some Christian girls started to come. They were happy in the courses. They had no other opportunity to socialize.

With very little means and a lot of resolve and creativity, Dr. Hala and her colleagues managed to open branches in two other areas of Baghdad as well as in Fallujah. When asked what her organization had been doing concretely to help poverty-stricken widows, Dr. Hala replied:

We gave them 25,000 dinars [about 17 U.S. dollars] monthly to help them. Before we gave them money, we gave them lectures about having to help themselves, not to depend on charity. We spoke about the need to work. So women came to us asking us to help them find work. We brought them cheap cloth and showed them how to sew. We sold the clothes in a charity market. Some women did not like sewing, so we thought about cooking. We had a big kitchen in the house. We thought about letting them make *kubba, burek* and other Iraqi foods, which was a very good project. Some girls asked for lectures in English. We have one member who graduated in languages, who volunteered to teach English. Some women did not like sewing, cooking or English, so we gave them lessons in memorizing the Qu'ran. Then they started to bring children. So we started a kindergarten. We have nine rooms, and each room has a different function. (Al-Ali 2007: 252)

Although many women activists have been forced to abandon their projects because of the escalation of violence and threats to their lives and those of the women who benefited from their services, Hala and her friends have managed to continue with their work, even while risking their lives on a daily basis. A successful fundraising campaign by a U.S.-based women's peace organization has boosted the financial status of the organization. Dr. Hala knows that she and her colleagues are at risk of violence, but being deeply religious and antisectarian at the same time, she is hoping that the hard work is being appreciated within the various communities where her organization is operating. Hala stresses her sense of Iraqiness and her wish to help Iraqi widows and orphans of all religious and ethnic backgrounds. She and her friends have participated in more overtly political campaigns and debates around the constitution and against sectarianism. Being rooted in a religious framework that finds expression in her modest dress code and support of the implementation of Islamic law, she and her colleagues may be less at risk than secular women activists, who, whatever their ethnic or religious background, have become major targets of Shi'i militias and Sunni insurgents alike. Then again, Dr. Hana's devout religious position may make her a target for sectarian violence, and she shares with all other Iraqis the risk of random shootings and violence by the occupation forces.

Our interviews with Iraqi women who continue to live inside Iraq have clearly shown that women have been particularly hard hit by poverty, inadequate health care, malnutrition, and lack of electricity and clean water as well as the daily violence and lack of security, all conditions that have deteriorated since the invasion. Women, however, have been at the forefront of trying to cope with and improve difficult living conditions, sharing their scarce resources, their expertise, and their professional skills to help those in even greater need. Yet unlike Dr. Hala's organization, which has been extremely adamant and principled about not accepting funding from any government sources, many organizations and groups have taken a different approach. Later on in this chapter we elaborate on the various attitudes toward and implications of foreign funding of women's initiatives.

Many women's organizations that started out focusing on providing charity, humanitarian assistance, and social services—practical gender issues—got involved in more political and strategic gender issues in 2004 and 2005. Women mobilized politically when their legal rights in relation to their roles within families became endangered. They even started to mobilize to demand participation in the political process, starting with a women's quota that would ensure political representation. But as violence and social conservatism have increased and as living conditions have deteriorated since mid-2005, the associated loss of political and social spaces for women's organizations has led many women activists to revert to a focus on welfare, charity, income generation, and training.

WOMEN'S POLITICAL MOBILIZATION

Many Iraqi women soon realized that despite the rhetoric of women's liberation and increased women's rights they could not rely on the Americans, the British, or their own male politicians to have a say and play a significant role in creating the "new Iraq." As discussed in the previous chapter, some Iraqi women linked to former exiled opposition parties and those of elite background clearly benefited from the early attempts by the United States to show its adherence to women's rights. Yet a broad range of women activists and organizations emerged in the aftermath of the invasion whose main sources of motivation were a great commitment to do something positive, even if this meant risking their lives. Samira Moustafa, secretary general of the Baghdad-based Iraqi Women's League, the oldest Iraqi women's rights group, said in 2003: "We want a real place on the political map of Iraq" (Khalil 2004). In an interview on *Woman's Hour* (BBC Radio 4) in April 2003, Shanez Rashid, another Iraqi woman activist, said emphatically: "We had an equal share of pain and we need an equal share of peace" (Abdela et al. 2003).

Many of the new women's organizations, such as the National Council of Women, the 1000 Women's Conference, the Iraqi Women's Higher Council, the Iraqi Independent Women's Group, and the Society for Iraqi Women for the Future, were founded either by members of the former INC or by prominent professional women with close ties to political parties. Several organizations, such as the Women's Alliance for a Democratic Iraq (WAFDI), the Iraqi Women's Network, and the Organization for Women's Freedom in Iraq, were initiated by returnees—that is, Iraqi women activists who had been part of the diaspora before 2003. The hundreds of women's organizations that proliferated in central and southern Iraq added to the already significant numbers in Iraqi Kurdistan, such as al-Amal, the Women's Empowerment Organization, the Rewan Women's Center, and Zhin, as well as the women's unions linked to different political parties there. However, as discussed in greater detail later in this chapter, Kurdish women's organizations are forming a Kurdish women's movement that is by and large separate from an Iraqi women's movement in central and southern Iraq.

The women involved in these numerous organizations tend to be urban-based, middle-class women of various ethnic and religious backgrounds. While many organizations are founded by elite women, some of the groups have a broad membership and have branches throughout the country. The Iraqi Women's Network (al-Shabaka al-Mar'a al-'Iraqiyya), for example, consists of over eighty women's grassroots organizations dispersed throughout Iraq. These organizations engage in humanitarian and practical projects, such as income generation, legal advice, free health care and counseling, and political advocacy and lobbying.

Women's rights activists have worked across political differences in terms of their political party ties or lack thereof, as well as their attitudes toward the occupation. Women inside Iraq and from the diaspora who were opposed to the invasion of Iraq have been working side by side with women who initially welcomed the invasion as the only possible means to change the political system and get rid of the dictatorship of Saddam Hussein. Shirouk Alabyachi told Nadje during a short visit to London in August 2007: "Dealing or not dealing with the Americans was not the decisive measure for us. We wanted to get things done. We wanted them [United States and United Kingdom] to work to our agenda. But of course there were different strategies in terms of contact with the Americans and funding." According to several women activists Nadje talked to, in the early period many Iraqi women activists, especially those from the opposition parties, "spent all their time thanking Bremer for getting rid of Saddam and bringing democracy. However, those of us who were critical from the beginning and said so openly were in the minority."

Shirouk explained the complex dynamics between coordinators of the Iraqi Women's Network and "the Americans":

> In April 2004, the U.S. embassy invited us to a meeting. We knew that they wanted to establish an Iraqi Women's Council and Bremer wanted to push some of "his women." These women were not really qualified, but some-

how he was supporting them. We decided to boycott the meeting, and it turned out to be a failure. A few days later, we got an invitation from someone else in the CPA telling us that they wanted to hear what our demands are. While some of the women present spent their time praising and thanking Bremer, our coordinator Hanaa Edwar went through a long list of criticisms and demands, including our demand to stop the military assaults in Fallujah and Najaf. She was so brave! You should have seen Bremer's face; it was getting redder and redder. At some point he interrupted Hanaa and told her that he wanted to reply to her criticisms. He was justifying his policies and actions with stereotypes and clichés about Iraqis.

A white paper produced by the National Conference for Empowering Women in Democracy in June 2004, which was attended by over 350 delegates from all over the country, demanded an "end to the occupation and conviction of all inhuman practices committed by the occupying forces against civilian people" (Iraqi al-Amal Association 2004). Over the past years, even those in favor of the invasion acknowledge that the situation under occupation has deteriorated beyond imagination and that women's rights have suffered tremendously. Sawsan A. was initially a fervent supporter of the U.S./U.K. invasion in 2003 but had changed her mind by 2006:

> I had so much hope in 2003. I thought, "The Americans and the British will make sure that women's rights will be protected." We worked so hard despite difficulties from the very beginning. There were conferences, meetings; we even organized demonstrations and sit-ins. Many educated women started projects to help poor illiterate women, widows, and orphans. Things were not great, but I believed that it was just a matter of time until we would manage to find a new way and live in a true democracy. But see what they have done to our country? Our politicians sit in the Green Zone while ordinary people are being killed every day. Terrorists control the streets and the Americans only watch. Women are targeted, especially those who have a public profile.

Though a very small minority of women continue to applaud the democratization and liberation efforts of the occupying forces and the elected government, the majority of women activists from central and southern Iraq are deeply disillusioned and disappointed. While generally critical of U.S./U.K. policies and Iraqi male politicians, women activists differ in terms of what strategies to adopt now: a few ask for a immediate withdrawal of troops, but others prefer to call for a definitive but phased timetable for withdrawal. Despite their misgivings, many women activists prefer U.S. and U.K. troops to remain until the threat of Islamist militancy, terrorist attacks, and sectarian violence has been controlled and Iraqi troops and police are ready to take over. Meanwhile, many women's organizations have opted to be part of the political process, despite their opposition to many of its aspects. Miriam H., who is active in a women's project in Baghdad, said: "We do not have a choice but to engage with the process. It is a reality whether we like it or not. But I have to admit we have spent most of the time campaigning and demonstrating against the way this process has taken place so far. One of our main objections is the exclusion of women and the incompetence of people involved." Another woman activist lamented that the Iraqi women's movement has been unable to develop its capacity and focus on the real needs and issues because of the way the political process was imposed: "We always had to follow the political agenda, which prevented us from expanding and building our capacity as a movement. We had to focus on the elections, which did not allow us much space to develop our own projects. It is an ongoing problem. Lots of money is spent on women's rights awareness training, but the money should be spent on improving the humanitarian situation. How can I talk to a poor woman in the countryside about her legal rights if she is worried about finding medicine for her sick son?" What engagement with the political process might mean is open to interpretation and varies from activist to activist. Some women and organizations are in regular contact with the Iraqi government and the occupying forces within the Green Zone, especially those women activists who are also part of political parties. But most of the women with whom we talked try to stay away from the Green Zone and avoid, as much as possible, close contact with the occupation forces while advocating for women's rights.

Among the most outspoken organizations against the occupation are OWFI, represented by Yanar Mohammed inside Iraq, and Iraqi Women's Will (IWW), founded by Hana Ibrahim. These two women's organizations have different political orientations: OWFI pursues radical secular, leftist, and feminist politics linked to the Workers' Communist Party of Iraq, and IWW has a nonpartisan anti-imperialist and Arab nationalist agenda. However, both organizations have consistently tried to raise awareness about the various ways women have been affected by the occupation. While IWW has focused on gender-specific violence by occupation forces, OWFI has also been trying to raise awareness about violence by Islamist groups, organizations, and political parties.

Nadeen El-Kassem (2007), whose ongoing research focuses on the external involvement in Iraqi women's NGOs, argues that while many of the women's groups who were less outspoken against the occupation were initially able to flourish, members of the antioccupation Cultural Club for Women, which focused on peace and antiwar education, were repeatedly verbally and physically threatened. According to Hana Ibrahim, they were finally forced to leave their headquarters when five men working for Ahmed Chalabi's party, the INC, wanted to confiscate the building for the party. Subsequently, Ibrahim and other members of the Cultural Club for Women established the IWW, which was much more politicized and openly antioccupation than the former organization (El-Kassem 2007).

Yanar Mohammed of OWFI is probably the Iraqi women's activist with the highest international public profile, especially after she received several death threats in 2004. OWFI has established good networking between members of the organization inside Iraq and in the diaspora and succeeded in lobbying internationally. A small popular basis has been established through OWFI's various programs of humanitarian assistance and provision of services, including a women's shelter and the provision of medicines, food, and clothes to displaced people living in camps in Baghdad. However, several Iraqi women activists we talked to have chosen to distance themselves from OWFI's radical secular and radical feminist politics, which they perceive as a liability and an obstacle to constructive dialogue between secular and Islamist women.

THE WOMEN'S QUOTA

One of the first issues to mobilize women politically was the campaign around the women's quota, which the previous chapter discussed in the context of the TAL and the elections. Souad R. was part of a delegation to visit Bremer in spring of 2004 to demand 40 percent representation in any future government, ministries, and state institutions. She was still outraged when she told Nadje in 2005:

> We were determined to get involved in the new institutions and government. We knew that Iraqi male politicians, even the more progressive ones, would try to sideline us. But we make up more than half of the population![2] And we women have been holding together Iraqi society during all these years of suffering. But Bremer told us: "We don't do quotas." We were so angry, especially because the Americans had used quotas with respect to ethnic and religious groups in the Iraqi Governing Council. The British ambassador, Jeremy Greenstock, was much more supportive. And we decided not to give up but continue our lobbying.

In the run-up to the transition from the appointed IGC to a provisional administration that took over in June 2004 and the drafting of the TAL,

Iraqi women activists organized demonstrations and sit-ins. As Hanaa Edwar, secretary general of al-Amal as well as co-coordinator of al-Shabaka (the Iraqi Women's Network), stated at the time: "It is a decisive time for Iraqi women to be represented in the democratization of our country. We have to have a guarantee in this law that the representation of women will not be less than 40 percent in all political decision making" (Agence France-Presse 2004).

Not all women activists, however, believed that a formal quota was the answer. Samira Moustafa of the Iraqi Women's League worried that the government was looking for women just to fill the quota: "Why should we set a number? Why close the door?" she asked. "Hiring should be based on qualifications. Maybe 60 percent of the female candidates are better than the men." But Safia al-Suhail, a U.S.-backed activist who had been part of the political opposition in exile, disagreed strongly and thought Moustafa's argument was far too idealistic. In her view, quotas were a necessary and temporary evil to help implant a "generation or two" of qualified women throughout the government. "If a man gets 150,000 votes and a woman gets 30,000 votes in the same district, I'd choose the woman because that's a more impressive accomplishment," she said. "It's a stage until we can adjust, then little by little we can return to the normal situation" (Khalil 2004).

Despite internal debates and Bremer's opposition, Iraqi women activists achieved the compromise of a 25 percent target for women's participation in elected assemblies in the TAL and the permanent constitution. For many observers of political developments inside Iraq, as well as for Iraqi women activists themselves, the 25 percent quota has been one of the major achievements of the Iraqi women's movement. Ann Clwyd, a U.K. politician who has long campaigned for the human rights of Iraqis and who was Prime Minister Tony Blair's special envoy on human rights in Iraq, told Nicola: "I think the 25 percent quota in parliament is good. We always say that this is more than in the U.K. parliament. So we still have to struggle in this country to ensure women's participation in politics. It is not just in Iraq." Similar systems have been instituted in South Africa and Rwanda; the latter reached the highest level of female participation of any government in the world when a 49 percent female parliament was elected in 2003. Rezan M., a member of the Islamic Union of Kurdistan and a provincial council, said: "The best thing that has happened is that the constitution gives women a 25 percent quota. The quota has helped us to get into parliament as women."

Not all women activists share the enthusiasm for the women's quota,

though. There has been a debate about the benefits and problems of stipulating a women's quota, especially since many of the conservative Islamist political parties have obviously appointed conservative Islamist
women who are not necessarily interested in the promotion of women's
rights. While secular women in parliament were determined to protect
women's rights within a secular framework, they were a minority in parliament. Nadia S., an Iraqi-Kurdish women's rights activist, described to
Nicola the first parliament after the elections in January 2005: "The vast
majority of the women in the national assembly cover themselves from
head to foot—they're not just wearing the *hijab* [headscarf]. The secular groups are the Kurdish parties and the Allawi list. Ghazi Yawar's list
is not secular because he presents himself as tribal and they are usually
religious. . . . Women in secular parties are not very strong. There are
some good, tough women there, but there are not very many of them."
In a similar vein, Sawsan H., another Baghdad-based women's rights activist, complained to Nadje: "Most of the women who are in parliament
or in the various ministries are the wives, daughters, and sisters of conservative Islamist politicians. They don't have any experience with politics, nor do they care about women's rights. In fact, I hardly see them
open their mouths to say anything. When there is a vote on something,
they first look at what the male politicians in their party vote for." The
party list system meant that women in parliament had been chosen by
the male leaders of political groups. Therefore, they were more beholden
to these male leaders than to the voters or even the goal of women's empowerment per se. Nadra B., a former *peshmerga* fighter and women's
rights activist, told Nicola: "It is important to have independent women
as opposed to women who are part of political parties. These types of
women are always defending their party." Many women's rights advocates we talked to complained that party lists have been stuffed with
women who have no experience of public affairs and simply do what
they are told by their party leaders. Jenan al-Ubaedey, a former pedia-
trician elected on the Shi'i UIA list, stated: "It's true that many of them—
maybe a third—have just been put there by the men. They are not aware
and don't come to meetings, so they don't know what's going on. . . .
About 10 percent of them are learning, but the others don't really care"
(Philip 2005: 152).

Jenan Al-Ubaedey is one of many women who were determined to
reform the personal status code in line with shari'a (Islamic law). This
brought her and her colleagues into conflict with those women and men
who wanted to maintain Iraq as a secular state. Nermine A., working

in an international agency concerned with women's empowerment, told Nicola: "It is commonly heard that there is a polarization between liberal and conservative women [in parliament] over the role of the shari'a. More conservative women see nothing wrong with introducing shari'a. Because of this polarization, many people said, 'Women don't know what they want, so let's keep the status quo.'"

Some women we have talked to argue, however, that in a general political climate of social conservatism a quota ensures at least some female presence in public life and may also allow those more committed to women's issues and social justice to enter government institutions. Several secular women activists we interviewed argued that conservative women parliamentarians may change their opinions with experience and that there are some attempts to build alliances between secular and Islamist women in parliament over issues such as the treatment of women prisoners and humanitarian issues.

CAMPAIGNING FOR WOMEN'S LEGAL RIGHTS

Iraqi women's perseverance was crucial in helping to stop the passage of Resolution 137 in early 2004. As discussed in the last chapter, the proposed law, suggested at the end of 2003 by members of the IGC under the rotating chairmanship of Abdul-Aziz al-Hakim, a leader of SCIRI (now renamed the Supreme Islamic Iraqi Council or SIIC), could have replaced Iraq's unified personal status code with laws rooted in more conservative interpretations of shari'a. The personal status code—the set of laws on family matters such as marriage, divorce, child custody, and inheritance—was codified in the postrevolutionary constitution in 1959, as we explained in the context of the history of Iraqi women's activism (for more details, see Efrati 2005). Although this set of laws, which was amended in 1978, was not secular but rooted in shari'a, it represented a relatively progressive and liberal interpretation of Islamic law. Being a unified law, it mitigated sectarianism by synthesizing Shi'i and Sunni interpretations of Islamic law into one code that was applied to all citizens regardless of sect. Crucially, the 1959 personal status code also replaced a system that gave judicial authority and control to religious clerics with a unified national judicial system under the authority of the state.

Many women's activists (though by no means all) vehemently opposed Resolution 137 as a step backwards for Iraqi women. Hundreds of Iraqi women demonstrated on the streets and lobbied the IGC, the CPA, and international bodies to prevent the proposal from passing into law.

Zeinab H., who was involved in the campaign at the time, told Nadje: "There was still the sense at the time that we could make a difference. It was still safe enough to actually go out on the streets and demonstrate. The women were of all religious and ethnic backgrounds. There were veiled women and unveiled ones. What united us was the fear of letting any of the increasingly more conservative and radical Islamists interpret Islamic law in a totally random way." It took ten weeks and intense protests by Iraqi women activists as well as international organizations before Paul Bremer repealed Resolution 137. The campaign not only brought together secular Iraqi women activists across the political spectrum and a variety of ethnic and religious backgrounds but also was one of the more successful instances of transnational feminist solidarity and activism. Iraqi women's rights activists managed to raise the issue internationally and gained support from women's organizations and networks throughout the world.

Unfortunately, the attempt to curtail women's rights and increase the authority of religious clerics has found its way into Iraq's new constitution. As we discussed earlier, neither the previous TAL nor the current constitution explicitly mentions women's rights in the context of marriage, divorce, child custody, and inheritance. Instead, Article 41 of the constitution states that "Iraqis are free in their adherence to their personal status according to their own religion, sect, belief and choice, and that will be organized by law." Many Iraqi women activists fear that Article 41, if retained in the constitution, will totally and irrevocably change the lives of Iraqi women. The old personal status code, which applied to everyone, would be replaced by family laws pertaining to specific religious and ethnic communities. Authority would reside in religious leaders, who could interpret the shari'a according to their own beliefs. Given precedents in Iraq before 1959 as well as in other Muslim countries in the region, secular Iraqi women activists fear that in some communities the marriage of girls as young as nine might be sanctioned; women might be forced into marriage or remarried against their will, if widowed, to a dead husband's male relative. Inheritance, custody of children, and divorce rights might be denied to women. Secular women activists also argue that the judiciary would certainly not be independent and that women, unprotected by any legal safeguards, would risk experiencing systematic oppression and discrimination.

Shari'a in and of itself is not to be equated with women's oppression, since much depends on the actual interpretation of Islamic law. Across the Muslim world there is a wide range of interpretations of Islamic family laws on marriage, divorce, child custody, and inheritance, from the conservative Wahabi interpretations in Saudi Arabia to the more progressive and egalitarian interpretation on which the Moroccan *moudawana* (personal status code) is based. Given the shift toward greater social conservatism and the rise of extremist Islamist forces in the shape of political parties, militias, insurgents, and religious and political leaders such as Muqtada al-Sadr, there is not much room for optimism regarding the way Islamic law would be interpreted, used, and misused in contemporary Iraq. It is probably no exaggeration for women to fear that in some communities self-appointed religious leaders as well as those linked to government institutions, militias, and insurgent groups might start to impose rules and regulations reminiscent of the Taliban regime in Afghanistan.

In the summer of 2005, Nadje was shocked to hear from a medical doctor and women's rights activist from Diwaniya, a city in the south of Iraq, about a new regulation issued by the Ministry of Health: female patients under full anesthesia would not be allowed to be operated on by male doctors or treated by male nurses. At the time, the ministry was controlled by supporters of Muqtada al-Sadr, whose Mahdi Army has become notorious for brutal sectarian killings and overzealous policing of public morality, as well as armed battles against rival Islamist Shi'i groups and occupation forces. Although the majority of Iraqi doctors did not take this directive seriously, it was a stark reminder of the possible future facing Iraqi women if religious leaders linked either to militant Shi'i or Sunni Islamists could dictate how to interpret Islamic law.

Ironically, the women's quota may help push through a conservative agenda on women's rights. Most of the women elected in parliament are linked to Shi'i political parties and support the implementation of shari'a, which includes the abolition of the codified and relatively progressive personal status code. Salama al-Khafagi, a conservative Shi'i woman politician from the UIA, argues: "Most people don't feel ownership to the existing secular family law, and we must change it to follow the sharia. Forcing secularism on our society is also a form of dictatorship" (Fassihi 2005). Jenan al-Ubaedey, another woman parliamentarian belonging to the UIA, is promoting not only Islamic law but conservative interpretations of it: "If you say to a man he cannot use force against a woman, you are asking the impossible. So we say a husband can beat his wife, but he cannot leave a mark. If he does that, he will be punished" (Philip 2005). Her vision of personal status laws includes allowing men to marry up to four wives, awarding women half the inheritance of men, and denying women custody of children over age two in the event of divorce (Philip 2005).

Yet secular Iraqi women activists inside the country and in the diaspora argue passionately that Article 41 does not merely erode the rights of women and deny them the rights they are entitled to under international law; it may also fuel and increase sectarianism. Replacing a previously unified and codified set of laws that applied equally to Sunni and Shi'i Iraqis with communally based laws that are wide open to interpretation will make new mixed marriages virtually impossible and will threaten existing ones. It will further a sense of communalism as opposed to unified citizenship and heighten the risk of continual sectarian violence and chronic civil war. Sherifa Zuhur explains how a system based on confessionalism inevitably leads to sectarianism: "In the sectarian system, women are merely a sub-category of other constituencies; they are female Kurds, Sunnis, Shi'a, or Assyrians. Sectarian interests rather than gender issues take precedence" (2006: 10).

The campaign to abolish Article 41 and keep a unified personal status code is linked to the previously mentioned wider campaign addressing women's rights within the new Iraqi constitution. The two main additional issues that the Iraqi women's movement has been particularly concerned about are the role of Islam in shaping legislation[3] and the significance of international conventions for human and women's rights—for example, the Convention on the Elimination of All Forms of Discrimination Against Women (CEDAW), which, at the time of this writing, was not explicitly recognized in the Iraqi constitution.

In the run-up to the referendum on the constitution on October 15, 2005, Iraqi women activists had tried to communicate their demands for a guarantee of women's rights to the constitutional drafting committee. Despite numerous conferences and workshops organized by various international organizations in the months prior to the referendum, women had had few official consultations with the drafting committee and few channels for discussing their concerns with them. Women activists had to resort to organizing demonstrations and sit-ins to get the attention of the drafting committee. In the middle of August 2005, members of the Iraqi women's movements organized a sit-in for the third time. Hanaa Edwar recalls:

> On Sunday 14 August, 40 Iraqi women converged at the convention centre in Baghdad, the site of drafting negotiations by the constitutional committee. They were immediately prevented from entering the lobby by a line of

red tape and armed guards, who had explicit orders to deny entry to any female demonstrators. The women, accompanied also by members of the media, tried fervently to get their messages across to participants in the main room of the negotiations, succeeding eventually in getting letters to the representatives of both the British and American embassies. As the tension mounted, the women began to sit on the floor, one by one, right under the red tape, linking their elbows and singing a traditional Iraqi song, considered one of the most cherished songs by all Iraqis. Emotions ran high and, eventually, the drafting committee agreed to meet with three women representing the group. Discussions with the representatives of the constitutional committee and with parliamentarians also present at the meeting proved largely futile, although there was a promise that all demands would be presented to the committee. (UNIFEM 2005)

Despite the deteriorating living conditions, widespread violence, and dangers to women activists' lives, the Iraqi women's movement has continued its campaign on the constitution and has managed to widen its support. In May 2007, more than 150 women's organizations signed a letter to U.S. Speaker of the House Nancy Pelosi and another to UN Secretary-General Ban Ki-moon expressing concern over the constitutional review process taking place and calling for international support for their effort to preserve women's rights in Iraqi law. The letter contains an urgent appeal for the support of international partners "to act upon obligations of UN Security Council Resolutions regarding Iraq to guarantee equality and preserve human rights," including the full implementation of UN Security Council Resolution 1325 on Women, Peace and Security (American Friends Service Committee 2007). In its tone, the letter in 2007 clearly differs from the more optimistic and hopeful statements by Iraqi women activists in 2005: "As women face escalating violence and exclusion in Iraq, they have been marginalized in reconciliation initiatives and negotiations for government positions. Even with the shy and insignificant pressure exerted by the U.N. and other international donors/players on the Iraqi government and politicians to fulfill minimum obligations of Security Council Resolution 1325, the action taken has been a sequence of disappointments" (Massey 2007). Much as they did before the referendum on the constitution in 2005, Iraqi women activists are trying to get international attention in order to put pressure on the constitutional review committee to take the views and demands of civil society organizations into consideration. However, by 2007 it has become increasingly obvious that women's rights are the first issues to be sacrificed and compromised by the various political factions as they address issues such as federalism and the status of Kirkuk in their constitutional review process. Although some Kurdish women's organizations and activists have been involved in the campaign on the Iraqi constitution, particularly with respect to Article 41 (concerning the personal status code), most of the Kurdish women activists we talked to in Erbil and Sulaymaniya state that they are not very much concerned with the Iraqi constitution. Sawsan H., a Kurdish activist working for a women's organization based in Erbil that is involved in welfare as well as lobbying for women's rights, told Nadje: "We are putting our energies and efforts into the Kurdish constitution and into lobbying our local Kurdish politicians. This is what is important for us! Yes, we work with our Iraqi sisters from time to time. I feel for them and what they have to go through. Fortunately, women in Kurdistan have managed to achieve a lot since '91. We don't want to lose what we have achieved, but we want to gain even more rights. We have been successful in inserting some positive articles into our constitution. This is what we need to focus on." According to the Iraqi constitution, the Kurdish regional constitution will take precedence so long as it does not contravene Iraqi law. One of the main differences is that the Kurdish regional constitution does not establish Islam as the main source of legislation. Most Kurdish women's rights activists we talked to argue that using Islam as the main source of legislation does not guarantee women's rights. But they stressed that women's rights were enshrined in the Kurdish regional constitution, even though much effort would have to be put into implementing those rights.

Yet many Kurdish women experienced a rude awakening when they discovered that some elements of the national legislation override the Kurdish constitution. This became obvious only with the announcement of a new administrative decree by the central government in April 2007 for the issuing of passports, according to which women need the permission of a male guardian *(mahram)* to apply for a passport. A Kurdish journalist from Sulaymaniya appeared rather frustrated, telling Nadje: "I argue all the time with my friends who do not seem to care about the Iraqi constitution. They are so short-sighted. And see what the result is: I need to get a new passport after the government announced that the old ones are invalid. I want to travel to Sweden for a conference. And now I have to ask permission from my husband, father, uncle, or brother. It is so humiliating!" Although no law in the Iraqi constitution stipulates this discriminatory passport policy, the constitution's ambiguity and space for interpretation allows for repressive decrees and policies to gain ground.

SECULAR VERSUS ISLAMIST POSITIONS

The campaign to preserve a unified and codified set of personal status laws and to recognize international conventions of human and women's rights has drawn together party-affiliated and independent women activists of different ethnic and religious backgrounds and has forged transnational links between activists inside and outside Iraq. However, a rift has emerged between secular women activists and those belonging to Islamist political parties. Jamelia R., a journalist who was linked to the Iraqi Women's League in the 1980s, told Nicola: "This division, between Islamist women and secular women, is new in Iraq. There were never these divisions before." Women associated with the Shi'i religious parties of the Da'wa and the SIIC (formerly SCIRI) have protested in favor of placing family law under religious jurisdiction (Al-Jazeera 2004), and women elected on the UIA list have also supported measures that Suzan R., a Kurdish-list member of parliament in Baghdad, sees as "against their interests [as women]."

During the campaign for women's legal rights prior to the referendum on the constitution in October 2005, Islamist women staged a counter-demonstration, as Hanaa Edwar of the Iraqi Women's Network reports:

> The sit-in that we've organized on July 19th in Al-Ferdaws Square was marvelous. Despite the fiery heat and the deteriorating security situation, brave women from different governorates have taken the initiative to raise their voices demanding to ensure women's rights and equality in the constitution and protesting against the attempt to marginalize the role of women and their human rights as well as the role of the civil society organizations in the process of writing the constitution. We stood there for three hours raising our demands and meeting with media and distributing flyers and posters to people in the street. During that time, a small group of women appeared in the street holding banners and slogans against "absolute" equality of women. They shouted slogans for Islam and Qur'an. One of them has clearly stated in an interview that they demand for Qur'an to be adopted as a constitution and for establishing an Islamic government. They stood for half an hour and left. (Edwar 2005)

On another occasion, however, Islamist women had a stronger presence and managed to divert some media attention. According to Zeinab G., one of the coordinators of the Iraqi Women's Network, the secular women made an effort to try to reach out to Islamist women:

> They were standing on the other side of Firdaws Square. We asked them to come to our tent and discuss the issue. Actually, from the beginning, we invited women from Islamic backgrounds. Not the fanatical figures, of

course. When we were dealing with women from the grassroots this was never an issue. But we sometimes have problems with women from the Islamist political parties. On this occasion, they came to our tent and we realized that our differences are actually not so big. We explained to them that the personal status code that we are supporting is not against Islamic law. Unfortunately, one of the more radical feminists came although we had asked her to stay away. She made one of her radical statements against religion, which then destroyed all the mediation and discussion between us and the Islamist women.

Many secular-oriented women rights activists have not been eager or, in some cases, able to find common ground and make strategic alliances with Islamist women, seeing the situation as a zero-sum game. Zana L., the founder of a women's organization in Iraqi Kurdistan, believes that the majority of women's organizations in the rest of Iraq want to introduce Islam into public life but says that "this threatens women's rights and democracy. . . . Now we are scared that the religious parties will take away our rights in Kurdistan." However, in central and southern Iraq, women's activists are also deeply concerned about the increasing encroachment of secular spaces and the increasing influence of Islamist conservative forces.

Suad F., an activist who was visiting Amman in June 2005, told Nadje while debating to return to Iraq or not: "There are some very active religious figures. We are competing with Islamists to provide a sack of rice. That is why we focus so much on the economics, and it works wonders. Women have a strong awareness, but only after their basic needs are met. Secular women have been approached by Islamist women to put on a *hijab*. The Islamists even promise women positions if they start to wear the *hijab*." Given the dire humanitarian situation and the widespread poverty and unemployment, it comes as no surprise that Islamist organizations and parties, which have managed to provide services and welfare, are gaining support among the increasingly impoverished population. This phenomenon has been documented in other countries in the region, such as Egypt, Palestine, and Lebanon, where the state fails to provide adequate services and humanitarian assistance to its populations.

Regarding the debate about the Iraqi constitution, it became obvious to us that some of the discrepancies between secular women's attitudes and women promoting Islamic law had more to do with lack of information about the content of the constitution and its implications than with deeply entrenched political differences (Al-Ali 2007: 256). On several occasions, women from inside Iraq who were just visiting Amman told Nadje that they were happy with the call for the implementation of the shari'a. Azza A., for example, said: "We are Muslims. Of course we want Islamic law" (256). However, when Nadje began to discuss the possible implications of this, such as the right to unilateral divorce, restrictions on freedom of movement, increased polygamy, and changes in existing child custody laws, most women expressed shock and acknowledged that they had been unaware of these potential implications.

Alia T. is a Palestinian American activist who has been working for Women to Women International for many years and who spent more than two years in Iraq before the deteriorating security situation forced her to move to Amman.[4] She expressed a great sense of frustration about not only the constitution itself but also the drafting process. Even more significantly, she was deeply concerned about the lack of dissemination and education concerning the contents of the constitution: "We were trying to bring the debate about secular versus religious onto a grassroots level. Overwhelmingly everyone said that they wanted religious law. When you explain to them what it means, explain the possible interpretations, when they start to understand the implications, they get upset."

However, as Sundus Abass points out, consciousness-raising about the constitution and the potential danger of Islamic law may not be so easy in the current context of Iraqi people's everyday lives: "People are not aware of the law and women in Iraq don't really know their rights. This is not a matter of ignorance as such, but has to do with the cruel circumstances of life in Iraq. In the context of this daily pressure, where your actual life is threatened at every moment, it sometimes feels beside the point to talk about duties and rights" (Al-Ali, Baban, and Abass 2006: 33). Except for some secular activists inside Iraq, many Iraqi women construct their differences as a contestation between "authentic" culture and values on the one side and the imposition of foreign values and political agendas on the other. The tendency to associate feminism and women's rights with Western agendas is, of course, not unique to the Iraqi context; it has been a continuous challenge and difficulty for women activists in the region since the beginning of women's movements at the turn of the twentieth century. Yet the polarization and construction of difference are particularly detrimental in the context of war and occupation. Increasingly, the discourses about women's rights and women's empowerment have been associated with the American and British occupation, or with "Western feminism," rather than with the long history of women's rights activism inside Iraq and a transnational feminist activism that unites women across the world.

THE KURDISH WOMEN'S MOVEMENT

In March and April of 2007 we visited Iraqi Kurdistan to try to understand the particular situation, struggles, and issues of Kurdish women activists and organizations. Because of various other commitments, we were not able to travel together, so we independently spent time in Erbil and Sulaymaniya, the two main cities under the Kurdistan Regional Government. During this trip we talked to numerous women who were members of the Kurdistan parliament or were associated with the women's unions linked to the main Kurdish political parties: the KDP, associated with Massoud Barzani and based in the area in and around Erbil (called Hawler in Kurdish), and the PUK, associated with Jalal Talabani, the president of Iraq, and based in Sulaymaniya. Other women activists we met with who were associated with political parties included members of the Kurdistan Communist Party, the Islamic Union of Kurdistan, and the Assyrian National Party. We talked to numerous women who were founders of or involved with one of the numerous civil society associations, such as Zhin, Pery, al-Amal, and Women's Empowerment, all based in Erbil, and the Asuda Organization for Combating Violence against Women, the Kurdistan Social Development Organization, the Civil Development Organization, Ghassem, the Breeze of Hope Organization, Reach, the Rewan Women's Center, the Children's Nest, the Democracy and Human Rights Development Center, and the National Center for Gender Research, all based in Sulaymaniya. We also spoke to women lawyers and journalists. These various women and civil society organizations are involved in a wide range of activities and campaigns spanning welfare and humanitarian assistance; education; income generation; legal aid and services; support and protection of victims of gender-specific violence; political lobbying for women's legal rights; and campaigns to stop the ever-increasing incidence of honor killings and female suicides.

We were both struck by the fact that a large number of women's activities, organizations, initiatives, or events could be linked to one of the main political parties: the KDP or the PUK. Even civil society organizations were largely far from independent, but most organizations had the financial and political support and protection of one of the political parties. This means that most civil society organizations are GNGOs (governmental NGOs), as is common in many countries in the region. The close relationship to political parties and to inevitably male political leaders clearly influences much of the rhetoric and many of the priorities of

Kurdish women's rights activists. Sherizaan M., who works for an independent women's organization in Erbil, complained to Nadje about the way the women of the main political parties influence the women's movement: "Those of us who are not backed by political parties are struggling to have a voice. It is also difficult to focus on women's issues, as other national political agendas related to Kurdish independence, the struggle around Kirkuk, and federalism are always perceived to have priority." The view that "women are only there for decoration" came up several times. Chiman A., a women's rights activist whom Nicola interviewed in Sulaymaniya, commented:

> We don't see so much progress at the national level. Political leaders are busy with issues to do with political balance, negotiations, and trading. They are not bothered with women's rights. Kurdish leaders forget about women's rights when they discuss Kirkuk. The Kurdish parties are afraid to accept 100 percent equality between men and women. They are worried about the Islamic parties in the Kurdish area, and members of their own parties are against women's rights. Women who believe in their rights think religion is the greatest obstacle to our rights. When we call for changes to the personal status code, some people say that it is against Islam.

This critical view of the role of the Kurdish political leadership stands in contrast to the views expressed by women closely linked to the political parties. Nazdar S., who used to be a militant *peshmerga* struggling for Kurdish independence, is now a prominent figure in the Kurdistan Women's Union, which is linked to Massoud Barzani's KDP. She told Nadje:

> I am very proud of what we have achieved since 1991. Women have advanced greatly in Kurdistan, and our political leaders have played an important role in helping women's rights. They have supported us in educating women, encouraging them to work and to get involved in politics. But our problem is culture and traditions. Some women listen to clerics more than they listen to university professors. We need to start in schools and educate our children about equality and human rights. Despite all the problems we have, every day is better than the previous one and we become more and more modernized.

Although Nazdar stresses that she is not against religion per se, only certain interpretations of it, her secular modernist discourse obviously constructs religious and tribal practices and cultural attitudes as the main obstacle to women's rights. Most of the women we talked to who are linked to the main political parties explained the increase in honor killings and female self-immolations—one of the most pressing and debated issues among Kurdish women activists—in terms of culture, religion, and "backward social customs and tradition." Yet those critical of the political leadership were not convinced by this argument. One outspoken activist in Erbil told Nadje: "It is too easy to blame culture. The truth is that politicians view honor killings as a family problem. Yes, according to the new Kurdish constitution honor killings are criminal and need to be punished. But the law is not implemented. They prefer family and tribal mediation instead of proper laws and courts, especially when political and economic interests are at stake." Kawther G., another activist Nadje talked to, added that social and economic realities are pushing women over the edge and have led to a situation where female suicides have become an epidemic: "People are fed up. We had so much hope after 1991, but now the middle classes are impoverished. We still have only two hours of electricity a day. There is lots of unemployment. And if you want to get a good position, you need to have connections within one of the parties." Yet despite her criticism of Kurdish leaders' corruption, lack of transparency, and incompetence, Kawther, like many Kurdish women we talked to, is optimistic about the future: "Hopefully, this is just a phase. Things will improve. And if we compare our situation to that of women in the other parts of Iraq, we should be very happy." Those focusing on the struggle to stop violence against women recognize that only a holistic approach will be successful, as honor killings and female suicides are expressions of social, economic, cultural, and political problems that do not go away merely through the issuing of laws.

One of the many obstacles facing Kurdish women activists is that they are often caught in the cross fire between the two main political parties, which, despite having formed a unified Kurdistan Regional Government, still view each other suspiciously. In July 2006 in Sulaymaniya, antigovernment demonstrations, during which over 350 people were arrested, were triggered by an ongoing lack of electricity, social services, and employment. During and after the demonstrations, several women activists tried to mediate between the government and demonstrators; the government retaliated by cutting its monthly stipend of $1,000 to the NGOs that had tried to help the demonstrators. We heard the same story from several activists in Sulaymaniya. One of them explained how she and other activists had gotten caught up in the tensions between the political parties:

> Omar Fatah, the deputy prime minister of the KRG [Kurdistan Regional Government], cut our funding. He is from the PUK, which is controlling Sulaymaniya. He is not afraid of anyone. So we went to Erbil to see Nechirvan Barzani, the Kurdish prime minister who is part of the KDP. He was very supportive and told us that he would like to pay us, but it

would become a problem between the two political parties. So the only thing he did was to read our complaint letter and to send it on to Omar Fatah. He never replied to it. Now we are afraid to make more complaints, as Fatah could take away our license or even imprison us, as he did with some other activists. And we are still not getting any money from the government now.

Tensions and rivalries spill over to the level of activists, who openly express their perceptions and misgivings about "the other side." But notwithstanding some prejudices, women activists worked across the political and geographical divide to organize and participate in joint events, workshops, conferences, and campaigns.

FUNDING WOMEN'S ACTIVISM

Given the political parties' corruption, political meddling, and influence in Iraqi Kurdistan, it comes as no surprise that many women's organizations prefer foreign funding, which they view as less problematic than funding from their own government. Several Kurdish women activists we talked to stated that linking with and obtaining financial support from international organizations makes them feel more autonomous from the Kurdistan Regional Government. The government's attempt to control civil society associations and activities is also evident in southern and central Iraq. Instead of supporting and facilitating the work of NGOs, the Ministry of Civil Society has issued a series of draconian laws that reflect the government's suspicion of civil society. Nermine A., who works for an international agency focusing on women's empowerment, told Nicola:

> We have focused our work on women's NGOs and some human rights NGOs. However, our work has faced difficulties because a November 2005 decree froze the bank accounts of all NGOs on the basis that there were too many fraudulent NGOs. While we agree that there is a lot of fraud, we do not think that this was the right way to go about this. The process to get the accounts unfrozen is very lengthy and difficult. A committee has to meet to review the NGO's request. NGOs are governed by the state, the Ministry for Civil Society, which is turning out to be quite powerful. They have proposed a new NGO law, and it is very restrictive.

The proposed draconian bill was not passed by the parliamentary Committee for Civil Society, but it clearly indicates that many of Iraq's male political leaders view civil society associations as a threat to their authority.

While many Kurdish activists did not seem to be concerned about their funding sources, the issue of foreign funding is, of course, vexed and has been debated in numerous other contexts. For example, both of us have studied the debates around the impact of foreign funding on women's rights organizations in Egypt (Al-Ali 2000; Pratt 2006). Yet the Iraqi context of extreme political authoritarianism, occupation, political divisions, and acute humanitarian crisis has created an even more complex situation than what we found in our previous research.

That women's rights activism can become not only a job but a career is most obvious in Iraqi Kurdistan, which has been able to develop women's organizations and civil society organizations since 1991. Shahrzad Mojab has studied the impact of neoliberal agendas for civil society on Kurdish women's organizations. She argues that the "NGOization" of the women's movement (also described by Jad 2004 for Palestine) has resulted in "bureaucratization, professionalization, institutionalization and depolitization" (Mojab 2007: 14) rather than the gathering of in-depth knowledge about the situation of "real Kurdish women" and the actual addressing of their needs. Lack of transparency, corruption, the emergence of a new economic elite, the increasing gap between elite women's agendas and activities and the actual situation of the majority of Kurdish women, and a lack of autonomy are among the negative side effects of the NGOization of women's rights activism. Mojab argues that most Kurdish women activists make up a "new transnational technocratic elite class with the power to create the best local conditions for transnational capitalist reconstruction projects" (14).

A similar argument is put forward by Nadeen El-Kassem (2007), who is studying the impact of foreign intervention, particularly foreign funding, on Iraqi women's organizations more broadly. Focusing on IWW, one organization that has strictly refused any foreign funding, El-Kassem argues that other organizations that are accepting foreign funding inadvertently contribute to "the maintenance of the external domination of Iraq." Haifa Zangana (2007), speaking of "colonial feminism," makes this point with regard to Iraqi American organizations, such as Women for a Free Iraq and WAFDI, which we discuss in greater detail below.

Although we agree with the underlying critique of neoliberal conceptions of women's empowerment and democracy as well as imperialist aspirations and attempts to control beyond military might, our respective research reveals a more nuanced situation in which women activists' attitudes and strategies regarding foreign funding vary widely. For example, many activists we talked to refuse any funding related to government bodies, whether Iraqi, American, or British, but would accept money from UN institutions. When Nicola interviewed several people in the British

Foreign Office about their funding practices, she was told that some women's organizations that had been approached by the Foreign Office during the drafting of the constitution had refused any financial support and had stated that the drafting of the constitution was an internal process that should not be interfered with by outside forces. Zeinab G., who returned to Iraq in 2003 and has been involved with al-Amal and the Iraqi Women's Network ever since, became clearly agitated as she spoke to Nadje about what she called a "mafia revolving around funding":

> We have refused to take money from the American or British government. We don't want them to interfere in our affairs or have any control of them. But I am also fed up with UN agencies. There is lots of corruption there as well. I keep telling them: "Please stop funding democracy training!" We have had enough of meetings in five-star hotels in Amman where we meet one expert from the outside. The money spent on a one-day conference could be used to build a water-cleaning facility in Iraq. These international agencies are like a mafia. They have their channels, and if you have the right connections you get the funding. They don't want Iraqis to build their own capacity. I even heard of people who managed to get funding for their proposals by paying commission to intermediaries to the EU Commission or the UN. And there are lots of false contracts and proposals with no proper follow-up.

Zeinab is clearly disillusioned with international organizations' lack of transparency, corruption, and imposition of a training agenda pertaining to democracy and human rights when, as she argues, more basic humanitarian needs need to be addressed. Other women we talked to were less critical of international funding organizations, instead stressing their ability to follow their own agendas without much interference. When Nadje asked Ferial H., who has been involved in a women's rights organization in Baghdad since 2004, about her relationship to foreign fund-ers, she replied:

> I have never had any problems with foreign funders. I have had money from UNIFEM, IRI [International Republican Institute], NDI, and USAID. We identify what programs we want to implement or which activities we want to work on. I write a proposal and then we might get their funding or not. So far, no one has tried to influence our organization on how to spend the money. I am actually not aware of all the political agendas linked to the various funding institutions. I know lots of people don't like some of the funders linked to the American government and political parties, like USAID and IRI. For me it does not really make a difference as long as they fund what we want to do.

Ferial's attitude might be naive in light of the widely documented impact of government-related funding institutions on development agendas and the development of civil societies more generally. Short term, there may, of course, be an overlap between the agendas and identified priorities of local organizations and those of U.S.-government-related funding bodies. But there are certainly many tensions and gaps between local needs, capacities, and priorities and the funding priorities of many international organizations and especially of organizations linked to the U.S. government. Funding organizations do vary widely: those belonging to Canada, the Netherlands, and Scandinavian countries generally rank high in terms of transparency and lack of interference. But our conversations with Iraqi women activists revealed a range of attitudes toward and strategies for dealing with funding organizations that illustrate not only the diversity among women activists but also the fact that they are not just passive victims of neoliberal agendas or agents of colonialism and that many try to use available resources to meet their own agendas.

One of the biggest criticisms of foreign funding bodies has been their emphasis on training programs pertaining to democracy, human rights, and women's rights when essential humanitarian needs related to health, nutrition, education, electricity, provision of clean water, and employment are not adequately addressed. Several women stress that although there is a place for training and capacity-building programs, these programs must be based on carefully researched needs in consultation with Iraqi women's rights activists rather than on generic prescriptions of how to build civil societies.

MOBILIZING IN THE DIASPORA

Anyone who spent time with diaspora Iraqis in the first couple of years after the invasion would have been struck by the amount of travel and the flurry of activities. Many women we talked to in late 2003 and throughout 2004 were seriously considering returning to Iraq permanently. The energy, enthusiasm, and hopefulness even reached some of those women who had fervently opposed the invasion. Many women wanted to be part of the "new Iraq." Sanaa M. told Nadje during a cultural event in London in the fall of 2003:

> You know, I was against this war. But now that Saddam is gone, I hope to be able to return and help my country. We have been waiting for this moment. I would like to set up a small project to help orphans in Baghdad. There are so many of them after all these wars. Throughout the sanctions period I used to send money and medicines to my relatives in Iraq. I want to continue my work, but now I can actually spend time within the country.

Maybe I will even return for good? I never felt at home in London, and I miss Iraq all the time.

Many women, like Sanaa, visited Iraq because they wanted to help rebuild the country and improve living conditions for ordinary Iraqis. While some went only for short visits, others had more long-term plans. However, it was mainly the proinvasion women who initially got involved in political processes and projects linked to reconstruction. On both sides of the Atlantic, those women who had advocated a military invasion to topple the regime of Saddam Hussein were sought after by government officials and institutions eager to show their commitment to "women's liberation." Iraqi diaspora activists were perceived to be the legitimate mediators who could reach a wider population within Iraq.

A flurry of meetings, workshops, and conferences bringing together diaspora women and women from inside Iraq marked the early phase of post–Saddam Hussein Iraq. Diaspora women became involved in charity organizations, humanitarian assistance, training programs, advocacy around women's issues, democracy and human rights, and wider political issues both inside Iraq and in their countries of residence. Several Iraqi diaspora organizations and individual activists based in the United States and the United Kingdom were instrumental in facilitating and encouraging Iraqi women's political mobilization inside Iraq in the early period.

In London, numerous meetings, workshops, and seminars brought together Iraqi women of different political, ethnic, and religious backgrounds. These meetings were often facilitated, if not initiated, by the U.K. government, particularly DFID and Britain's former secretary of state for trade and industry and minister for women's affairs, Patricia Hewitt. In the beginning of July 2003 nearly one hundred women participated in a conference entitled "Voice of Women of Iraq," which was sponsored and supported by Hewitt as well as the U.S. undersecretary of state for global affairs, Paula Dobriansky. Although uninvited, Nadje and other members of Act Together: Women's Action for Iraq attended one of the preparatory meetings in London, during which most of the women present expressed their gratitude and thankfulness to the British government for "liberating Iraq." Those few women activists, like members of Act Together, who expressed more critical views and questioned the idea that diaspora women could either represent or liberate Iraqi women were clearly sidelined.

As discussed in chapter 2, many prowar Iraqi women activists in the United States received high-profile support and media attention in the run-up to the war and the immediate aftermath. In April 2005, Sumaya R., who was involved with WAFDI, described the close cooperation with U.S. government bodies and agencies with much enthusiasm and hope:

> Our group is part of a network that was established in 2002. My husband was very active and involved in this. It is a network of Iraqi American organizations, now consisting of about seventeen or eighteen organizations, including Kurdish and Islamist organizations. The first time we had a conference was in June 2002. Kanan Makiya[5] was involved, and people from the State Department. After the conference the State Department established a working group on Iraq. Then Iraq was liberated. In September 2003, we organized another conference and Al-Ja'fari [Ibrahim Al-Ja'fari, head of the Da'wa Party] came. There were many senators and again people from the State Department. . . . For the first time now, women are able to spread their wings. They are forming groups, they are speaking their minds. They are expressing themselves. We are organizing together with the Higher Council of Women inside Iraq. You can't imagine how our women are excited about these events. A lot of them are going outside the country for training. Now they have their freedom!

Aside from organizing conferences, seminars, and workshops inside Iraq and within the United States or the United Kingdom, the initial period after the invasion was characterized by a wave of training programs—mainly training for democracy and human rights—that brought a small number of Iraqi women to the United States or the United Kingdom. The women we talked to were divided about their attitudes toward these programs. Those women activists who had actually participated in one or several of them were generally enthusiastic. Amal K., a young woman who spent several months in the United Kingdom in a training program about political participation, was grateful about her experience: "I learned so much from it. Actually, I managed to use every single bit of information I received during my time in the U.K. when I returned to Iraq. It really helped me in my work." Others were much more cynical and expressed anger about the "training tourism which enables a small group of elite women to travel the world, stay in five-star hotels, and get training in how to do democracy," as one woman complained to Nadje. The few accounts we managed to get about different training programs indicated huge differences in terms of their relevance, seriousness, and applicability.

Not all diaspora women who got involved in the initial hype of diaspora activities had been politically active prior to the invasion. Widad F., who had left Iraq as a teenager in the eighties, explained to Nicola how she had gotten involved:

In the spring of 2003, I attended a meeting organized by Women Waging Peace. The meeting was to come up with objectives for women in postwar Iraq. The meeting energized us. For most of us, it was the first time to ever meet. We wanted to build on this energy and take things forward. That is why we founded WAFDI in summer of 2003. We had to do all the legal work and decide on by-laws, et cetera. About this time, I heard about the Iraqi Reconstruction and Development Council. It coordinates between Iraqis and the U.S. It was mainly men on the council. We wanted to have a woman on the council. You know, I'm not your typical activist. I don't look like an activist. I work out every day. I look like a woman who goes for a latte.

Supported by her husband, Widad took a leave of absence from her job and went to Iraq in October 2003. She continued:

I arrived on October 26; we were staying at the al-Rasheed hotel. It was the same night that it was bombed. It was quite a welcome for me! I was seeing Baghdad for the first time in years. I saw the beauty of the people. They were great. I stayed until the end of January and then I had to return. But after I came back, I felt like I couldn't turn my back on these people. I felt I could really do something to help. I started to talk to the troops stationed in Tennessee who would soon be going out to Iraq. I gave them some Arabic lessons. While I was in Iraq, [Decree] 137 came out. I was sitting in my office when my colleague came to me and said, "Here, read this." I couldn't believe my eyes. We spoke to the media. We went to speak to Bremer to ask him not to ratify it. Over the following forty-eight hours, we contacted a lot of groups and we spoke to the BBC. The following week, a protest was organized. In the end, Bremer didn't ratify it.

At the time Nicola interviewed Widad, she had just finished a media tour around the United States and was involved in organizing an exchange program between Iraqi and U.S.-based schools. She was also trying to help set up an education center in the north that was to include a carpet factory as an income-generating venture for women. She said: "Through this experience, I rejoined Iraq. It was like joining myself together."

RESTRICTIONS ON DIASPORA ACTIVITIES

As we were comparing notes, we were both astonished by the huge differences between countries in diaspora mobilization. Not surprisingly, Iraqi women in Jordan have been most limited in their diaspora mobilization and activism because of the restrictions on political spaces for civil society in general as well as the difficult economic, legal, and political conditions facing refugees within Jordan. But more astonishing to us have been the restrictions on the activism of Iraqi women residing in the United States in comparison with those on women's activism in the United Kingdom. Aside from the scarcity of independent Iraqi women's organizations in the United States—independent from both the U.S. government and from Iraqi political parties—we noticed the relatively narrow political spectrum of Iraqi activism within the United States compared to the diverse political views and forms of mobilization and activism found in the United Kingdom. While ethnic and religious divisions exist in both countries, the large presence of secular political parties in Britain such as the ICP and INA and of nonpolitical Iraqi professional, intellectual, and artistic associations has contributed to the building of more nonsectarian alliances and organizations.

Moreover, the political climate in the United States, particularly since September 11, has limited the political spaces and resources available for those who disagree with U.S. Middle East policy. Several Iraqi women we interviewed in the United States mentioned their fear of expressing dissent from U.S. policy, especially since the stringent PATRIOT Act of 2001. Dr. Zeinab N., a sympathizer, though not a member, of the Shiʿi Daʿwa Party and an active community leader within the Shiʿi community in Dearborn, Michigan, has a high profile among the religiously inclined Iraqi Shiʿi community in the United States. Shortly after the downfall of the Baʿth regime in 2003, Dr. Zeinab returned to Baghdad to help with reconstruction and share her acquired expertise and skills in a health-related profession. For a while, she went back and forth between Iraq and the United States, until, late in 2004, immigration officers unexpectedly took away her green card when she returned from one of her visits to Iraq:

> Even now I don't have U.S. citizenship. They gave citizenship to my three children but not to me because I have been politically active. They asked me a few weeks ago: "Have you ever opposed your government?" This is a trick question. If I say no, they will accuse me of having been a Baʿthist; if I say yes, they might not give me U.S. citizenship because I am a troublemaker. Am I allowed to be active here? This is a double standard. If you are not a U.S. citizen, you do not have the right to speak. They took my green card away after I came back from Iraq in 2004. I went back and forth for a while, but I never stayed for more than three months. Then they told me to stay here for six months, and they said they would give it back to me. Today I had to go to court, but they still refuse to give me back my green card.

In the United States, Iraqi women Nadje talked to, especially those who had more recently migrated or fled to the United States, frequently complained about their difficult economic circumstances and the need to work extremely hard, sometimes at more than one job, just to be able to pay the bills. This not only had a negative impact on their family and social lives but prevented many of them from getting involved in community activities and political mobilization. Others also mentioned the difficulty of mobilizing Iraqis, who make up about 2 percent of the overall Arab American community and are dispersed throughout the entire United States (U.S. History Encyclopedia 2006). However, huge clusters of Iraqis live in certain areas, such as metropolitan Detroit, Chicago, and Los Angeles, as well as Nashville and San Diego for Iraqi Kurds.

Historically, the United Kingdom has been the political and cultural center of the Iraqi diaspora, with Iraqi migrants and refugees having constituted the majority of asylum seekers for many years (UNHCR 2003). Although no reliable statistics are available, estimates for numbers of Iraqis residing in the United Kingdom range between two hundred thousand and three hundred thousand. In addition, the U.K. government's involvement in Iraq and many of its policies have implications for the ability of Iraqi migrant/refugee networks to influence political processes inside Iraq. A thriving civil society of Arab dissidents and intellectuals, a strong antiwar/peace movement, and a diverse women's movement have constituted the backdrop against which Iraqi women's organizations and individual activists have flourished in Britain.

Women's groups affiliated to political parties, such as the ICP, the Iraqi Worker's Communist Party, the KDP, the PUK, the Da'wa Party, the INC, and the Iraqi Democratic Party, exist side by side with independent groups, such as the Iraqi Women's Rights Organization, the Iraqi Women's League, Iraqi Women for Peace and Democracy, and Act Together: Women's Action on Iraq. Women activists also work through mixed groups like the Iraqi Prospect Organization, which mainly consists of young professional Iraqi Shi'i based in and around London. In addition, women are active within their respective ethnic and religious communities, such as the Assyrian Club of London, Kurdish community associations, and the Shi'i al-Khoei Foundation. These various groups and organizations represent a wide range of activism, from charity to advocacy and direct engagement with British government and with significant political actors inside Iraq. Significantly, Iraqi diaspora activism in the United Kingdom is extremely varied in terms of the attitudes toward the war, the occupation, and recent political developments in Iraq.

These differences are not easily attributable to distinct variables, such as ethnic and religious backgrounds, since previous political experiences, education, actual experiences of war and conflict, socialization, and experience of a current political milieu as well as personality are all part of women's political trajectories. Alliances and links with women's or antiwar organizations in the country of residence might shape the attitudes toward homeland politics. Members of the London-based group Act Together: Women's Action on Iraq, for example, have been very closely allied with Women in Black, a worldwide network of women opposing war and campaigning for peace with justice. While Women in Black is not homogeneous in terms of the political orientation and background of its members, it does project and mobilize around nonviolent resistance to war.

Iraqi women's associations in the United States have been influential with respect to U.S. policies on Iraq and the various interim Iraqi governments. U.S.-based Iraqi women activists and organizations have been intensively involved in shaping emerging women's organizations and groups inside Iraq. As we have shown in chapter 2, organizations like WAFDI are receiving grants for this purpose from the U.S. government. The centrality of the U.S. administration in directing Iraq's political development, including building political institutions, drafting the constitution, and allocating resources, places Iraqi women activists in the United States in a crucial position.

Yet the United States, unlike the United Kingdom, contains few Iraqi women's groups. The most prominent was Women for a Free Iraq (WFFI), which then formed WAFDI. The majority of Iraqi women activists in the United States, except for those affiliated to peace groups like Women in Black, have been working closely with the U.S. government and have been instrumental in justifying the invasion and projecting a neoliberal agenda of women's rights. The U.K.-based Iraqi writer and activist Haifa Zangana points out that women's organizations and activists, such as WFFI and WAFDI, have remained suspiciously silent about the suffering of Iraqi women under occupation while engaging in "transparently thin rhetoric about 'training for democracy'" (2006b: 225). Women's organizations, or "colonial feminists" as she calls them, are in her view one of the "three cyclops of empire building" and present a form of "soft occupation" (225).

While organizations such as WFFI/WAFDI have directly fed into U.S. government policies and have played a role in convincing the public of the U.S. commitment to women's rights, most diaspora organizations and activists have much more complex and ambiguous relationships with their respective governments. In the United States itself some women activists work through established political parties, especially the Kurdish parties, including the KDP and the PUK, as well as Shiʻi political parties like the Daʻwa Party. Several women activists who were members or sympathizers of the Daʻwa Party and were living in Dearborn felt ambiguous and uncomfortable about their relationship with the U.S. government: "We were hesitant to participate in the invasion because the U.S. betrayed the Iraqi people in 1991. We could not be sure. We had mixed feelings and did not know where to go. But our hatred for Saddam was so great, and we felt the only way to get rid of him was through an invasion. But I do not appreciate women's organizations such as WAFDI who all of a sudden appeared out of nowhere. Who are these women who are being promoted by the American government?"

As we have discussed earlier, there are huge differences among women's organizations in Iraq with regard to attitudes and strategies toward the occupation as well as toward government and foreign funding. While clearly some individual activists and organizations have been co-opted by the United States and its imperialist aspirations in Iraq, the majority of women activists and organizations we have come across are far too sophisticated, critical, and aware to be pawns of the occupation. They have, however, taken the strategic and pragmatic decision to engage in political processes under the occupation and in foreign attempts to address the growing humanitarian crisis.

TENSIONS OF TRANSNATIONAL ACTIVISM

Since middle-class professionals as well as foreign passport holders have been key targets of both frequent kidnappings for ransom and targeted assassinations, Iraqi women returnees have been particularly vulnerable. Moreover, the lack of credibility of the many former exiles holding key political positions and the disproportionate representation of former exiles in the various interim governments have contributed to a growing resentment toward women returnees who "want to get involved." Najwa R., a middle-aged professional woman who had been living in exile for over thirty years, first in London and then Amman in order to be closer to Baghdad, her hometown, told Nadje: "Many Iraqis who lived outside wanted to come inside to help rebuild the country, but we faced this hatred, this anger: 'You did not see it! You did not live it! Why should you come now?' They are very bitter about it. I even felt it with my own family. There is a bitterness towards those of us who did not live through the misery. I understand their position. I always thought that those who should go back should not look for positions, but should go as advisors" (Al-Ali 2007: 50). Others were much less understanding in their assessment and their account of their experiences inside Iraq. Widad M., a doctor and activist in her fifties who had lived in London for the past twenty-five years and had worked for the CPA in 2003 and 2004, said:

> It was very shocking, even my family had problems accepting me as I am. Their characters changed, they seem to have closed up. At one time, I organized a meeting between students and the Ministry of Education. They wanted to discuss things. The first thing they wanted to discuss was young girls turning up at the university with short sleeves or short skirts or dresses. The mentality went so wrong. Why is this so important to them? They do not know how to run an organization. They are not used to taking any initiative. And everyone has this strong sense of entitlement, which is not very constructive if you want to rebuild a country. (Al-Ali 2007: 255)

Like many other women Nadje spoke to, Widad feels very disillusioned. She was not the only one who told us that she was giving up because her efforts were not appreciated by people inside Iraq and also because things had just gone from bad to worse. Leila A., a researcher in her midforties, had once been very active in promoting health issues among the Iraqi refugee population in London and had initially been one of the most outspoken diaspora women trying to influence U.K. policies on Iraq in 2003. She told us, "I am totally fed up. Why am I giving up? Because I am boiling with anger. There is so much corruption, so much undermining of local initiatives. International NGOs are trying to project themselves instead of trying to support local initiatives. DFID and USAID are spending lots of money on useless things. I put my life at risk every time I go, and all I see is things getting worse, and I get criticism on top of it." In turn, several women who had never left Iraq complained about "all these women who lived outside for forty years and now want to tell us what we should do." Many, although not all, diaspora women are perceived to be patronizing and detached from realities on the ground. Amal R., a pharmacist who had not left Iraq and who had started a women's welfare organization in late 2003 that provided literacy and English classes, computer training, and Qur'anic recitation classes, complained:

> I participated in a workshop on the constitution. They asked us to come to Amman. There was a big problem: most of the women who participated were women who have lived outside for forty years. This was the first time I spoke about this subject with Iraqi women who had been abroad. I was surprised to hear what they were saying. They said women had no rights before. They have not been to school, not to university. I asked them whether

they lived in Iraq. Most had just returned after forty years. I told them: "Look, all the women here are over thirty-five years old. We all have college degrees, our education was free. I was in the college of pharmacy. In that college, women were in the majority." They were saying all the bad things about Saddam. I said: "We have to tell the truth. Not everything was bad." (Al-Ali 2007: 51–52)

Some prowar diaspora women have been involved in a widely publicized campaign supported by the U.S. government stressing the previous regime's poor record on women's rights. We do not wish to belittle the atrocities of Saddam Hussein and his regime, which engaged in the systematic abuse of human rights, including violence, torture, and sexual abuse of women, but some of the alleged claims contradict the accounts of the majority of women we interviewed as well as documented records. One especially absurd example is the assertion of some U.S.-based prowar activists that women were not allowed to enter university under the Ba'th regime.

Some Iraqi women activists who were living in exile prior to the invasion have managed to gain the trust and respect of women who lived in Iraq throughout the regime of Saddam Hussein. Through their genuine commitment to women's rights and the welfare of Iraqi people more generally, they have managed to overcome any existing tensions between Iraqi women of the diaspora and Iraqi women who have continued to live inside the country. Despite increasingly difficult and dangerous circumstances, these women have managed to stay in Iraq by the time of this writing in 2007 and have courageously built alliances with women activists across ethnic, religious, and political divides.

STRUGGLING WITH VIOLENCE ON MANY FRONTS

The most pressing issue in postinvasion Iraq is lawlessness, chaos, and increasing violence. While men constitute the majority of victims of violence, the lack of security affects women in particular ways. Violence against women has increased since the immediate postinvasion chaos, when an alarming number of cases of sexual violence and abductions of women and girls were identified in Baghdad alone (Human Rights Watch 2003). Women have been abducted by gangs, raped, and beaten; their bodies have been dumped; they have been sold into prostitution. If they manage to survive the ordeal, the stigma attached to rape deters many women from coming forward to report cases of sexual violence. They could be killed by their families to protect their "honor."

The sources of violence in Iraq are multiple. Much of the violence targeted at the middle classes is perpetrated by criminal gangs, who exploit the lawlessness of postinvasion Iraq and have easy access to small arms. Such violence includes kidnappings, carjackings, burglaries, and sexual assault. Women are also victims of political violence between the U.S. military and Iraqi police forces, on the one hand, and ex-regime loyalists, jihadists, nationalists, foreign fighters, and militia groups, such as the Mahdi Army, on the other. The increasing sectarian violence has led to ethnic cleansing in certain parts of Iraq and is responsible for the killing of Iraqis of all ethnic and religious backgrounds and political persuasions. While men have been the main target of mass killings across sectarian lines, women have been targeted as well, and those women who have lost loved ones are struggling to survive in a situation of extreme poverty, hardship, and lack of state provision.

The lawlessness, chaos, and widespread violence are a direct responsibility of U.S. and U.K. troops and governments, who under international law are obliged to provide security to the Iraqi population and have failed to do so. The occupation forces, particularly U.S. forces, have also been engaged more directly in various forms of violence against women. In addition to killing innocent women, men, and children through aerial bombardment and random shootings, troops are carrying out gender-specific violence. Several women we talked to reported that they had been verbally or physically threatened and assaulted by soldiers during searches at checkpoints or house searches. Further, female relatives of suspected insurgents have been literally taken hostage by U.S. forces. *Newsweek* reports that "the U.S. military is holding dozens of Iraqi women as bargaining chips to put pressure on their wanted relatives to surrender. These detainees are not accused of any crimes, and experts say their detention violates the Geneva Conventions and other international laws. The practice also risks associating the United States with the tactics of countries it has long criticized for arbitrary arrests" (Bazzi 2004). Iman Khamas was head of the International Occupation Watch Centre, a nongovernmental organization that gathered information on human rights abuses under the occupation, before she was forced to flee the country. She stated: "One former detainee had recounted the alleged rape of her cellmate in Abu Ghraib. Her cellmate had been rendered unconscious for forty-eight hours. She had been raped seventeen times in one day by Iraqi police in the presence of American soldiers." Khamas also reported that "since December 2003 there are around 625 women prisoners in Al-Rusafah prison in Umm Qasr and 750 in Al-Kazimah alone. They range from girls of twelve to women in their sixties" (Hassan 2004). British Labour MP Ann Clwyd, the U.K. Prime Minister's human rights envoy to Iraq, highlighted the humiliation last year of an Iraqi woman in her seventies detained by U.S. soldiers at Abu Ghraib for about six weeks without charge. The elderly woman had been abused, insulted, and ridden like a donkey by U.S. soldiers (Hassan 2004).

Aside from the violence related to the arrests themselves, women detained by the troops may suffer from shame associated with detention. Since women are regarded as bearers of the moral purity of their families and even their communities, they experience violence and the threat of violence differently than men do. Women are afraid to travel to seek health care or education, to work, or even to leave the house to do shopping (CSIS 2004: 69–75), let alone to participate in public activism.

Increasingly, Iraqi women are being threatened and assassinated by powerful Islamist militias and insurgent groups. Women have been caught in the cross fire between these various factions. For women activists the risk is higher because their involvement in public life challenges the views of Islamist militia and insurgent groups on appropriate gender relations and gender roles. In winter 2006, Souad al-Jazaeiri, a longtime women's rights activist and prominent journalist, told a group of Iraqi and British activists, NGO workers, and policy makers about the dangers and obstacles facing the Iraqi women's movement:

> The Iraqi women's movement expects even greater setback[s]. This can already be seen in Iraqi daily life. Iraqi women's rights are not only subject to violations in the constitution or in their representation in government and parliament. Personal freedoms of Iraqi women are also violated. Women activists have received direct threats, to stop working in women's organizations and leave the country or be killed. Many women who do not wear the veil or do drive cars have been attacked. Some practices, previously unknown in Iraqi society, have emerged, such as the segregation between males and females in public institutions and places, allocating an entrance for women and another for men. In other words, manifestations of an extremist religious society are becoming widespread in Iraq. (Al-Jazaeiri 2006)

Women's participation in the public sphere is seen by some extremist forces to symbolize Western cultural encroachment on Iraq and is associated with the perceived secular nature of Saddam Hussein's regime. Many activists have been forced to flee the country or have sought refuge in Iraqi Kurdistan after receiving death threats.

Those who remain in central and southern Iraq fear for their lives and those of their families and friends on a daily basis. According to several women's rights activists we spoke to in 2006, incidents of women being killed on the streets have risen and have started to become a noticeable and extremely worrying pattern. "Even veiled women who are seen to be out alone or driving a car started to be targeted," Zeinab G. told Nadje. She continued:

> Women are being assassinated, just because they are women. And we don't even know whom to turn to. The police is scared itself by the militia, and many units are actually infiltrated by the Mahdi Army or Badr Brigade. Others would like to help but are not in a position to do so because they are just not enough and they are ill-equipped. The Islamists are targeting women who have a public profile even more, but they have started to even kill women who are not in any way politically active and do not work in an NGO. Those of us who do live in constant fear. Several of my colleagues have already been shot, and I received several death threats.

Another leading Iraqi women's rights activist told Nadje during a visit to London in July 2006 that she had had to escape from Baghdad a few weeks before:

> I have been active for the past two years, but after I mentioned the targeted killing of women on TV, I received a death threat via e-mail. I was asked to stop all my activities or expect to be killed. I ignored this for some time and then received another e-mail, basically telling me that the group had noticed that I had continued with my political activism and that I had ten days to leave the country. One of my close affiliates was shot a few days after that, and I realized that this was really serious. I left Iraq the following night. I really want to go back, but I am not sure that it would be safe for me.

Meetings have become virtually impossible because of security concerns, and women activists are forced to risk their lives to travel to neighboring Jordan to participate in meetings and conferences. Iraqi men (e.g., university professors and journalists) are also targeted by Islamist militia and insurgents. However, the perception that women are somehow more vulnerable makes it more likely that threats of violence will lead women to abandon public participation.

Obviously, this greatly hampers the ability to sustain women's activism in Iraq. Women activists in southern and central Iraq perceive the ongoing violence as the biggest obstacle to their work. Even in Iraqi Kurdistan, which, at the time of this writing, is largely unaffected by violence, women activists emphasize the ongoing conflict in the rest of Iraq as a barrier to networking with women there.

The struggle against violence has become one of the priority issues for women's rights activists inside Iraq since 2005. Women activists see different reasons behind the violence, including the U.S./U.K. occupation, the conflicts among militias, the sectarianism of political leaders, the ineffectiveness of the police, the poor socioeconomic conditions that drive young men to join armed groups, and the terrorism perpetrated by former regime loyalists and al-Qaeda. To this we must add that the political competition between communally based groups, the growth in conservative gender ideologies, the availability of small arms, and high unemployment have contributed to the militarization of masculinities and the increase in violence.

OBSTACLES TO WOMEN'S ACTIVISM

This book has highlighted the various ways the occupation has hindered rather than promoted women's liberation. Aside from problems intrinsic to imposing rights and democracy in the context of an illegal military occupation, we are addressing the obstacles to a woman's movement that is struggling on many fronts as sectarian and extremist violence threatens to tear Iraq apart. One major challenge relates to the accusation of aping the West (especially Western feminism) and buying into neocolonial schemes. These accusations are not new but have consistently accompanied women's rights activists in most countries in the region as conservative male political actors have tried to discredit challenges posed by women activists. However, in the context of an occupation that has used the rhetoric of women's liberation and democracy as a means of justification, these accusations become particularly fierce and burdensome.

In a film based on a discussion about the personal status law among three women activists of different generations, Bdoor Zaki Mohammed, a London-based Iraqi lawyer, stated:

> This occupation was forced on us! We don't want it, but what we do want is to build our country. Let everyone who is against this occupation work to build the country. Let them place a brick to help build the country and not throw stones at its people, or kill them, or form militias, no—let them build the country. The presence of an occupation doesn't mean we do nothing. If I don't make a constitution it means I can do nothing; I'll have no law, no army, I can't do anything, no economy—so if we really want to fight this occupation, and we're honest, honorable people who love their country, we have to work to build the Iraqi state. (Al-Ali, Baban, and Abass 2006: 34)

Mohammed's words reveal one of the major political dilemmas for Iraqi women activists: Should they engage in the struggle for human and women's rights within a system established under illegal occupation and fraught with corruption, or should they avoid any kind of engagement that might lead inadvertently to the legitimization of the occupation?

For most women activists inside Iraq, engagement in the political process as well as the provision of humanitarian assistance, welfare, education, literacy programs, income-generating projects, and a media awareness campaign that links the struggle of national unity with the struggle against sectarianism and violence are the only channels of resistance to the systematic destruction of Iraq's social fabric. And here many Iraqi-based activists would agree that the diaspora might have a different role to play than women inside the country. As Sundus Abass stated during her visit to London in the summer of 2006: "The vicious cycle of violence can only be broken by an end to the occupation. British people, activists and NGOs have a crucial role to play. I ask the peace groups in Britain to put pressure on Bush and Blair to stop the war. They have to seriously announce a timetable for withdrawal from Iraq before the whole world" (Gill 2006). Women activists inside Iraq do not have the luxury to squabble over their specific attitude and demands vis-à-vis the occupation. No one likes it and everyone would like to end it. But women differ as to when and how. Given the chaotic situation on the ground, the women we talked to who still live inside Iraq are as concerned about the increasing influence of extremist militia and insurgents as they are about the incompetence, recklessness, and violence of the occupation.

FIVE

TOWARD A FEMINIST AND
ANTI-IMPERIALIST POLITICS OF PEACE

During the summer of 2007, as we were busy writing the last chapters of this book, the stark realities of life under occupation—its lawlessness, chaos, and escalating violence—hit very close to home. On August 1, 2007, Nadje's uncle and her sixteen-year-old cousin were killed in their home in the al-Mansour neighborhood of Baghdad. Unmasked gunmen entered the house and shot both as they were having their lunch. While the motivation for the killing—whether political or sectarian—remains unclear, the consequences of their deaths went beyond the tragic loss of two family members. The wife of Nadje's uncle, Hana, became one of the many Iraqi widows, estimated to be well over three hundred thousand in Baghdad alone (UN-OCHA 2006b), who are living in hardship and are struggling to survive. Hana, her surviving children, and several other relatives decided to leave the country and join the over two million people who have become refugees or displaced since the invasion (UNHCR 2007a). While many of Nadje's relatives ended up as refugees in Amman, three male cousins were stuck in Damascus, unable to join the rest of their families because of increasingly strict border controls. Since they cannot make a living in Damascus, they may be forced to return to Baghdad. Several other family members became internally displaced within Baghdad.

During 2006 and 2007, over ninety civilians died violently every day (UNAMI 2007b). Men have been the main victims of these violent deaths. Although it is impossible to come by reliable statistics,[1] it is clear that

Iraq is becoming a nation of widows (Zangana 2007). Aside from trauma and grief, Iraqi widows are experiencing severe hardships trying to provide for their families. The Ministry of Labor and Social Affairs is currently paying $100 in emergency aid to households headed by widows. This is only half the $200 average monthly wage of an Iraqi family, which in and of itself is not enough for a family to get by. Over four million Iraqis are dependent on food assistance, but only 60 percent of those have access to rations through the government-run Public Distribution System (NGO Coordinating Committee in Iraq [NCCI] and Oxfam 2007: 3).[2] Some help is on offer to widows through governmental and nongovernmental groups such as the Iraqi Red Crescent, the Islamic Party, the Muslim Scholars Association, and the Women and Knowledge Society (Jamail and Al-Fadhily 2006). But this support is insufficient to help the growing number of widows and their families. Many widows are forced to beg or engage in prostitution in order to feed their children.

According to a report by NCCI and Oxfam (2007: 3), "Eight million people are in urgent need of emergency aid; that figure includes over two million who are displaced within the country, and more than two million refugees. Many more are living in poverty, without basic services, and increasingly threatened by disease and malnutrition." While the sheer scale of violence in Iraq is widely recognized to be unparalleled by any other emergency in the world today (UNAMI 2007: 1), Iraq's humanitarian crisis has received less public attention. Yet entire communities are extremely vulnerable and need immediate protection and humanitarian assistance. Paradoxically, humanitarian aid has fallen alarmingly over the past years despite the widespread evidence of an increase in need (NCCI and Oxfam 2007: 5).

Poverty has become extremely widespread and endemic, with 54 percent of Iraqis living on less than US$1 per day. Food is scarce and malnutrition rampant. Forty-three percent of children aged six months to five years are suffering from malnutrition. Of these children, 18 percent suffer from stunted growth (NCCI and Oxfam 2007: 2). Seventy percent of Iraqis have to survive without an adequate water supply, and 80 percent lack effective sanitation (11). Water is frequently contaminated because of poor sewage systems and the discharge of untreated sewage into rivers. The increase in diarrheal diseases is acutely lethal to children.

Health services are in total shambles: already crippled by thirteen years of economic sanctions, they have significantly deteriorated since 2003. Ninety percent of the 180 hospitals in Iraq do not have key resources such as basic medical and surgical supplies (NCCI and Oxfam 2007). Since the 2003 invasion, over 12,000 of Iraq's 34,000 doctors have left Iraq, 250 have been kidnapped, and 2,000 have been killed (UNAMI 2007b: 2). Hospitals are not equipped to deal with the large numbers of injured people. Doctors and nurses are overextended and must improvise in a situation of absolute chaos and deprivation.

Like doctors, teachers and university professors have left the country in huge numbers, since professionals and intellectuals have been primary targets in assassinations. Many schools have been damaged and lack supplies. Some have become shelters for internally displaced people or have been occupied by armed groups. According to Save the Children UK (2007), over eight hundred thousand children may be out of school. Girls and young women are especially vulnerable in a context where kidnappings and sexual abuse are rampant, and some parents keep their daughters at home out of fear.

Everyone in Iraq—everyone outside the Green Zone, that is—suffers in this escalating humanitarian crisis. But while men bear the main brunt of the armed violence, women are particularly hard hit by the harsh living conditions: poverty, malnutrition, lack of adequate health services, and lack of adequate infrastructure, including electricity, which in some areas of Iraq works for only about two hours per day. Over 70 percent of the more than two million displaced people inside Iraq are women and children. Many have found shelter with relatives who share their limited space, food, and supplies. But this, according to UNHCR (2006), has created a "rising tension between families over scarce resources." Many displaced women and children find themselves in unsanitary and overcrowded public buildings under constant threat of being evicted. It is no surprise that issues related to women's legal rights, the constitution, the imposition of certain dress codes, including the *hijab* (headscarf), and changing gender ideologies rooted in conservative or religious extremist ideologies are not priorities for the majority of Iraqi women, whose main worry is to provide for their families and get through the day alive (Zangana 2005).

THE ROLE OF ISLAM AND CULTURE

There is a widespread tendency, even among progressive antiwar activists and feminists, to explain the deteriorating situation of Iraqi women by reference to Islam and culture. Many of our audiences, especially in the

United States, refer to a growing body of literature by Muslim women when making statements about Islam and the poor track record of women's rights in Muslim countries. Irshad Manji's *The Trouble with Islam* (2003) and Ayaan Hirsi Ali's *Infidel* (2005) are the most well known and popular exemplars of a genre of literature that is promoted and sensationalized in the West.[3] Although we in no way wish to deny the hardships, oppression, and discrimination that these individual authors report having experienced, or to fall into the trap of becoming apologists for oppressive practices in the name of fighting Islamophobia, we are dismayed by both the sweeping generalizations that these authors make from their own experiences and their use of religion and culture to explain complex developments and trends that are rooted in concrete political, economic, and social conditions. It is much easier to condemn Islam and "oppressive Muslim men" than to unpack the intricate relationships between global policies related to empire building and capitalist expansion as well as regional and national struggles revolving around political and economic power and resources.

To put it simply, Iraqi women are not suffering because of anything specific to Islam. They are suffering because there is a staggering amount of violence on all levels and no functioning state to provide security, services, and adequate humanitarian assistance. No one is willing or able to guarantee and implement women's legal rights. The legal rights enshrined in the contested constitution are flawed to start with and do not promote equal citizenship. Iraqi women are also deprived because of widespread and crippling poverty, large-scale unemployment, and lack of access to adequate resources.

And, yes, women are suffering because Islam is used by various political parties, factions, militias, and insurgent groups to gain credibility and legitimacy. Iraqi politicians, Islamist militants, and insurgents are pursuing gender ideologies and policies that are conservative at best and extremist in most instances. As is the case with any religion, Islam and Islamic law are wide open to interpretation and have manifested in different practices, traditions, and rights throughout history and in different cultural and national contexts. Although one might argue that all religions are inherently patriarchal, nothing is set in stone about Muslim societies' specific articulations and practices with regard to women and gender relations (Leila Ahmed 1992). Yet in Iraq we are witnessing a radicalization of armed groups and their political leadership in which women are central to the attempt to gain control, impose rules, and inscribe a new order rooted in narrow interpretations that are based on political-strategic considerations and ideological righteousness rather than a learned approach to religious texts and traditions.

A glance at Iraq's history shows that its culture is not inherently opposed to women's rights and participation in public life. As we showed in chapter 1, Iraqi women were once at the forefront of the region with regard to women's education, labor force participation, and political activism. Understandings of culture and religion are not uniform throughout Iraq and very much depend on social class, education, political orientation, place of residence, and family and personal values. A shift toward greater social conservatism started in the 1990s in the context of economic sanctions, an economic crisis, and a weakening state that tried to co-opt tribal and religious leaders to make up for its dwindling financial basis and support among the population. Saddam Hussein, the very political leader who had promoted women's inclusion in the public sphere, championed modernization and development, and persecuted religious authorities in the early decades of the Ba'th regime, began to promote "Islam" and "Iraqi tribal culture" opportunistically just as the "clash of civilizations" thesis started to get attention and support in "the West."

In the current context of occupation, the United States has exploited the issue of women's liberation to justify its military intervention. The consequence is that Iraqi women are experiencing a tremendous backlash. On one level, a strong knee-jerk reaction is taking place across many sectors of Iraqi society that are opposing and resisting military occupation and Western cultural encroachment. "Our culture is different from yours" often translates into "Our women are different from yours." Political and religious leaders speak about a supposedly "authentic culture" that has deep roots in society. But they are actually constructing new notions of Iraqi culture rooted in particular interpretations of Islam by emerging Islamist movements and militia.

In this attempt to create and harden an authentic Iraqi or Muslim culture different from the culture of "the West," culture is reconfigured in far more exclusive ways than historically was the case. Western commentators often argue that communal identities and sectarian hatred and violence are inherent aspects of Iraqi culture, but this disregards Iraqi history. We recognize that the seeds of sectarianism and religious extremism were planted prior to the invasion by the former dictatorship of Saddam Hussein and also within Iraqi diasporic communities. Yet again it is the occupation, rather than Iraqi culture, tradition, or some primordial aspect of "the Iraqi mind," that has systematically eroded the structures and institutions that could have contributed to national unity.

Sectarian and communal sentiments and violence have been encouraged by policies that promote the fragmentation of Iraqi society and polity into ethnic and religious communities.

Another factor exacerbating sectarianism and violence has been the failure to secure Iraq's borders. This has produced a steady influx of foreign fighters whose ideology views Shi'is as even greater infidels and enemies than the occupiers. By targeting mainly Shi'i neighborhoods, religious shrines, and religious processions, these foreign extremists have contributed to the increasing sectarian strife and tit-for-tat killing that has taken up a life of its own since the bombing of the Shi'i al-Askari mosque in Samarra on February 22, 2006. Simultaneously, the policies of the U.S.-led CPA institutionalized sectarian and ethnic differences through the emerging political system, while disenfranchising Sunnis on the mistaken belief that they were all Ba'thists (Hashim 2006). As we have tried to show throughout this book, while men have been the main victims of sectarian killings, Iraqi women have suffered from the rise in communal and sectarian identities in different ways as tribal, religious, communal, and militia leaders have used women symbolically to demarcate difference and display control.

CAN MILITARY INTERVENTION LIBERATE WOMEN?

The resort to military intervention to "liberate" women, as well as men who are suffering under repressive dictatorships, is a seductive idea because it appears to succeed where other means—diplomacy, economic sanctions, and covert actions—have failed. The rationale of liberation was obvious in the case of Iraq, where Saddam Hussein withstood over a decade of crippling sanctions, defied UN resolutions, survived assassination attempts, and brutally suppressed an internal uprising in 1991. It is possible to point to specific examples elsewhere in which military intervention saved lives, such as Tanzania's intervention against Ugandan dictator Idi Amin and Vietnam's intervention against Pol Pot in Cambodia. There are also examples where the *failure* to intervene militarily caused horrific numbers of casualties—namely the Rwandan genocide, as well as the wars in the former Yugoslavia.

"Liberal interventionists" have argued that it is the obligation of humanity to protect human rights and human lives, irrespective of borders (Arend and Beck 1993: 133). In the United Kingdom, it was not neoconservatives but many within the Labour Party who supported the 2003 invasion of Iraq. In the run-up to the war, Ann Clwyd, Labour Party MP and long-standing campaigner for human rights in Iraq, told parliament, "I believe in regime change, and I say that without any hesitation at all, and I will support the government tonight because I think it's doing a brave thing" (Wintour 2003). With a U.S.-led invasion on the cards, many Iraqis had resigned themselves to outside force as the only way of freeing them from the tyranny of Saddam Hussein, although most were skeptical about the motivations of the invaders (International Crisis Group 2002).

In the wake of the disaster that has unfolded in Iraq since the toppling of Saddam Hussein, many have sought to demonstrate the mistakes that the United States and its allies made, as we briefly noted. This book has shown that the resort to military intervention, rather than freeing the people of Iraq from tyranny, has led to the emergence of new forms of tyranny, with devastating consequences for the everyday security of women and men as well as their human rights.

Meanwhile, we have seen how U.S. military and security interests have trumped the security of ordinary men and women. The United States failed to stem the lawlessness that erupted in the wake of the fall of the Ba'th regime and even contributed to it by dismantling the police and army and engaging in countless acts of human rights abuses themselves. The United States has prioritized combating the insurgency over preventing the harassment of women by armed militias. Iraqi civilians have been killed and maimed by the U.S. military, not only because they have been caught in the cross fire, but also because the military has failed to discriminate between civilians and "insurgents." In the political process, the United States has empowered sectarian and communal political forces, and these in turn have further fueled the violence. In the reconstruction process, the United States has given multi-billion-dollar contracts to U.S. companies rather than to Iraqi companies, failed to provide sufficient oversight of reconstruction funds, and reallocated a significant portion of these funds to "security" (i.e., the security of U.S. personnel and contractors). This has all been to the detriment of rebuilding the Iraqi state, infrastructure, and basic services.

Yet it is not enough to identify the negative consequences of military intervention or even to argue that the United States made mistakes in its occupation of Iraq. This would assume that there is a "right way" to intervene militarily for the sake of liberating women. Military intervention cannot liberate women because it is embedded within a set of assumptions, beliefs, and social relations that reinforce and reproduce gender inequality (Enloe 1988), as well as other social inequalities within and across nation-states. Military intervention depends upon a belief in the legitimacy of armed violence in resolving political problems, which in turn depends upon our adherence to particular ideas about what it means to be a man or a woman.

Across time and space, the majority of societies have created notions of masculinity that motivate men to fight (Goldstein 2001: 264). The use of violence is intrinsically linked with predominant notions of "masculine strength" and "feminine weakness," and the military is one of the most important institutions for reinforcing those ideas (265). Men are encouraged to prove their manhood for the sake of the "thewomenandchildren" (Enloe 1993). Linked to the reinforcement of gender identities is the creation of a gendered division of labor around the social institution of the military, whereby women "service" the military behind the scenes as wives, mothers, nurses, and prostitutes, while men take on the "frontline" role of soldier (Enloe 1988).[4]

Ideas of masculinity and femininity intersect with other markers of social difference so that different men and women experience the military in different ways, based not only on their gender but also on their class background, race/ethnicity, or sexual orientation (D'Amico 2000). Some have argued that the incorporation of increasing numbers of women, as well as other traditionally excluded social groups, into the military will challenge gender and other social inequalities. However, adding more women (or people of color or people who are gay) into an institution whose raison d'être is the use of violence against an "other," whoever that may be, for the purpose of securing the interest of one's own state is neither a peaceful nor a just solution to inequality and injustice.

More significantly with regard to the subject of this book, militarism at home contributes to reproducing social inequalities in countries that are the target of military intervention. If military intervention is a tool of U.S. empire building, and if militarism legitimizes the use of armed force for this end, the flip side is that armed force is considered a legitimate means of resistance to empire. We see this in Iraq, where resistance to occupation has become almost synonymous with armed resistance. Many groups with different ideological orientations make up the armed resistance, including jihadist Salafi groups, Ba'thists, loyalists of the former regime, and nationalists.[5] It is estimated that the fastest-growing wing of the resistance is what Toby Dodge calls "Iraqi Islamism"—a blend of nationalism and Islamism "that preaches the defense of the *Watan,* the Iraqi homeland, against foreign and non-Muslim invaders" (2006: 216).

Just as militarism is embedded within social inequalities and simultaneously helps to reproduce those inequalities, so armed resistance depends

upon the mobilization of particular notions of masculinity and femininity, linked to notions of race, ethnicity, religion, and class and the re-
shaping of gender relations. Even where armed resistance groups adopt
progressive ideologies, incorporate women fighters, and address issues of
gender inequality, experiences demonstrate that tensions exist between
national liberation and women's liberation (Enloe 1988: 160–72).
Women may gain new avenues of political participation within anticolonial struggles, but this participation is often circumscribed within nationalist discourses that represent women as the "custodians and trans-
mitters of national culture" (Jayawardena 1986: 257). The militarization
of societies to support the armed struggle "puts a premium on communal unity in the name of national survival, a priority which can silence
women critical of patriarchal practices and attitudes" (Enloe 2001: 57–
58). Women's involvement in armed struggle may simply expand notions
of women's roles without challenging masculine privilege.

These tensions between national liberation and women's liberation are
amplified in Iraq, where people have suffered years of deprivation and
humiliation under dictatorship, sanctions, war, and occupation. Feelings
of humiliation are gendered in that they have different impacts on women
and men. Predominant notions of masculinity are intrinsically linked to
strength and power over others, so victims of occupation and other forms
of oppression may feel "emasculated." Their resistance to oppression is
likely to be expressed in terms of reasserting a masculinity that is indige-
nized through links to national, religious, sectarian, or ethnic symbols and
that depends upon notions of women as custodians of culture.[6] We agree
with Nira Yuval-Davis that "as long as the struggle of the powerless is to
gain power rather than to transform power relations within the society,
so-called 'national liberation' often brings further oppression to women
and other disadvantaged groups within the new social order" (2004: 187).

This is particularly relevant to Iraq, where armed resistance, despite
its patriotic rhetoric, is overwhelmingly localized or tied to particular sectarian or ethnic agendas (International Crisis Group 2006a). Moreover,
the ideologies of the armed resistance to the U.S. occupation are predom -
inantly socially conservative. These characteristics are also mirrored in
the various militias that are linked to different groups within the national
government. As we have highlighted here, the combination of socially
conservative and sectarian or ethnic agendas has particularly negative
consequences for women's public participation, as well as for gender relations in general and the situation of ethnic and religious minorities. Harassing women into wearing the *hijab,* forbidding women to drive, en-

forcing gender segregation in public, and targeting ethnic and religious minorities are some examples of how different groups have sought to create constructions of particular religious or ethnic gender identities and relations in support of military actions by one group or another.

That is not to say that people should not resist occupation and injustice. In some cases, where lives are threatened, violence may be necessary to protect oneself, one's family and friends, and one's community. However, there is a difference between the resort to violence in self-defense and a sustained mobilization for the purpose of armed resistance, embedded within ideologies and social institutions that create further injustice, misery, and destruction. Moreover, armed resistance against U.S.-led militarism fails to address a whole range of processes sustaining the occupation. As we have discussed here, the U.S.-led occupation of Iraq not only depends upon the deployment of military personnel but is embedded within a range of discourses and practices that seek to establish U.S. hegemony. These include the promotion of women's empowerment, democracy, and neoliberal economics abroad, as well as the curtailment of civil liberties and Islamophobia at home, all in the name of the "War on Terror."

THE TROUBLE WITH "GENDER MAINSTREAMING"

This book demonstrates the limitations and dangers of "gender mainstreaming"—not only as a practice but also as a concept—in the context of war and occupation. The concept of "mainstreaming" attention to gender into policy arenas was first introduced to the United Nations at the Nairobi World Conference on Women in 1985. Since then, the idea has spread throughout international, governmental, and nongovernmental agencies working in "developing countries." The term *gender mainstreaming* refers to evaluating policies, programs, and funding allocations in terms of their impacts on women and men. It is based on the assumption that processes of development affect each gender differentially. More recently, and as we briefly mention in the introduction, gender has been "mainstreamed" into international peace and security arenas with the passing of UN Security Council Resolution 1325 in 2000. This resolution seeks to recognize women's contribution to peace building and conflict resolution, ensure women's inclusion in postconflict decision making, and channel resources to the protection of women and children in conflict and postconflict situations.

In the case of Iraq, there have been some limited attempts to introduce the concept of gender mainstreaming into postinvasion reconstruction and political transition. We have seen that a range of agencies, including governmental agencies (e.g., USAID and DFID), NGOs (e.g., Save the Children, Oxfam, and USIP), and international agencies (e.g., the United Nations and the World Bank), have addressed the issue of women's particular needs in their programs by setting target numbers of women beneficiaries or by allocating a proportion of funds to women-centered projects. In chapter 2 we saw that in the context of war and occupation, particularly a war over which the international community was divided, gender mainstreaming has been limited in practice by the slow disbursement of funds, the security situation, and, most significantly, the lack of attention to planning gender mainstreaming immediately following the invasion. Moreover, as we have demonstrated, there has been a distinct lack of support from the United States (the major international player in Iraq) to address the recommendations in Resolution 1325, such as the inclusion of women in (post)conflict decision-making bodies and the recognition of violence against women.

The problems encountered in the practice of gender mainstreaming in Iraq to some degree mirror those of other situations in which agencies attempt to mainstream gender into their policies and programs. However, the problem with gender mainstreaming is not only its erratic implementation. The concept becomes problematic because it has been co-opted into the foreign policy objectives of the United States and at least one of its allies—the United Kingdom. The Bush administration does not use the term *gender mainstreaming,* but, as we have discussed here, officials have asserted a commitment to women's empowerment in U.S. foreign policy. Reference to women in U.S. foreign policy discourse is actually part of empire building and reconfiguring relations of power internationally. In chapter 2 we discussed how the rhetoric of women's empowerment helps strengthen the United States in its bid for superpower status. Women are targeted as the building blocks of a new state and society that is pro–United States and neoliberal.

However, the greatest drawback of gender mainstreaming is that it concentrates the attention and resources of those who seek to improve women's rights and women's situation on measures and programs that leave intact the foreign policy decisions of the United States and its allies. This book has demonstrated that war and occupation have not liberated women but instead have subjected them to new and often more violent forms of oppression. In chapter 3, we saw the major limitations of measures aimed at empowering women within a political process designed to meet the needs of the United States and its Iraqi political allies. Women's rights have been sacrificed at the expense of sectarian and ethnic political agendas, which in turn have fueled the violence engulfing most of Iraq and prevented independent actors from making a stand. It is essential to emphasize that the deterioration in women's rights following the fall of the Ba'th regime was not inevitable but rather the result of particular political decisions. Paying attention to gender helps us understand why those particular political decisions were taken.

SUPPORTING WOMEN'S RIGHTS AND RESISTING EMPIRE

The United States has instrumentalized women for its own security ends. But does that mean we should not speak about women's rights in Iraq, lest we be co-opted into the U.S. project of empire? On the contrary, it is essential that antiwar movements address the issue of women's rights rather than marginalizing it. This is because building empires is not only about guns and bombs, the exploitation of resources by multinational corporations, and cultural invasion. It is also about shaping gender roles and gender relations and promoting particular notions of masculinity (Enloe 2004: 270, 304).

The continuation of the U.S.-led occupation of Iraq depends upon maintaining the alliances between the United States and the major political groups making up the national government. As we have described here, the United States carried out many measures and negotiated many deals that privileged its political allies over their rivals, at the expense of women's rights as well as the establishment of a transparent and democratic state and a functioning system of law and order. These measures include the introduction of sectarian and ethnic quotas into the IGC, de-Ba'thification and the dismantling of the Iraqi army, the training and arming of Badr Brigade and Mahdi army militias responsible for death squad activity, and the decision to establish a short time line for holding elections and writing a constitution. Attention to gender roles and relations alerts us to the links between alliances of various (male) political leaders and the erosion of women's rights. Women's public participation is severely curtailed by the rapid growth in violence—whether perpetrated by militia groups linked to parties in government or resisting occupation or by criminal gangs that have flourished in the context of lawlessness—coupled with the spread of conservative ideologies that call on women to stay at home or face the consequences. Simultaneously, women's voices are marginalized by the competition between sectarian and ethnic-based political interests while their constitutional rights are used as a bargaining chip in political negotiations.

Together, the United States and its allies have constructed what we have already described as an extreme and violent form of patriarchy. Given the dependence of the United States and its allies upon this "hyperpatriarchy" to underpin the U.S. occupation and domination of Iraq, opposing patriarchy is a significant component of undermining U.S. empire as well as building a democratic Iraq for all its citizens (Susskind 2007). This fact has not been lost on the many Iraqi women activists who have campaigned to guarantee women's rights in the constitution and denounced violence against women by a whole range of actors.

Pointing to the long history of Iraqi women's rights activism and the wider context of women's and feminist movements in the Middle East and other predominantly Muslim societies challenges the idea that women's rights—or human rights, for that matter—belong to Western civilizations. Ironically, in the current Iraqi context, as in many other places historically, the argument that women's rights belong to "the West" is put forward simultaneously by the occupiers and by the resistance to the occupation. Yet Iraqi women's rights activists are not merely imitating "Western agendas"; rather, they are responding to issues relevant to women within a specific national and local context. As many non-Western feminists have argued, women's rights activism and feminism have been part of the national political landscape of many formerly colonized countries as well as those experiencing colonial ventures today (Narayan 1997). Cultural contexts are internally contested, and women's rights activists all over the world challenge patriarchal and authoritarian interpretations of what a specific culture should be. This is also evident in Iraq, where contestations over Iraqi and/or Muslim culture are an element of a wider struggle over power, control, and resources. Conservative Islamist and tribal leaders are engaged in often violent contestations about resources and control that are regularly fought in the name of religion, culture, and traditions. Women's bodies, gender norms, and relationships between men and women become central to these struggles.

AN ANTI-IMPERIALIST, DEMOCRATIC, AND FEMINIST POLITICS

Throughout this book we have shown that gender identities and relations are not just peripheral issues to war and violence in Iraq. Inspired by the works of feminist scholars like Cynthia Cockburn (2007) and Cynthia Enloe (2005), we argue that gender ideologies and gender relations are part of the bigger picture. As Cockburn argues (2007: 231–32), "Gender relations are right there alongside class relations and ethno-national relations, intersecting with them, complicating them, sometimes even prevailing over them, in the origins, development and perpetuation of war." Many people would agree that we cannot understand the processes and developments inside Iraq without paying attention to neoliberal agendas and globalizing capitalism, neoconservative notions of empire building, and the so-called War on Terror. Many people also recognize the logic of the arms industry, which creates a perpetual demand for war and armed conflict. But what feminist scholars bring to the big picture is the argument that economics, politics, and the military are all gendered structures that not only are sustained by prevailing notions of masculinity and femininity but also produce them.

Any analysis of what went wrong in Iraq must put gender firmly on the agenda, from challenging the very premise that military intervention will lead to women's liberation to exploring the various ways war, violence, occupation, armed resistance, humanitarian crisis, and poverty affect men and women. A gendered analysis focuses our attention on the security of individual men, women, and their families and subverts state-centered notions of security, which mostly disregard human rights and human welfare. It demonstrates how the security concerns of one state can create unimagined insecurities for ordinary people of another state. It also shows how these insecurities can fuel gender and other social inequalities, with devastating consequences for society.

Given the level of violence and lack of security, the cessation of armed conflict must be a priority and a first step for establishing a more lasting peace. However, the cessation of armed conflict does not in and of itself signify peace. Cynthia Enloe (1988) famously stated over two decades ago that peace for women requires more than the cessation of armed conflict. Sustainable peace requires an absence of the factors that lead to conflict. Johan Galtung argues that conflict entails much more than direct violence: "There is also the violence frozen into structures, and the culture that legitimizes violence" (1996: viii). We have indicated here the "structures" fueling the conflict in Iraq, which include the U.S.-led occupation, and, relatedly, the lack of basic services, infrastructure, employment, and security as well as the growth of sectarian and ethnic-based politics and the legitimization of violence as a means of achieving certain political outcomes. While ending direct violence will enable the reconstruction of Iraq, this must not take place at the expense of the rights of one part of the population. All-out violence may be suppressed through an end to the occupation, along with the elimination of some armed groups and the co-optation of others, but the potential for violence will remain unless reconstruction also addresses social inequalities and injustices, including inequitable gender relations.

A gendering of political processes and reconstruction does not merely take a liberal "rights approach"; rather, it recognizes the significance of power relations rooted in class, ethnicity, race, religion, nationality, and gender. In other words, a focus on women's "empowerment" and "women's rights" is not sufficient in contexts where women often lack the political and economic power to take advantage of their rights. As Nira Yuval-Davis argues, "The construction of feminist agendas as a discourse of 'rights' can be partial at best" (2006). A legalistic focus on rights allows policy makers to forget about both the implementation of rights and women's abilities to take advantage of legal rights. Women's capabilities, political economies, and everyday life experiences must be considered in the drafting of constitutions, laws, reconstruction programs, and policies.[7]

However, we are not arguing that human rights and women's rights are not worth struggling for. Quite the opposite. In the Iraqi context, implementing international law would have prevented an illegal invasion and occupation from occurring in the first place. In the wake of the invasion, abiding by human rights conventions and the Geneva Conventions would have forced the occupation to prevent the looting, lawlessness, and spread of violence and to ensure not only the safety of the Iraqi population but also its well-being in terms of basic infrastructure and services. Meanwhile, constitutional guarantees of women's equal rights in all areas of public and private life represent an important tool for activists attempting to improve the situation of Iraqi women.

Those who are concerned to improve women's rights all over the world are challenged to make the links between various forms of discrimination and oppression, the abuse of rights, and gender-specific violence on the one hand and the abuse of human and civil rights and military interventions in the name of the War on Terror on the other. We cannot credibly and coherently argue for women's liberation, or even the narrower concept of women's rights, without simultaneously addressing the wider context entailing a whole array of human and civil rights abuses as well as forms of exclusion. Torture, for example, is a feminist issue. Whether it takes place in Abu Ghraib, Guantánamo Bay, or local detention centers in the United States and the United Kingdom, we need to challenge the systematic abuse of civil and human rights and reconceptualize the continuum of violence to include the War on Terror, U.S.-led military interventions in the Middle East, and the abuse and oppression inherent within these.

Those who are concerned to bring an end to the war in Iraq and to oppose U.S. empire building must also address the full continuum of violence. This involves not only conflict and war between armed groups (whether militaries or militias) but also the harassment and intimidation of women, as well as of ethnic, religious, and sexual minorities in their communities and their homes, often by the same actors. Violence against women and other vulnerable groups is not marginal to the bigger picture of conflict in Iraq. It is not a "natural" consequence of Iraqi or Muslim "patriarchal culture." Rather, it is indicative of the absence of a functioning state that can ensure law and order, basic services, and socioeconomic development, together with the construction of a political system that rewards sectarian and ethnic politics. While an end to the occupation is a necessary step toward ending the conflict, it will not bring about peace. Antiwar activists must also advocate for more international resources to rebuild state institutions and to provide humanitarian relief. Meanwhile, they must recognize that a significant proportion of the Iraqi groups engaged in armed resistance against the occupation are simultaneously engaged in harassing, intimidating, and even murdering ordinary Iraqis, particularly women and other vulnerable groups.

As we conclude this book, it has become obvious that there are no quick-fix solutions to what has been happening in Iraq. Even most of those in favor of the invasion in 2003 agree that the military intervention has damaged the future of Iraq in general and women's rights in particular. We believe that the end of the occupation is a necessary first step toward a long-term solution to the violence, chaos, and misery currently experienced by the majority of Iraqis. As long as the United States and the United Kingdom occupy Iraqi land and intervene in Iraqi politics, a violent resistance not only is fueled but also gains greater legitimacy within Iraq and outside its borders. Meanwhile, the corrupt and ineffective national government in Baghdad holds on to power. As we have shown throughout the book, the occupying forces have not prevented but contributed to the rise in communal identities and the escalation of sectarian hatred and violence, lawlessness, and widespread criminal activities. In addition, the occupation authorities have not engaged in any meaningful reconstruction process. Instead, the Iraqi population is experiencing a humanitarian crisis of unprecedented scale, worse even than during thirteen years of economic sanctions.

Nevertheless, we are under no illusion that a withdrawal of American and British troops would mean an end to violence, sectarian hatred, political incompetence, corruption, and the abuse of human and women's rights. We strongly believe that it is the responsibility of the international community, led by a reformed United Nations that is able to act independently of the interests and whims of the U.S. administration, to address the basic needs of the Iraqi population in terms of the worsening humanitarian crisis. This must involve a greater investment of funds in Iraqi organizations and the employment of Iraqi professionals where possible, rather than foreign contractors, to rehabilitate Iraq's electricity grid, water, and sewage systems and the health and education sectors. In addition, there should be a rapid and coordinated international response to the Iraqi refugee crisis within the region, most notably in Jordan and Syria but also in Western countries such as the United Kingdom, where over eight thousand Iraqi asylum seekers are destitute because they are denied access to basic services (Doward and Townsend 2007). Ultimately, the reconstruction of Iraq and the solution of the refugee crisis depend upon a properly functioning Iraqi state. But this is not a likelihood in the near future. In the longer term, a critical mass of Iraqis must be able to choose an alternative to the political parties that currently preside over the fragmenting and failing state.

Any cease-fire or end of violence by current armed groups should not be negotiated on the basis of compromising human rights and women's rights. Nor should it exclude or disadvantage a segment of the population, whether on the basis of religious affiliation, ethnicity, gender, or class. In our view, national reconciliation is possible only if Iraqis of all ethnic and religious backgrounds and political persuasions can take part in a process that allows for real discussion of the variety of experiences under the previous regime. Certainly, Iraqi Kurds and Shi'is bore the brunt of the atrocities linked to the Ba'th regime, but other ethnic and religious groups, including the Arab Sunni population, also suffered, and many Iraqi Sunnis actively opposed the dictatorship of Saddam Hussein. Simultaneously, a cross section of Iraqi society benefited from socioeconomic development and a generous welfare system until the imposition of economic sanctions in August 1990.

Although we do not want to essentialize women as natural peacemakers, we see that in Iraq, as in conflict zones all over the world, women activists and women politicians have been more willing and able to work

across ethnic, religious, and political differences, as well as those pertaining to secular and religious positions. This is not to deny tensions
and conflicts within the women's movement or to ignore the fact that
many women activists and politicians echo the communal and sectarian
voices of the male political leadership. Yet we do see rays of hope in the
grassroots-based activities and campaigns of Iraqi women activists across
the country.

Notes

INTRODUCTION

1. Until now, no book has systematically analyzed Iraqi women's participation in postinvasion political transition and reconstruction, although Riverbend's blog, compiled into two books (2005, 2006), often discusses the impact of the U.S.-led occupation on women's lives. Other books that address women in Iraq in the modern period include Zangana (2007), Al-Ali (2007), Al-Jawaheri (2008), Mojab (2001), and Al-Khayat (1990). Also of note are Kamp (2003) and Efrati (2004) on the prerevolutionary women's movement in Iraq, as well as Efrati (2005) on reforms of the personal status code and gender roles during the Iran-Iraq War.

2. Other contributions to the field of feminist analyses of conflict and post conflict moments include Rostami-Povey (2007), C. Cockburn (1998, 2004b), and Lentin (1997), as well as several edited volumes with chapters covering most countries in (post)conflict but those in the Middle East least of all: e.g., Mazurana, Raven-Roberts, and Parpart (2005), Giles and Hyndman (2004), Meintjes, Pillay, and Turshen (2001), Cockburn and Zarkov (2002), and Jacobs, Jacobson, and Marchbank (2000).

3. We differentiate between two critiques of multiculturalism: one arguing that it prevents Muslims from assimilating or integrating into the supposed majority culture and society and the other arguing that it constructs difference based on ethnicity and privileges certain groups of elites within so-called ethnic communities, usually at the expense of women and other less powerful groups. For the latter, see Anthias and Yuval-Davis (1992, ch. 6).

4. The link between nationalist projects and constructions of femininities and masculinities has been increasingly discussed in various historical and cultural contexts (Alexander and Mohanty 1997; Anthias and Yuval Davis 1989;

Kandiyoti 1991; Moghadam 1994; Mohanty, Russo, and Torres 1991; Parker et al. 1992; Yuval-Davis 1997).

1. IRAQI WOMEN BEFORE THE INVASION

1. For an in-depth discussion of the modern history of Iraqi women, see Al-Ali (2007).

2. The principal ideological foundations of Ba'thism were formulated by Michel 'Aflaq, a Syrian Christian, born 1910. It originated in the context of anticolonial struggles in the post–World War II period and promoted Arab unity and independence. It was secular in nature and extremely hierarchical and centralized in organization. The creation of the state of Israel and the pan-Arab ideology of Nasser fueled pan-Arab sentiments and boosted the membership of the Iraqi Ba'th, which was a branch of the pan-Arab party.

3. We have made a few cosmetic changes (in spelling, capitalization, and punctuation) to quotations from our interviews with Iraqi women that are drawn from this book.

4. Al-Bazzaz was the first civilian prime minister after the overthrow of the monarchy in 1958.

5. It seems ironical today, but Iraq also funded a UNESCO-related Iraq literacy prize, established in 1978.

6. For a detailed and in-depth discussion on the debates about the personal status laws of 1959 and 1978, see Efrati (2005).

7. The Da'wa Party was founded toward the end of the 1950s to resist secularizing trends within politics and society and to defend the Shi'i religious establishment against state encroachment. Throughout the 1970s, there were major clashes between the regime and the religious Shi'i movement, leading to a massive clampdown on Shi'i religious leaders, scholars, and their students. This included the regime's ban on the annual ceremony commemorating the martyrdom of Husayn (Aziz 1993).

8. One of the first victims of systematic Ba'thi repression and Arabization policies were the Fayli Kurds, who represent a minority within a minority: as Kurds within a predominantly Arab state and as Shi'i among otherwise Sunni Kurds. From 1969 onwards, tens of thousands of Fayli Kurds who had been living in the southern section of the Zagros Mountains near the Iraq-Iran border were deported to Iran.

9. For more details on this campaign, see Human Rights Watch (1993) and Hiltermann (2007).

10. For an in-depth study on the impact of economic sanctions on women and gender relations, see Yasmin Husein Al Jawaheri (2008).

11. The research project was carried out between Nadje and Yasmin Husein Al Jawaheri and focused on the everyday lives of teenagers in Iraq during the sanctions period. Yasmin Husein Al Jawaheri spent six months in Iraq between 2000 and 2001.

12. For statistics and case studies on violence against women, see Rahim and Shwan (2003).

2. THE USE AND ABUSE OF IRAQI WOMEN

1. Remarks by U.S. officials on U.S. commitment to women in Iraq can be accessed from the index of remarks on international women's issues at www.state .gov/g/wi/c6322.htm.

2. Emergency Supplemental Appropriations Act for Defense and for the Reconstruction of Iraq and Afghanistan (2004), H.R. 3289, 108th Congress, www .govtrack.us/congress/bill.xpd?bill=h108-3289.

3. IBWA has a Web site at www.ibwa-iraq.org/index.html.

4. Coalition Provisional Authority, "De-Ba'athification of Iraqi Society" (2003), CPA/ORD/16 May 2003/01, www.cpa-iraq.org/regulations/20030516 _CPAORD_1_De-Ba_athification_of_Iraqi_Society_.pdf, pp. 1–2.

5. According to the Brookings Institution, in April 2007, Iraqis received a national average of 11.7 hours/day (O'Hanlon and Campbell 2007, 39). This was not the experience of people in northern Iraq with whom we met.

6. For further discussion of casualty figures in Iraq, see Reif (2006).

7. See also Human Rights Watch (2003); Amnesty International (2004); Al-Jazeera (2006). The Al-Jazeera article is based on a study by the Organisation of Women's Freedom in Iraq.

8. For more details on the assassination of Fern Holland, alongside her co-worker, Robert Zangas, and her translator, Salwa Oumashi, see E. Rubin (2004).

9. This is not to deny the pleasure, comfort, and/or security that particular women may enjoy within their particular families.

3. ENGENDERING THE NEW IRAQI STATE

1. We do, however, note the achievements with regard to women's participation in the Scottish and Welsh assemblies in the United Kingdom.

2. According to the BBC Radio 4 program *Woman's Hour,* the number of women was one. Ziba H. told Nicola that the number was four—though this may refer to the number of women invited to the Baghdad Big Tent meeting later on in May 2003. It was also reported that six women in total were invited to both the Nasiriyya and Baghdad meetings (Westcott 2003).

3. Ahmed Chalabi was the head of the Iraqi National Congress, an umbrella group of exiled opponents of Saddam's regime, which had received funding from the U.S. Congress and had been in talks with the Pentagon in the run-up to the invasion.

4. The woman who was assassinated was Aqila al-Hashimi, a diplomat under the former regime. She was killed on September 25, 2003, when her convoy was ambushed near her home in Baghdad. She was replaced on the IGC by Salma al-Khafaji, a dentist, in November 2003.

5. For further discussion of the 1959 personal status laws, see chapter 1.

6. For text of the TAL, see www.cpa-iraq.org/government/TAL.html.

7. The women's movement called for a quota for women in all elected bodies of between 30 and 40 percent. See the next chapter for details. The United States was against the idea of a quota. The United Kingdom supported a com-

promise figure of 25 percent. The final text called for a "goal" with regard to the percentage of seats for women in the Transitional National Assembly.

8. For details of how particular legislation discriminates against women in the Middle East, see Nazir and Tomppert (2005).

9. The actual wording of the CPA order in question is: "No fewer than one out of the first three candidates on the list must be woman; no fewer than two out of the first six candidates on the list must be woman; and so forth until the end of the list." The Electoral Law, No. 96, CPA/ORD/7 June 04/96, June 7, 2004, sec. 4, no. 3. www.cpa-iraq.org/regulations/20040615_CPAORD_96_The_Electoral_Law.pdf.

10. Foreign and Commonwealth Office, e-mail to Nicola Pratt, February 22, 2006.

11. We thank Nathan Brown for pointing out that personal status laws are not designated as among the areas decided by central government (pers. comm. to Nicola Pratt, September 2005).

12. Independent Electoral Commission of Iraq, "Allocation of Seats," IECI Regulation 13-2005, December 6, 2005, www.ieciraq.org/final%20cand/Regn 13-2005AllocationofSeats_English-Dec6_[1].pdf.

4. THE IRAQI WOMEN'S MOVEMENT

1. Nadje is one of the founding members of Act Together, which consists of Iraqi and non-Iraqi women who initially came together to raise consciousness about the impact of economic sanctions and dictatorship on women and families in Iraq. In recent years, Act Together has focused on the effects of war and occupation. In addition to consciousness-raising and lobbying, the group has worked to support Iraqi women activists inside Iraq. See www.acttogether.org.

2. Because of a series of wars (1980–88, 1991, 2003), political assassinations, and mass executions by the former regime, as well as migration by a greater number of men than women, Iraq started to experience a significant demographic imbalance by the 1990s. Statistical estimates of the female population vary between 55 and 65 percent.

3. The debate revolves around the question of whether Islam should be a major source of legislation, a source of legislation, or the source of legislation.

4. Women to Women International is a U.S.-based NGO founded by Zeinab Salbi, a feminist activist of Iraqi origin. It has been active all over the world trying to address women's needs in the context of conflict and postconflict societies.

5. Kanan Makiya is the author of *Republic of Fear* (1998) and *Cruelty and Silence* (1993), books documenting the brutality of the Saddam Hussein regime.

5. TOWARD A FEMINIST AND ANTI-IMPERIALIST POLITICS OF PEACE

1. According to government officials within the Ministry of Labor and Social Affairs and NGOs devoted to women's issues such as the Women's Rights Association, the Knowledge for Iraqi Women Society, and groups linked to the

Iraqi Women's Network, more than ninety women become widows each day due to continuing violence countrywide. Another source (UN-OCHA 2006) states that there are eight million widows throughout the country. Given that the entire population of Iraq prior to the invasion was estimated to be around twenty-three million people, eight million seems an impossible figure.

2. In 2004 the figure was much higher: 96 percent of the extremely vulnerable and poor population had access, through the Public Distribution System, to food baskets that included staples such as wheat, rice, dried milk, sugar, tea, and soap.

3. Both authors are of Muslim origin and are extremely critical of Islam as a religion inherently oppressive to Muslim women. Taking their own life stories as a starting point, both authors engage in vast generalizations, essentialisms, and stereotypes of Islam, Muslims, and Muslim culture much like those promulgated in the Western media. Their background as women of Muslim origin has granted them authority and celebrity status for speaking out against the ills of their own religion and culture.

4. The terms *masculine* and *feminine* are not synonymous with the terms *male* and *female*. Not all men conform to predominant notions of masculinity, and not all women conform to predominant notions of femininity. However, men who are seen to resist notions of masculinity are often singled out for ridicule—such as being called "pussy" or "gay." Meanwhile, women who fail to conform to notions of femininity face differing responses. Women who have been included in militaries—only recently as direct combatants—are encouraged to join not as a means of proving their sexual identity, but as a means of obtaining a more glamorous life than they could through the pathways presented to them by a patriarchal system (Enloe 1988: 132–33). Yet once enlisted they are often typecast by male soldiers as either "whores" or "lesbians," depending on how sexually available they make themselves (see, e.g., Enloe 1988: 140–41; C. Cockburn 2007: 223), and they face a significant risk of being raped or sexually harassed by male soldiers (Regan 2007).

5. *Salafi* is Arabic for "predecessors" or "early generations." The term refers to the Prophet Muhammad, his companions, and two following generations. More broadly, it refers to groups that seek to revive a practice of Islam that is supposed to more closely resemble the religion during the time of Muhammad and that rejects any innovations within the religion since that time. *Jihadist* refers to groups that believe in armed struggle (which represents one form of jihad) as a means of defending the Muslim community. Not all Salafis are jihadists and vice versa.

6. For a study of similar processes in relation to resistance to globalization, see Kimmel (2003).

7. For a detailed discussion of a "capabilities approach" as opposed to a legalistic "rights approach," see Nussbaum (2000).

Bibliography

Abdela, Lesley, et al. 2003. "Interview with Woman's Hour." BBC Radio 4, April 15.

Abdul-Ahad, Ghaith. 2006. "Inside Iraq's Hidden War." *Guardian,* May 20.

Abdullah, Thabit. 2003. *A Short History of Iraq.* London: Pearson-Longman.

Agence France-Presse. 2004. "Iraqi Women Demand Equal Rights." February 18. http://iafrica.com/news/worldnews/303500.htm.

Ahmed, Huda. 2006. "Women in the Shadows of Democracy." *Middle East Report* 36: 24–26.

Ahmed, Leila. 1992. *Women and Gender in Islam: Historical Roots of a Modern Debate.* New Haven, CT: Yale University Press.

Akbar Mahdi, Ali, ed. 2003. *Teen Life in the Middle East.* Westport, CT: Greenwood Press.

Al-Ali, Nadje. 2000. *Gender, Secularism and the State in the Middle East: The Egyptian Women's Movement.* Cambridge: Cambridge University Press.

———. 2003. "Women and Economic Sanctions in Iraq." In *Iraq: History, People and Politics,* edited by Shams Inati. Philadelphia: Prometheus Press.

———. 2005. "Gendering Reconstruction: Iraqi Women between Dictatorship, Wars, Sanctions and Occupation." *Third World Quarterly* 26 (4–5): 739–58.

———. 2006. "'The Enemy of My Enemy Is Not My Friend': Women's Rights, Occupation and Reconstruction in Iraq." In *Situating the Politics of Belonging,* edited by Nira Yuval-Davis, Kalpana Kannabiran, and Ulrike M. Vieten, 191–204. New York: Routledge.

———. 2007. *Iraqi Women: Untold Stories from 1948 to the Present.* London: Zed Books.

Al-Ali, Nadje, Mubejel Baban, and Sundus Abass. 2006. *Iraq Women's Rights under Attack: Occupation, Constitution and Fundamentalism.* Women Living

Under Muslim Law, Occasional Paper No. 15. December. www.wluml.org/english/index.shtml/.

Al-Ali, Nadje, and Yasmin Husein. 2003. "Iraq." In *Teen Life in the Middle East,* edited by Ali Akbar Mahdi. Westport, CT: Greenwood Press.

Al-Ali, Nadje, and Nicola Pratt. 2006. "Women in Iraq: Beyond the Rhetoric." *Middle East Report* 36: 18–23.

———. 2008. "Researching Women in Post-invasion Iraq: Negotiating 'Truths' and Deconstructing Dominant Discourses." *Bulletin of the Royal Institute for Inter-faith Studies* 8 (1–2): 1–22.

Alexander, M. Jacqui, and Chandra Talpade Mohanty, eds. 1997. *Feminist Genealogies, Colonial Legacies, Democratic Futures.* New York: Routledge.

Al-Jawaheri, Yasmin Husein. 2008. *Women in Iraq: The Gender Impact of International Sanctions.* Boulder, CO: Lynne Reinner.

Al-Jazaeiri, Souad. 2006. "How Can We Guarantee Iraqi Women's Rights Now?" Paper presented at Seminar on Iraqi Women's Rights, London, October.

Al-Jazeera. 2004. "Iraqi Women Divided over Family Law." May 10. http://english.aljazeera.net/English/archive/archive?ArchiveId=973.

———. 2006. "After Saddam, Iraqi Women Used as Sex Objects." March 14. www.globalresearch.ca/index.php?context=va&aid=2118.

Alkadiri, Raad, and Chris Toensing. 2003. "The Iraqi Governing Council's Sectarian Hue." August 20. www.merip.org/mero/mero082003.html.

Al-Khayat, Sana. 1990. *Honour and Shame: Women in Modern Iraq.* London: Saqi Books.

Allen, Chris. 2007. "Down with Multiculturalism, Book-Burning and Fatwas." *Culture and Religion* 8 (2): 125–38.

Al-Marashi, Ibrahim. 2005. "Iraq's Constitutional Debate." *Middle East Review of International Affairs* 9 (3): 136–72.

Al-Radi, Nuha. 1998. *Baghdad Diaries.* London: Saqi Books.

Al-Sharqi, Amal. 1982. "The Emancipation of Iraqi Women." In *Iraq: The Contemporary State,* edited by Tim Niblock. London: Croom Helm.

America.gov. 2006. "Bush Says Women's Empowerment Strengthens Emerging Democracies." March 7. www.america.gov/st/washfile-english/2006/March/20060307142624eaifaso.3840906.html.

American Friends Service Committee. 2007. "Working to Preserve Their Legacy: The Iraqi Women's Movement." www.afsc.org/iraq/personal_stories/iraqi-womens-movement.htm.

Amnesty International. 2000. "Iraq: Fear of Further Extra-judicial Executions." November 3. http://web.amnesty.org/library/Index/ENGMDE140152000?open&of=ENG-IRQ.

———. 2004. "Violence against Women Increases Sharply." News Amnesty. March 31. http://news.amnesty.org/index/ENGMDE143103200042004.

Amos, Valerie, and Pratibha Parmar. 1984. "Challenging Imperial Feminism." *Feminist Review* 17: 3–19.

Anderlini, Sanam Naraghi. 2000. *Women at the Peace Table: Making a Difference.* New York: UNIFEM. www.unifem.org/filesconfirmed/8/226_peacebk.pdf.

Anthias, Floya, and Nira Yuval-Davis. 1989. *Woman, Nation, State.* New York: Macmillan.

————. 1992. *Racialized Boundaries: Race, Nation, Gender, Colour and Class and the Anti-racist Struggle*. London, Routledge.

Arend, Anthony C., and Robert J. Beck. 1993. *International Law and the Use of Force*. London: Routledge.

Ayubi, Nazih. 1991. *Political Islam: Religion and Politics in the Arab World*. London: Routledge.

Aziz, T. M. 1993. "The Role of Muhammad Baqir al-Sadr in Shʻi Political Activism in Iraq from 1958 to 1980." *International Journal of Middle East Studies* 25: 207–22.

Batatu, Hana. 2004. *The Old Social Classes and the Revolutionary Movement of Iraq*. 3rd ed. London: Saqi Books.

Bazzi, Mohammed. 2004. "U.S. Using Some Iraqis as Bargaining Chips." *Newsweek*, May 26, 2004.

BBC News Online. 2003. "Flashback: 1991 Gulf War." March 20. http://news.bbc .co.uk/2/hi/middle_east/2754103.stm.

————. 2005a. "Iraq Constitution: Sticking Points." August 25. http://news.bbc .co.uk/1/hi/world/middle_east/4155860.stm.

————. 2005b. "Iraq Election Log: 30 January." January 30. http://news.bbc .co.uk/1/hi/world/middle_east/4220307.stm.

Blanford, Nicholas. 2004. "The Specter of Sectarian and Ethnic Unrest in Iraq." January 7. www.merip.org/mero/mero010704.html.

Brenner, Johanna. 2003. "Transnational Feminism and The Struggle for Global Justice." *New Politics* 9 (Winter 2003). www.wpunj.edu/~newpol/issue34/brenne34.htm.

Brown, N. J. 2004. "Transitional Administrative Law: Commentary and Analysis." March 7–8. www.geocities.com/nathanbrown1/interimiraqiconstitution .html.

————. 2005. "Iraq's Constitutional Process Plunges Ahead." *Carnegie Policy Outlook,* July. www.carnegieendowment.org/files/PO19Brown.pdf.

Burnham, G., R. Lafta, S. Doocy, and L. Roberts. 2006. "Mortality after the 2003 Invasion of Iraq: A Cross-Sectional Cluster Sample Survey." *Lancet* 368 (9545): 1421–28.

Bush, George W. 2001. "Statement of the President in His Address to the Nation." September 11. www.whitehouse.gov/news/releases/2001/09/20010911-16 .html.

————. 2003. "Remarks by the President at the 20th Anniversary of the National Endowment for Democracy." November 6. www.whitehouse.gov/news/releases/2003/11/20031106-2.html.

————. 2005. "State of the Union Address." February 2. www.whitehouse.gov/news/releases/2005/02/print/20050202-11.html.

Cainkar, Louise. 1993. "The Gulf War, Sanctions and the Lives of Iraqi Women." *Arab Studies Quarterly* 14 (2): 14–49.

————. 2002. "No Longer Invisible: Arab and Muslim Exclusion after September 11." *Middle East Report* 224 (Fall): 22–29.

Carroll, Rory. 2005. "Clerics Push for Shiastan in Southern Iraq: Sunni Dismay at Power Pitch in Constitution Countdown." *Guardian,* August 12.

Cartier, Cyrille. 2006. "Iraqi Kurdish Women Voice Hopes for the Constitution."

Women's Enews, April 26. www.womensenews.org/article.cfm/dyn/aid/1703/context/archive.

CASI. 1999. "North vs. South: Professor Garfield's Comments on the UNICEF Survey and the State Department." CASI discussion list. August 16. www.casi.org.uk/discuss/1999/msg00450.html.

———. 2000. *Sanctions on Iraq: Background, Consequences, Strategies.* Cambridge: CASI.

———. 2002a. "Guide to Sanctions: What Is 'Oil for Food' and Isn't It Enough?" www.casi.org.uk/guide/off.html.

———. 2002b. "Non-conventional Weapons, Sanctions and the Threat of War." *CASI Newsletter,* July. www.casi.org.uk/newslet/0207weapons.html.

———. 2002c. "UN Watch." *CASI Newsletter,* July. www.casi.org.uk/newslet/0207reform.html.

Charlesworth, Hilary, and Christine Chinkin. 2002. "Sex, Gender and September 11." *American Journal of International Law* 96 (3): 600–605.

Chatterjee, Pratap. 2004. *Iraq, Inc.: A Profitable Occupation.* New York: Seven Stories Press.

Chinkin, Christine, and Kate Paradine. 2001. "Vision and Reality: Democracy and Citizenship of Women in the Dayton Peace Accords." *Yale Journal of International Law* 26: 103–78.

Chowdhry, Geeta, and Sheila Nair. 2004. Introduction to *Power, Postcolonialism and International Relations: Reading Race, Gender and Class,* edited by Geeta Chowdry and Sheila Nair, 1–31. New York: Routledge.

Civil Society Groups and Concerned Citizens of Iraq. 2003. "Letter to Ambassadors Bremer and Greenstock and Interim Governing Council Members." December 18. Baghdad. www.ncwo-online.org/pages.cfm?ID=62.

Cobbet, Deborah. 1986. "Women in Iraq." In *Saddam's Iraq: Revolution or Reaction?* Edited by Committee against Repression and for Democratic Rights in Iraq. London: Zed Books.

Cockburn, Cynthia. 1998. *The Space between Us: Negotiating Gender and National Identities in Conflict.* London: Zed Books.

———. 1999. "Gender, Armed Conflict and Political Violence." World Bank Background Paper. June. www.genderandpeacekeeping.org/resources/3_Gender_Armed_Conflict_and_Political_Violence.pdf.

———. 2002. "Women's Organization in the Rebuilding of Postwar Bosnia-Herzegovina." In *The Postwar Moment: Militaries, Masculinities and International Peacekeeping,* edited by Cynthia Cockburn and Dubravka Zarkov, ch. 5. London: Lawrence and Wishart.

———. 2004a. "The Continuum of Violence: A Gender Perspective on War and Peace." In *Sites of Violence: Gender and Conflict Zones,* edited by Wenona Giles and Jennifer Hyndman, 24–44. Berkeley: University of California Press.

———. 2004b. *The Line: Women, Partition and the Gender Order in Cyprus.* London: Zed Books.

———. 2007. *From Where We Stand: War, Women's Activism and Feminist Analysis.* London: Zed Books.

Cockburn, Cynthia, and Dubravka Zarkov, eds. 2002. *The Postwar Moment:*

Militaries, Masculinities and International Peacekeeping. London: Lawrence and Wishart.

Cockburn, Patrick. 2002a. "Iraqi Opposition Gathers to Plot Saddam's Fall." *Independent,* December 16, 9.

———. 2002b. "Opposition Summit Papers over Rivalries." *Independent,* December 18, 11.

———. 2005. "Iraq's Election Result: A Divided Nation." *Independent,* December 23, 1, 2.

———. 2006. "Destruction of Holiest Shia Shrine Brings Iraq to the Brink of Civil War." *Independent,* February 23, 2.

———. 2007. "UN Warns of Five Million Iraqi Refugees; Half of Displaced People Have No Access to Food Aid." *Independent,* June 10.

Cohn, Carol. 2008. "Mainstreaming Gender in UN Security Policy: A Path to Political Transformation?" In *Analysing and Transforming Global Governance: Feminist Perspectives,* edited by S. Rai and G. Waylen. Basingstoke: Palgrave. 185–206.

Colás, Alejandro. 2007. *Empire.* Cambridge: Polity Press.

Colás, Alejandro, and Richard Saull. 2005. *The War on Terror and the American "Empire" after the Cold War.* London: Routledge.

Cole, Juan. 2003. "Shiite Religious Parties Fill Vacuum in Southern Iraq." April 22. www.merip.org/mero/mero042203.html.

———. 2004a. "Kurds Threaten Boycott." Informed Comment, June 8. www.juancole.com/2004_06_01_juancole_archive.html.

———. 2004b. "Maneuvering over Transitional Government Continues." Informed Comment, June 1. www.juancole.com/2004_06_01_juancole_archive.html.

———. 2004c. "The New Improved Iraq." Informed Comment, June 30. www.juancole.com/2004_06_01_juancole_archive.html.

———. 2004d. "UN Security Council Vote Expected Tuesday; Sistani Weighs in against Interim Constitution." June 8. www.juancole.com/2004_06_01_juancole_archive.html.

Cole, Shahin, and Juan Cole. 2004. "Veil of Anxiety over Women's Rights." *Los Angeles Times,* March 7.

Coleman, Isobel. 2006. "Women, Islam and the New Iraq." *Foreign Affairs* 85 (January/February 2006): 24–38.

Cordesman, Anthony. 2004. "Inexcusable Failure: Progress in Training the Iraqi Army and Security Forces as of Mid-July 2004." July 20. Report, CSIS, Washington, DC. www.csis.org/media/csis/pubs/iraq_inexcusablefailure.pdf.

Corrin, Chris. 1996. Introduction to *Women in a Violent World: Feminist Analyses and Resistance across "Europe,"* edited by Chris Corrin. Edinburgh: Edinburgh University Press.

Cox, Michael. 2004. "Empire, Imperialism and the Bush Doctrine." *Review of International Studies* 30 (4): 585–608.

CSIS. 2004. *Progress or Peril? Measuring Iraq's Reconstruction.* September. Washington, DC: CSIS. www.reliefweb.int/rw/RWFiles2004.nsf/FilesByRWDoc UNIDFileName/MHII-64N9CP-csis-irq-1sep.pdf/$File/csis-irq-1sep.pdf.

D'Amico, Francine. 2000. "Citizen Soldier? Class, Race, Gender, Sexuality and the US Military." In *States of Conflict: Gender, Violence and Resistance,* edited by Susie Jacobs, Ruth Jacobson, and J. Marchbank, 105–22. London: Zed Books.

Daragahi, Borzou. 2003. "Iraqis Face a Daily Toil Just Getting By." *Pittsburgh Post-Gazette,* September 14.

Davis, Eric. 2005. *Memories of State: Politics, History, and Collective Memory in Modern Iraq.* Berkeley: University of California Press.

Diamond, Larry. 2004. "What Went Wrong in Iraq." *Foreign Affairs* 83 (September/October): 34–56. www.foreignaffairs.org/20040901faessay83505/larry-diamond/what-went-wrong-in-iraq.html.

———. 2005. *Squandered Victory: The American Occupation and the Bungled Effort to Bring Democracy to Iraq.* New York: Times Books.

Dobriansky, Paula J. 2003a. "Taking Exception: Standing up for Iraqi Women." *Washington Post,* July 2.

———. 2003b. "Women and the Transition to Democracy: Iraq, Afghanistan, Beyond." Speech delivered at the Heritage Foundation, April 11, 2003. www.state.gov/g/rls/rm/2003/19583.htm.

———. 2005. Preface to *Working for Women Worldwide: The US Commitment.* Washington, DC: State Department. http://usinfo.state.gov/products/pubs/women/.

Dobriansky, Paula J., Tanya Gilly, Zainab Al-Suwaij, Maha Alattar, and Esra Naama. 2003. "Human Rights and Women in Iraq: Voices of Iraqi Women." U.S. Department of State, Foreign Press Center Briefing, March 6. www.state.gov/g/rls/rm/2003/18477.htm.

Dodge, Toby. 2003. *Inventing Iraq: The Failure of Nation-Building and a History Denied.* New York: Columbia University Press.

———. 2005. *Iraq's Future: The Aftermath of Regime Change.* Adelphi Paper 372. London: International Institute for Strategic Studies.

———. 2006. "War and Resistance in Iraq: From Regime Change to Collapsed State." In *The Iraq War: Causes and Consequences,* edited by Rick Fawn and Raymond Hinnebusch, 211–24. Boulder, CO: Lynne Rienner.

———. 2007. "U.S. Failure in Iraq and the Return of Primordialism to the Social Sciences." Unpublished paper, London.

Dodge, Toby, and Steven Simon. 2003. *Iraq at the Crossroads: State and Society in the Shadow of Regime Change.* Adelphi Paper 354, International Institute for Strategic Studies. London: Oxford University Press.

Doward, Jamie, and Mark Townsend. 2007. "Just One in Six of Iraq's Refugees Is Accepted." *Observer,* October 7. www.guardian.co.uk/uk/2007/oct/07/iraq.immigration.

Edwar, Hanaa. 2005. "Latest Update from the Iraqi Women Network, 21 July 2005." www.whrnet.org/fundamentalisms/docs/action-iraq-sitin-0507.html.

Efrati, Noga. 2004. "The Other 'Awakening' in Iraq: The Women's Movement in the First Half of the Twentieth Century." *British Journal of Middle Eastern Studies* 31 (November 2004): 153–73.

———. 2005. "Negotiating Rights in Iraq: Women and Personal Status Law." *Middle East Journal* 59 (August 2005): 577–95.

Eisenstein, Zillah R. 2004. *Against Empire: Feminisms, Racism and the West.* New York: Zed Books.

El-Kassem, Nadeen. 2007. "Organising Women or Women Organising? 'Reconstruction' and Women's NGOs in Iraq." Paper presented at the Eighth Mediterranean Social and Political Research Meeting, Robert Schuman Centre for Advanced Studies, European University Institute, Italy, March 21–25.

Elshtain, Jean Bethke. 2003. *Just War against Terror: The Burden of American Power in a Violent World.* New York: Basic Books.

Eltahawy, Mona. 2005. "Iraq's Elections II: Will Women Be the Biggest Losers?" *International Herald Tribune,* January 29.

Engels, Friedrich. 1972. *Origin of the Family, Private Property and the State.* New York: Pathfinder Press.

Enloe, Cynthia. 1988. *Does Khaki Become You? The Militarization of Women's Lives.* London: Pandora.

———. 1990. *Bananas, Beaches and Bases: Making Feminist Sense of International Politics.* London: Pandora Press.

———. 1993. *The Morning After: Sexual Politics at the End of the Cold War.* Berkeley: University of California Press.

———. 2000. *Maneuvers: The International Politics of Militarizing Women's Lives.* Berkeley: University of California Press.

———. 2001. *Bananas, Beaches and Bases: Making Feminist Sense of International Politics.* 2nd, rev. ed. Berkeley: University of California Press.

———. 2004. *The Curious Feminist: Searching for Women in a New Age of Empire.* Berkeley: University of California Press.

———. 2005. "What If Patriarchy Is 'the Big Picture?'" In *Gender, Conflict and Peacekeeping,* edited by Dyan Mazurana, Angela Raven-Roberts, and Jane Parpart. Lanham, MD: Rowman and Littlefield.

Fanon, Frantz. 1990. *The Wretched of the Earth.* Harmondsworth: Penguin.

Farouk-Sluglett, Marion. 1993. "Liberation or Repression? Pan-Arab Nationalism and the Women's Movement in Iraq." In *Iraq: Power and Society,* edited by Derek Hopwood, 51–73. Reading: Ithaca Press.

Farouk-Sluglett, Marion, and Peter Sluglett. 2003. *Iraq since 1958: From Revolution to Dictatorship.* 4th ed. London: I. B. Tauris.

Fassihi, Farzan. 2005. "Iraqi Shiite Women Push Islamic Law on Gender Roles." *Wall Street Journal,* March 9.

Fischer, Jeff. 2004. "Iraq's Electoral System: A Strategy for Inclusiveness." *Arab Reform Bulletin,* September. www.carnegieendowment.org/publications/index.cfm?fa=view&id=15783#iraqsuccess.

Flanders, Laura, ed. 2004. *The W Effect: Bush's War on Women.* New York: Feminist Press.

Foreign and Commonwealth Office. 2002. "Saddam Hussein: Crimes and Human Rights Abuses." November. www.fco.gov.uk/Files/kfile/hrdossier.pdf.

Galtung, Johan. 1996. *Peace by Peaceful Means: Peace and Conflict, Development and Civilization.* Thousand Oaks, CA: Sage Publications.

Garfield, Richard. 1999. "Mortality Changes in Iraq, 1990–1996: A Review of Evidence." Occasional Paper, Fourth Freedom Forum.

———. 2000. "Changes in Health and Well-Being in Iraq during the 1990s: What

Do We Know and How Do We Know It?" In *Sanctions on Iraq: Background, Consequences, Strategies.* Cambridge: CASI.

Giacaman, Rita, Islah Jad, and Penny Johnson. 1996. "For the Common Good? Gender and Social Citizenship in Palestine." *Middle East Report* 198 (January-March): 11–16.

Giles, Wenona, Malathi de Alwis, Edith Klein, Neluka Silva, and Maja Korac, eds. *Feminists under Fire: Exchanges across War Zones.* Toronto: Between the Lines.

Giles, Wenona, and Jennifer Hyndman, eds. 2004. *Sites of Violence: Gender and Conflict Zones.* Berkeley: University of California Press.

Gill, Joe. 2006. "Sundus Abbass Was in Iraq Fighting for the Rights of Women—Until She Was Threatened with Death, That Is." *Morning Star,* August 28.

Goetz, Anne Marie. 2005. "Against Daunting Odds: Women Fight for Gender Equality Rights in Iraq's New Constitution." *IDS News,* April 8. www.ids .ac.uk/ids/news/Archive2005/AnneMarieIraq.html.

Goldstein, Joshua S. 2001. *War and Gender: How Gender Shapes the War System and Vice Versa.* Cambridge: Cambridge University Press.

Gordan, E. 2005. "Our Friend in the Gallery: Safia al-Suhail and the New Iraq." *National Review Online,* February 4.

Graham-Brown, Sarah. 1999. *Sanctioning Saddam: The Politics of Intervention in Iraq.* London: I. B. Tauris.

Hainsworth, Zarin, and Claire Hughes. 2004. "Iraq: Scoping Study to Identify Needs of Emerging National Iraqi Women's Organisations." Visit report. DFID, London.

Hajaj, Claire, and Ban Dhayi. 2007. "Lack of Safe Water Endangers the Health of Baghdad's Most Deprived Children." UNICEF, Iraq Newsline, March 22. www.unicef.org/emerg/iraq_39172.html.

Hajjar, Lisa. 2004. "Religion, State Power and Domestic Violence in Muslim Societies: A Framework for Comparative Analysis." *Law and Social Inquiry* 29 (1): 1–38.

Hamzeh, Karim Mohammed. 2004. *Evaluating the Status of Iraq Women in Light of the Beijing Platform for Action.* Amman: UNIFEM Arab States Regional Office.

Harding, Sandra. 1993. "Rethinking Standpoint Epistemology: What Is 'Strong Objectivity'?" In *Feminist Epistemologies,* edited by Linda Alcoff and Elizabeth Potter, 127–40. New York: Routledge.

Hartsock, Nancy. 1985. *Money, Sex and Power: Toward a Feminist Historical Materialism.* Boston: Northeastern University Press.

Hashim, Ahmed S. 2006. *Insurgency and Counter-insurgency in Iraq.* London: Hurst.

Hassan, Ghali. 2004. "Colonial Violence against Women." *Countercurrents,* May 31. www.countercurrents.org/iraq-hassan310504.htm.

Helms, Christine Moss. 1984. *Iraq, Eastern Flank of the Arab World.* Washington, DC: Brookings Institute.

Hendessi, Mandana. 2005. "Women's Civil Rights and Governance in Iraq." Report. DFID, London.

Herring, Eric, and Glen Rangwala. 2006. *Iraq in Fragments: The Occupation and Its Legacy*. London: Hurst.

Hiltermann, Joost. 2005. "Make-up or Break-up? The Impact of the Draft Constitution on Iraq's Divided Communities." Paper presented at a conference organized by Women for Women International, "Our Constitution, Our Future," Erbil, September 25. www.crisisgroup.org/home/index.cfm?id=3707.

———. 2007. *A Poisonous Affair: America, Iraq and the Gassing of Halabja*. Cambridge: Cambridge University Press.

Hinnebusch, Raymond. 2003. *The International Politics of the Middle East*. Manchester: Manchester University Press.

Hirsi Ali, Ayaan. 2007. *Infidel*. New York: Free Press.

Human Rights Watch. 1993. *Genocide in Iraq: The Anfal Campaign against the Kurds*. New York: Human Rights Watch.

———. 2003. *Climate of Fear: Sexual Violence and Abduction of Women and Girls in Baghdad*. July. New York: Human Rights Watch.

———. 2005. "Iraqi Elections: Human Rights Concerns." www.hrw.org/english/docs/2005/01/21/iraq10058.htm.

———. 2006. "Human Rights Overview: United States." January. http://hrw.org/english/docs/2006/01/18/usdom12292_txt.htm.

———. 2007a. "Caught in the Whirlwind: Torture and Denial of Due Process by the Kurdistan Security Forces." July 3. Report, Human Rights Watch. http://hrw.org/reports/2007/kurdistan0707/.

———. 2007b. "UK: Brown Should Adopt New Approach against Terrorism." June 21. http://hrw.org/english/docs/2007/06/21/uk16210.htm.

Hunt, Krista. 2002. "The Strategic Co-optation of Women's Rights." *International Feminist Journal of Politics* 4 (1): 116–21.

Huntington, Samuel P. 1993. "The Clash of Civilizations?" *Foreign Affairs* 72 (3): 22–49.

Hussein, Saddam. 1981. *The Revolution and Women in Iraq*. Translated by Khalid Kishtany. Baghdad: Translation and Foreign Languages Publishing House.

IMIE. 2006. "Final Report: Assessment of the January 30, 2005, Election Process." January 19. www.imie.ca/rep_Jan30.html.

Inati, Shams, ed. 2003. *Iraq: Its History, People, and Politics*. Amherst: Humanity Books.

Independent Electoral Commission of Iraq. 2005. "Certification of the Constitutional Referendum Final Results." February 10. www.ieciraq.org/English/Frameset_english.htm.

Ingrams, Doreen. 1983. *The Awakened: Women in Iraq*. London: Third World Center.

Institute for War and Peace Reporting. 2005. "Female Deputies Trying to Promote Women's Rights Face Uphill Struggle." August 3. www.peacewomen.org/news/Iraq/Aug05/WomenlosingParliament.htm.

International Committee of the Red Cross. 2007. "Civilians without Protection: The Ever Worsening Humanitarian Crisis in Iraq." Report, April 11, International Committee of the Red Cross, Geneva. www.icrc.org/Web/eng/siteengo.nsf/htmlall/iraq-report-110407/$File/Iraq-report-icrc.pdf.

International Crisis Group. 2002. "Voices from the Iraqi Street." Middle East Briefing No. 3. December 4. www.crisisgroup.org/home/index.cfm?id=1825&l=1.

———. 2003. "Governing Iraq." Middle East Report No. 17. August 25. www.crisisgroup.org/home/index.cfm?l=1&id=1672.

———. 2004a. "Iraq's Transition on a Knife Edge." Middle East Report No. 27. April 27. www.crisisgroup.org/home/index.cfm?id=2679&l=1.

———. 2004b. "Reconstructing Iraq." Middle East Report No. 30, September 2. www.crisisgroup.org/home/index.cfm?id=2936&l=1.

———. 2005. "Unmaking Iraq: A Constitutional Process Gone Awry." Middle East Briefing No. 19. September 26. www.crisisgroup.org/home/index.cfm?id=3703.

———. 2006a. "In Their Own Words: Reading the Iraqi Insurgency." Middle East Report No. 50. February 15. www.crisisgroup.org/home/index.cfm?id=3953.

———. 2006b. "The Next Iraqi War? Sectarianism and Civil Conflict." Middle East Report No. 52, February 27. www.crisisgroup.org/home/index.cfm?id=3980.

Iraq Body Count. 2007. "Iraq Body Count Project." www.iraqbodycount.org/background.php.

Iraqi al-Amal Association. 2004. "The National Conference for Empowering Women in Democracy (White Paper)." June 16–17, Baghdad.

Ismael, Jacqueline S. 1980. "Social Policy and Social Change: The Case of Iraq." *Arab Studies Quarterly* 2 (3): 235–48.

Ismael, Jacqueline S., and Shereen T. Ismael. 2000. "Gender and State in Iraq." In *Gender and Citizenship in the Middle East,* edited by Suad Joseph, 185–211. New York: Syracuse University Press.

IWF. 2006. "Our Mission." www.iwf.org/about_iwf/default.asp.

———. 2007. "IWEI Women Leaders Conference—'The Principles and Practices of Democracy' (Dead Sea, Jordan, April 2005)." www.iwf.org/iraq/women_conference.asp.

Jabar, Faleh. 2003. *The Shi'ite Movement in Iraq.* London: Saqi Books.

Jacobs, Susie, Ruth Jacobson, and Jennifer Marchbank, eds. 2000. *States of Conflict: Gender, Violence and Resistance.* London: Zed Books.

Jad, Islah. 2004. "The NGOization of the Arab Women's Movement." *Review of Women's Studies* 2: 42–56.

Jamail, Dahr, and Ali Al-Fadhily. 2006. "IRAQ: Widows Become the Silent Tragedy." December 7. www.globalresearch.ca/index.php?context=va&aid=4085.

Jayawardena, Kumari. 1986. *Feminism and Nationalism in the Third World.* London: Zed Books.

Jones, Adam. 2004. "Humiliation and Masculine Crisis in Iraq." *Al-Raida* 21 (104–5): 70–73.

Joseph, Suad. 1991. "Elite Strategies: Iraq and Lebanon." In *Women, Islam and the State,* edited by Deniz Kandiyoti. Philadelphia: Temple University Press.

Kamp, Martina. 2003. "Organizing Ideologies of Gender, Class, and Ethnicity:

The Pre-Revolutionary Women's Movement in Iraq." In *Women and Gender in the Middle East and Islamic World Today,* edited by Sherifa Zuhur. Berkeley: University of California International and Area Studies.

Kandiyoti, Deniz, ed. 1991. *Women, Islam and the State.* Philadelphia: Temple University Press.

———. 2007. "Between the Hammer and the Anvil: Post-conflict Reconstruction, Islam and Women's Rights." *Third World Quarterly* 28 (3): 503–17.

Kaufman, Stephen. 2004. "Iraqi Women Receiving Democracy Training Ahead of Elections." September 27. http://usinfo.state.gov/mena/Archive/2004/Sep/27-387029.html.

Khalil, Ashraf. 2004. "Women Call for Equal Representation in Parliament." Women's Enews, February 6. www.womensenews.org/article.cfm/dyn/aid/1703/context/archive.

Kimmel, Michael S. 2003. "Globalization and Its Mal(e)contents: The Gendered Moral and Political Economy of Terrorism." *International Sociology* 18 (3): 603–20.

Korac, Maya. 1998. *Linking Arms: Women and War in Post-Yugoslav States.* Uppsala: Life and Peace Institute.

KPMG Bahrain. 2004. "Development Fund for Iraq, Report of Factual Findings in Connection with Disbursements for the Period from 1 January 2004 to 28 June 2004." September. http://news.findlaw.com/hdocs/docs/iraq/cpa101304audit.pdf.

Kubba, Laith, Rend Al-Rahim, Nijyar Shemdin, and Gayle Smith. 2005. "Countdown to a Constitution: Iraqis Debate Their Country's Future." Center for American Progress, Washington, DC, March 22.

Kurdistan Regional Government. 2006. "Members of the Kurdistan National Assembly." August. www.krg.org/uploads/documents/KNAMembers__2006_11_30_h12m44s8.pdf.

Lantos, Tom. 2002. "Discrimination against Women and the Roots of Global Terrorism." *Human Rights,* July 1, 7–8.

Larserud, Stina, and Rita Taphorn. 2007. *Designing for Equality: Best-Fit, Medium-Fit and Non-favourable Combinations of Electoral Systems and Gender Quotas.* Stockholm: International IDEA.

Lentin, Ronit, ed. 1997. *Gender and Catastrophe.* London: Zed Books.

Lorentzen, Lois Ann, and Jennifer Turpin, eds. 1998. *Women and War Reader.* New York: New York University Press.

MacDonald, Neil, and Dhiya Rasan. 2005. "Constitution May Reduce Women's Rights, Iraqi Campaigners Say." July 26. www.ft.com/cms/s/eda83f4e-fd71-11d9-b224-00000e2511c8.html.

Mackenzie, Meredith. 2006. "Iraqi Women Seek Leadership Position." United Press International, January 24. www.spacewar.com/reports/Iraqi_Women_Seek_Leadership_Positions.html.

Mahmoud, Houzan. 2005. "Iraqi Women Find Election a Cruel Joke." *Seattle Post-Intelligencer,* January 30. http://seattlepi.nwsource.com/opinion/209809_iraqiwomanvote.html.

Makiya, Kanan. 1993. *Cruelty and Silence: War, Tyranny, Uprising, and the Arab World.* New York: Norton.

———. 1998. *Republic of Fear: The Politics of Modern Iraq.* Berkeley: University of California Press.

Malik, Kenan. 2005. "Islamophobia Myth." *Prospect,* February, 107.

Manji, Irshad. 2003. *The Trouble with Islam: A Wake-Up Call for Honesty and Change.* New York: Random House.

Massey, Ellen. 2007. "Iraq: Women Resist Return to Sectarian Laws." Inter Press Service, June 25. www.ipsnews.net/news.asp?idnews=38304.

Mazurana, Dyan, Angela Raven-Roberts, and Jane Parpart, eds. 2005. *Gender, Conflict and Peacekeeping.* Lanham, MD: Rowman and Littlefield.

McDowall, David. 2000. *A Modern History of the Kurds.* London: J. B. Tauris.

Mehryar, Amir H., Akbar Aghajanian, Shirin Ahmad-Nia, Muhammad Mirzae, and Mohsen Naghavi. 2005. "Primary Health Care System, Narrowing of Rural-Urban Gap in Health Indicators, and Rural Poverty Reduction: The Experience of Iran." Paper presented at the 25th General Population Conference of the International Union for the Scientific Study of Population, Tours, France, July 18–23.

Meijer, Roel. 2005. "The Association of Muslim Scholars in Iraq." *Middle East Report* 237 (Winter): 12–19. www.merip.org/mer/mer237/meijer.html.

Meintjes, Sheila, Anu Pillay, and Meredeth Turshen, eds. 2001. *The Aftermath: Women in Post-conflict Transformation.* London: Zed Books.

Melia, Thomas O., and Brian M. Katulis. 2003. "Iraqis Discuss Their Country's Future: Post-war Perspectives from the Iraqi Street." July 28. National Democratic Institute for International Affairs. www.peacewomen.org/resources/Iraq/FullNDI.pdf.

Moghadam, Valentine, ed. 1994. *Gender and National Identity: Women and Politics in Muslim Societies.* London: Zed Books.

———. 2003. "Globalizing the Local: Transnational Feminism and Afghan Women's Rights." Peuples et Monde, December 26. www.peuplesmonde.com/article.php3?id_article=20.

———. 2005. *Globalizing Women: Transnational Feminist Networks.* Baltimore: John Hopkins University Press.

Mohanty, Chandra Talpade. 1991. "Under Western Eyes: Feminist Scholarship and Colonial Discourses." In *Third World Women and the Politics of Feminism,* edited by Chandra Talpade Mohanty, Ann Russo, and Lourdes Torres, 51(80. Bloomington: Indiana University Press.

Mohanty, Chandra Talpade, Ann Russo, and Lourdes Torres. 1991. *Third World Women and the Politics of Feminism.* Bloomington: Indiana University Press.

Mojab, Shahrzad. 1996. "Nationalism and Feminism: The Case of Kurdistan." *Simone de Beauvoir Institute Bulletin* 16: 65–73. http://fcis.oise.utoronto.ca/~mojabweb/publications/english/NationalismFeminism.pdf.

———. 2000. "Vengeance and Violence: Kurdish Women Recount the War." *Canadian Women's Studies* 19 (4): 89–94.

———, ed. 2001. *Women of a Non-state Nation: The Kurds.* Costa Mesa, CA: Mazda.

———. 2003. "Kurdish Women in the Zone of Genocide and Gendercide." *Al-Raida* 21 (Fall 2003): 25.

———. 2004. "No 'Safe Haven': Violence against Women in Iraqi Kurdistan."

In *Sites of Violence: Gender and Conflict Zones,* edited by Wenona Giles and Jennifer Hyndmann. Berkeley: University of California Press.

———. 2007. "Women's NGOs and Post-war Reconstruction." Paper presented at the Eighth Mediterranean Social and Political Research Meeting, Florence, Montecatini Terme, March 21–25.

———. n.d. "Women's NGOs under Conditions of Occupation and War." *Against the Current,* July 6. www.solidarity-us.org/node/576.

Morrow, J. 2006. "Weak Viability: The Iraqi Federal State and the Constitutional Amendment Process." Special Report No. 168, July, USIP, Washington, DC.

Nader, Talal. 2004. "Kurds Still Seeking Lost Women." Iraq Crisis Report no. 69, June 21. http://iwpr.net/?p=ic&s=f&o=167693&apc_state=heniicr2004.

Narayan, Uma. 1997. *Dislocating Cultures: Identities, Traditions, and Third World Feminism.* New York: Routledge.

Nazir, Sameena, and Leigh Tomppert, eds. 2005. *Women's Rights in the Middle East and North Africa: Citizenship and Justice.* New York: Freedom House.

NCCI and Oxfam. 2007. "Rising to the Humanitarian Challenge in Iraq." Briefing paper, July. www.oxfam.org/en/policy/briefingpapers/bp105_humanitarian_challenge_in_iraq_0707.

Norris, Pippa. 2004. "Increasing Women's Representation in Iraq: What Strategies Would Work Best." Briefing Document for the National Endowment for Democracy, February 16. John F. Kennedy School of Government, Harvard University, Boston. http://ksghome.harvard.edu/~pnorris/Acrobat/Iraq%20—%20Options%20for%20Women's%20Representation.pdf.

Nussbaum, Martha. 2000. *Women and Human Development: A Capabilities Approach.* Cambridge: Cambridge University Press.

Office of International Women's Issues. 2003. "Iraqi Women under Saddam's Regime: A Population Silenced." March 20. www.state.gov/g/wi/rls/18877.htm.

Office of the Inspector General. CPA. 2004. "Quarterly Report to Congress." October 30. Washington, DC. www.globalsecurity.org/military/library/report/2004/cpaig_30oct2004_report.pdf.

Office of the Senior Coordinator for International Women's Issues. 2004. "U.S. Commitment to Women in Iraq." September 23. www.state.gov/g/wi/rls/36751.htm.

O'Hanlon, Michael E., and Jason H. Campbell. 2007. "Iraq Index: Tracking Variables of Reconstruction and Security in Post-Saddam Iraq." December 21. Brookings Institution, Washington, DC. www.brookings.edu/saban/~/media/Files/Centers/Saban/Iraq%20Index/index20071221.pdf.

Ong, Aiwha. 1999. *Flexible Citizenship: The Cultural Logics of Transnationality.* Durham: Duke University Press.

Pachachi, Maysoon, dir., prod. 2004. *Return to the Land of Wonders.* London: Oxymoron Films.

Pankhurst, Donna. 2004. "The 'Sex War' and Other Wars: Towards a Feminist Approach to Peace Building." In *Development, Women, and War: Feminist Perspectives,* edited by Haleh Afshar and Deborah Eade. Oxford: OXFAM.

Parker, Andrew, Mary Russo, Doris Sommer, and Patricia Yaeger, eds. 1992. *Nationalisms and Sexualities.* New York: Routledge.

Pateman, Carole. 1989. *The Disorder of Women: Democracy, Feminism, and Political Theory.* Oxford: Polity Press.

Peterson, V. Spike. 1992. *Gendered States: Feminist (Re)visions of International Relations Theory.* Boulder, CO: Lynne Rienner.

———. 1998. "Gendered Nationalism: Reproducing 'Us' versus 'Them.'" In *The Women and War Reader,* edited by Lois Ann Lorentzen and Jennifer Turpin. New York: New York University Press.

———. 2003. *A Critical Rewriting of Global Political Economy: Reproductive, Productive and Virtual Economies.* New York: Routledge.

———. 2007. "Gendering Coping, Combat and Criminal Economies." Paper presented at the Eighth Mediterranean Social and Political Research Meeting, Florence, Montecatini, Terme, March 21–25.

Peterson, V. Spike, and Anne Sisson Runyan. 1993. *Global Gender Issues.* Boulder, CO: Westview Press.

Philip, Catherine. 2005. "Iraq's Women of Power Who Tolerate Wife-Beating and Promote Polygamy." *Times,* March 31.

Phillips, David L. 2005. *Losing Iraq: Inside the Postwar Reconstruction Fiasco.* Boulder, CO: Westview Press.

Pollack, Kenneth M. 2002. "Next Stop Baghdad?" *Foreign Affairs* 81 (2): 32–47.

Pratt, Nicola. 2006. "Human Rights NGOs and the 'Foreign Funding Debate' in Egypt." In *Human Rights in the Arab World: Independent Voices,* edited by Anthony Tirado Chase and Amr Hamzawy, 114–26. Philadelphia: University of Pennsylvania Press.

———. 2007. *Democracy and Authoritarianism in the Arab World.* Boulder, CO: Lynne Rienner.

Project for the New American Century. 2001. "Letter to President Bush." September 20. www.newamericancentury.org/Bushletter.htm.

Prothero, Mitchell. 2005. "Iraqi Women on the Verge of a Revolution." *Salon,* February 22. http://dir.salon.com/story/news/feature/2005/02/22/women/index.html.

Raha, Maria. 2004. "Veiled Intentions: The U.S. Media's Hug and Run Affair with Afghan Women." In *The W Effect: Bush's War on Women,* edited by Laura Flanders, 177–80. New York: Feminist Press.

Rahim, Runak Faraj, and Hana Shwan. 2003. *Statistics on Violence against Women with an Article.* Translated by Tanea Abdulkhadir. Publication No. 4. Sulimaniya: Women Information and Culture Center.

Rand Corporation. 2005. *Developing Iraq's Security Sector: The Coalition Provisional Authority's Experience.* Washington, DC: Rand Corporation. www.rand.org/pubs/monographs/2005/RAND_MG365.pdf.

Rangwala, Glen. 2005. "Democratic Transition and Its Limitations." In *The Iraq War and Democratic Politics,* edited by Alex Danchev and John MacMillan. New York: Routledge.

Rassam, Amal. 1982. "Revolution within the Revolution? Women and the State in Iraq." In *Iraq: The Contemporary State,* edited by Tim Niblock. London: Croom Helm.

————. 1992. "Political Ideology and Women in Iraq." In *Women and Development in the Middle East and North Africa,* edited by Joseph D. Jabbra and Nancy W. Jabbra. Leiden: E. J. Brill.

————. 2003. "Iraq." In *Women's Rights in the Middle East and North Africa: Citizenship and Justice,* edited by Sameena Nazir and Leigh Tomppert, 87–104. Washington, DC: Freedom House.

Reardon, Betty. 1985. *Sexism and the War System.* New York: Teachers College Press.

Recknagel, Charles. 2005. "Iraqi Women See Challenges, Opportunities to Vote." RadioFreeEurope/RadioLiberty, January 18.

Regan, Tom. 2007. "Sexual Assault of Women Soldiers on Rise in US Military." *Christian Science Monitor,* March 19.

Reif, Kingston. 2006. "Iraq Health Update." Medact, Spring. www.medact.org/content/wmd_and_conflict/iraqupdate2006.pdf.

Richards, Janet R. 1990. "Why the Pursuit of Peace Is No Part of Feminism." In *Women, Militarism and War: Essays in History, Politics and Social Theory,* edited by Jean Bethke Elshtain and Sheila Tobias, 211–26. Savage, MD: Rowman and Littlefield.

Richter, Paul. 2004. "Costs Whittle Funds to Iraqis." *Los Angeles Times,* September 26.

Riverbend. 2005. *Baghdad Burning: Girl Blog from Iraq.* New York: Feminist Press.

————. 2006. *Baghdad Burning II: More Girl Blog from Iraq.* New York: Feminist Press.

Rohde, Achim. 2006a. "Facing Dictatorship: State-Society Relations in Ba'thist Iraq." PhD diss., Freie Universität Berlin.

————. 2006b. "Opportunities for Masculinity and Love: Cultural Production in Iraq during the 1980s." In *Islamic Masculinities,* edited by Lahoucine Ouzgane, 184–201. London: Zed Books.

Rosen, Ruth. 2006. "The Hidden War on Women in Iraq." July 13. www.commondreams.org/views06/0713-33.htm.

Rostami-Povey, Elaheh. *Afghan Women: Identity and Invasion.* London: Zed Books, 2007.

Rubin, Elizabeth. 2004. "Fern Holland's War." *New York Times Magazine,* September 19.

Rubin, Michael. 2004. "Iraq's Electoral System: A Misguided Strategy." *Arab Reform Bulletin,* September. www.carnegieendowment.org/publications/index.cfm?fa=view&id=15783#iraqfailure.

Ruddick, Sara. 1989. *Maternal Thinking: Toward a Politics of Peace.* New York: Ballantine Books.

Runnymede Trust. 1997. *Islamophobia: A Challenge for Us All.* London: Runnymede Trust.

Russell, Ben. 2002. "Blair Hears Iraqi Women's Stories of Abuse and Suffering." *Independent,* December 3.

Russo, Ann. 2006. "The Feminist Majority Foundation's Campaign to Stop Gender Apartheid." *International Feminist Journal of Politics* 8 (4): 557–80.

Saghieh, Hazim. 2000. "Saddam, Manhood and the Image." In *Imagined Masculinities: Identity and Culture in the Middle East,* edited by Mai M. Ghoussoub and Emma Sinclair-Webb. London: Saqi Books.

Said, Edward. 1978. *Orientalism.* London: Penguin Books.

———. 2001. "The Clash of Ignorance." *Nation,* October 22.

Salbi, Zainab. 2003. "'Please Tell Mr. Bush . . .' Diaries from Iraq, 9–20 May 2003." Women for Women International.

———. 2006. *Between Two Worlds—Escape from Tyranny: Growing Up in the Shadow of Saddam.* New York: Gotham Books.

Samra, Dina Abou. 2007. "Military-Induced Displacement." *Forced Migration Review,* June, 37–38.

Save the Children UK. 2007. "Last in Line, Last in School: How Donors Are Failing Children in Conflict-Affected Fragile States." Report Briefing, July 27. Save the Children UK, London. www.savethechildren.org.uk/en/54_2525.htm.

Sen, Amartya. 2006. *Identity and Violence: The Illusion of Destiny.* New York: Norton.

Sengupta, Kim. 2005. "New Iraqi Constitution Must Follow Islam on Women's Rights, Say Shia." *Independent,* July 21.

Shepherd, Laura. 2006. "Veiled References." *International Feminist Journal of Politics* 8 (1): 1–23.

Sideek, Nasreen M. 2003. "Women in Iraq, Future Prospects: Role of Women in Reconstructing Iraq." Paper presented at the conference "Winning the Peace: Women's Role in Post-conflict Iraq." Woodrow Wilson International Center, Washington, DC, April 22.

SIGIR. 2005. "Oversight of Funds Provided to Iraqi Ministries through the National Budget Process." Report 05-004. January 30. Washington, DC. www.sigir.mil/reports/pdf/audits/dfi_ministry_report.pdf.

———. 2007a. "Quarterly and Semiannual Report to Congress." January 30. Washington, DC. www.sigir.mil/reports/quarterlyreports/Jan07/pdf/Report_-_January_2007_Complete.pdf.

———. 2007b. "Quarterly Report to Congress." April 30. Washington, DC. www.sigir.mil/reports/quarterlyreports/Apr07/pdf/Report_-_April_2007_Complete.pdf.

Simmel, Georg. 1921. "The Sociological Significance of the 'Stranger.'" In *Introduction to the Science of Sociology,* edited by Robert E. Park and Ernest W. Burgess. Chicago: University of Chicago Press.

Sjoberg, Laura. 2006. *Gender, Justice, and the Wars in Iraq: A Feminist Reformulation of Just War Theory.* Lanham, MD: Lexington Books.

Spivak, Gayatri. 1988. "Can the Subaltern Speak?" In *Marxism and the Interpretation of Culture,* edited by Cary Nelson and Lawrence Grossberg, 271–313. New York: Macmillan.

Stabile, Carol A., and Deepa Kumar. 2005. "Unveiling Imperialism: Media, Gender and the War on Afghanistan." *Media, Culture and Society* 27 (5): 765–82.

Staff and Agencies. 2004. "US Hands Over Power in Iraq." June 28. www.guardian.co.uk/Iraq/Story/0,2763,1248928,00.html.

Steele, Jonathan. 2003. "Delegates Agree New Talks on Government." *Guardian,* April 29.

————. 2005. "Iraqi Cabinet Approval Ends Deadlock." *Guardian,* April 29.

Stoetzler, Marcel, and Nira Yuval-Davis. 2002. "Standpoint Theory, Situated Knowledge and the Situated Imagination." *Feminist Theory* 3 (3): 315–33.

Sturken, Marita. 2002. "Masculinity, Courage, and Sacrifice." *Signs: Journal of Women in Culture and Society* 28 (1): 444–45.

Susskind, Yifat. 2007. "Promising Democracy, Imposing Theocracy: Gender-Based Violence and the US War on Iraq." March 6. Report, MADRE, New York. http://madre.org/articles/me/iraqreport.html.

Sylvester, Christine. 1994. *Feminist Theory and International Relations in a Postmodern Era.* Cambridge: Cambridge University Press.

Thayer, Millie. 2000. "Travelling Feminisms: From Embodied Women to Gendered Citizenship." In *Global Ethnography: Forces, Connections, and Imaginations in a Postmodern World,* edited by Michael Burawoy et al. Berkeley: University of California Press.

Tickner, J. Ann. 1992. *Gender in International Relations: Feminist Perspectives on Achieving Global Security.* New York: Columbia University Press.

Tinsley, Becky. 2004. "America's Own Goal in Iraq." *New Statesman,* August 16.

Transparency International. 2005. *Global Corruption Report 2005.* Berlin: Transparency International. www.transparency.org/publications/gcr.

Tripp, Charles. 2000. *A History of Iraq.* Cambridge: Cambridge University Press.

Turshen, Meredeth, and Clotilde Twagiramariya, eds. 1998. *What Women Do in Wartime: Gender and Conflict in Africa.* London: Zed Books.

Tyler, Patrick E. 2003. "New Iraqi Governing Council Meets for First Time." *New York Times.* July 13.

UNAMI. 2005. "Some Political Entities Take Advantage of Religious Symbols—Al-Dustur." Iraqi Media Monitoring, January 17. www.globalsecurity.org/wmd//library/news/iraq/2005/01/imm-050117-unami.htm.

————. 2007a. "Human Rights Report, 1 January–31 March 2007." www.uniraq.org/FileLib/misc/HR%20Report%20Jan%20Mar%202007%20EN.pdf.

————. 2007b. "Humanitarian Briefing on the Crisis in Iraq." May 2. www.uniraq.org/documents/UN-Iraq%20Humanitarian%20Briefing%20Fact%20Sheet%20May%2007.pdf.

UNDP. 2000. "Iraq Country Office, 1999–2000 Report." June. http://mirror.undp.org/iraq/pdf/REPORT.PDF.

————. 2004. "Iraq Living Conditions Survey." www.iq.undp.org/ILCS/women.htm.

UNFAO. 2000. "Assessment of the Food and Nutrition Situation: Iraq." Technical Report. www.reliefweb.int/library/documents/iraqnutrition.pdf.

UNHCHR. 2004. "The Present Situation of Human Rights in Iraq." June 4. www.reliefweb.int/rw/rwb.nsf/AllDocsByUNID/50ed076dd543d1e249256ea c001f9da5.

UNHCR. 2003. "Iraqi Refugee and Asylum Seeker Statistics." March. www.unhcr.org/cgi-bin/texis/vtx/home/opendoc.pdf?tbl=SUBSITES&id=3e79b00b9.

————. 2006. "Iraq Displacement." Briefing Note, November 3. http://www.unhcr.org/cgi-bin/texis/vtx/iraq?page=briefing&id=454b1f8f2.

————. 2007a. "Growing Needs amid Continuing Displacement." www.unhcr.org/cgi-bin/texis/vtx/iraq?page=intro.

———. 2007b. "Statistics on Displaced Iraqis around the World." September. www.unhcr.org/cgi-bin/texis/vtx/home/opendoc.pdf?tbl=SUBSITES&id=470387fc2.

UNICEF. 1993. *Children and Women in Iraq: A Situation Analysis.* Baghdad: UNICEF.

———. 2001. "UNICEF Humanitarian Action: Iraq Donor Update." July 11. www.unicef.org/infobycountry/iraq_31597.html (no longer accessible).

———. n.d. "Iraq Country Statistics." www.unicef.org/infobycountry/iraq_statistics.html.

UNIFEM. 2004. "Gender Profile—Iraq." www.utoronto.ca/wwdl/bibliography_war/UNIFEM%20-%20Iraq%20-%20women%20war%20and%20peace.htm.

———. 2005. "Iraqi Women Hold Third Sit-In Demonstration to Demand Rights in New Constitution." August 19. www.reliefweb.int/rw/rwb.nsf/db900SID/EVOD-6FHCZ5?OpenDocument.

———. 2007. "Announcing the Formulation of Women Caucus in the Iraqi Parliament." October 7. www.unifem.org.jo/pages/articledetails.aspx?aid=1228.

United Nations. 2005. "Iraq Electoral Fact Sheet." www.un.org/news/dh/infocus/iraq/election-fact-sht.htm#current.

UN-OCHA. 2003. "Iraq: Focus on Widows." IRIN News, July 16. www.irinnews.org/report.asp?ReportID=35434&SelectRegion=Iraq_Crisis&SelectCountry=IRAQ.

———. 2004. "Iraq: Rights Groups—Mixed Reaction to New Government." IRIN News, June 1. www.peacewomen.org/news/Iraq/June04/mixed.html.

———. 2005. "Iraq: Focus on Constitutional Concerns." IRIN News, August 14. www.reliefweb.int/rw/RWB.NSF/db900SID/KHII-6FA8CZ?OpenDocument.

———. 2006a. "Iraq: Unemployment Forces Female Professionals into Domestic Work." IRIN News, July 25. www.peacewomen.org/news/Iraq/July06/women_forced_to_domestic.html.

———. 2006b. "Iraq: Widow Numbers Rise in Wake of Violence." IRIN News, April 26. www.irinnews.org/report.aspx?reportid=26320.

———. 2007. "Violence Taking Toll on Pregnant Mothers, Infants." IRIN News, August 14. www.irinnews.org/Report.aspx?ReportId=73719.

UNSC. 1999. "Security Council Humanitarian Panel Report." March 30. www.casi.org.uk/info/panelrep.html.

UNWFP. 2004. "Baseline Food Security Analysis in Iraq." WFP/VAM-MOPDC/CSO-MOH/NRI. www.wfp.org/country_brief/middle_east/iraq/assessments/0409_foodsecurity.pdf.

USAID. n.d. "Assistance for Iraq: Support to Iraqi Women." www.usaid.gov/iraq/accomplishments/women.html (accessed June 20, 2007).

U.S. Bureau of Democracy, Human Rights, and Labor. 2007. "Country Reports on Human Rights Practices, 2006: Iraq." U.S. Department of State, Washington, DC.

U.S. Department of State. 2006. "Selection of Shirin Tahir-Kheli as Senior Adviser to the Secretary of State on Women's Empowerment." Press release, April 6. www.state.gov/r/pa/prs/ps/2006/64162.htm.

————. n.d. "Middle East Partnership Initiative." http://www.mepi.state.gov/.

U.S. History Encyclopedia. 2006. "Iraqi Americans." www.answers.com/topic/iraqi-american.

U.S. House. Committee on the Judiciary. Subcommittee on Crime, Terrorism, and Homeland Security. 2007. "War Profiteering and Other Contractor Crimes Committed Overseas." June 19. Washington, DC. http://judiciary.house.gov/Oversight.aspx?ID=338.

USIP. 2003. "Immediate Imperatives in Post-war Iraq." April 18. www.usip.org/newsmedia/releases/2003/0418_NBiraq.html.

Various. 2003. "Concluding Statement, the Voice of Women of Iraq Conference, Baghdad." July 9.

Voice of America. 2005. "Women and the Iraqi Constitution." August 4. www.voanews.com/uspolicy/archive/2005-08/2005-08-05-voa2.cfm?CFID=1090 45901&CFTOKEN=31889661.

Wadley, Jonathan D. 2006. "Reclaiming Manhood: The Connection between State-Level Emasculation and Foreign Policy." Paper presented at the annual meeting of the International Studies Association, San Diego, CA, March 22.

Waite, Lisa. 2000. "How Is Household Vulnerability Gendered? Female-Headed Households in the Collectives of Suleimaniyah, Iraqi Kurdistan." *Disasters* 24 (2): 53–172.

Westcott, Kathryn. 2003. "Where Are Iraq's Women?" BBC News, May 8. http://news.bbc.co.uk/1/hi/world/middle_east/3007381.stm.

White House Office of the Press Secretary. 2003. "President Bush Meets with Iraqi Women Leaders." November 17. www.whitehouse.gov/news/releases/2003/11/20031117-4.html#.

————. 2004. "President, Mrs. Bush Mark Progress in Global Women's Human Rights." March 12. www.whitehouse.gov/news/releases/2004/03/20040312-5.html.

Wintour, P. 2003. "Ann Clwyd: 'I Support the Government. It's Doing a Brave Thing.'" *Guardian,* February 27.

Wolfowitz, Paul. 2004. "Women in the New Iraq." *Washington Post,* February 1.

Women for Women International. 2005. "Windows of Opportunity: The Pursuit of Gender Equality in Post-war Iraq." Briefing paper, January. Washington, DC. www.womenforwomen.org/Downloads/Iraq_Paper_0105.pdf.

World Bank. 2005. "Iraq Trust Fund Data Sheet." July 31. www.iraqanalysis.org/info/334.

World Bank and UNDP. 2003. "Joint Iraq Needs Assessment." October. http://siteresources.worldbank.org/IRFFI/Resources/Joint+Needs+Assessment.pdf.

Yildiz, Kerim. 2004. *The Kurds in Iraq: The Past, Present and Future.* London: Pluto Press.

Younes, Kristele, and Sean Garcia. 2007. "Iraqi Refugees: Time for the UN System to Fully Engage." July 27. Refugees International, Washington, DC. www.refugeesinternational.org/content/article/detail/10126/.

Yuval-Davis, Nira. 1997. *Gender and Nation.* Thousand Oaks, CA: Sage Publications.

————. 2004. "Gender, the Nationalist Imagination, War, and Peace." In *Sites of*

Violence: Gender and Conflict Zones, edited by Wenona Giles and Jennifer Hyndman, 170–89. Berkeley: University of California Press.

———. 2006. "Human/Women's Rights and Feminist Transversal Politics." In *Transnational Feminisms: Women's Global Activism and Human Rights,* edited by Myra Marx Ferree and Aili Mari Tripp, 291. New York: New York University Press.

Zangana, Haifa. 2004. "Quiet, or I'll Call Democracy." *Guardian,* December 22.

———. 2005. "Chewing on Meaningless Words." *Guardian,* August 17.

———. 2006a. "Colonial Feminists from Washington to Baghdad: 'Women for a Free Iraq' as a Case Study." In *Barriers to Reconciliation: Case Studies on Iraq and the Palestine-Israel Conflict,* edited by J. Ismael and W. Haddad, 63–84. Lantham, MD: University Press of America.

———. 2006b. "The Three Cyclops of Empire Building: Targeting the Fabric of Iraqi Society." In *Empire's Law: The American Imperial Project and the War to Remake the World,* edited by Amy Bartholomew. London: Pluto Press.

———. 2007. *City of Widows: An Iraqi Woman's Account of War and Resistance.* New York: Seven Stories Press.

Zubaida, Sami. 1991. "Community, Class and Minorities in Iraq Politics." In *The Iraqi Revolution of 1958: The Old Social Classes Revisited,* edited by Robert Fernea and William Roger Louis. New York: I. B. Tauris.

———. 2002. "The Fragments of the Nation: The Case of Iraq." *International Journal of Middle East Studies* 34 (2): 205–15.

Zuhur, Sherifa. 2006. "Iraq, Women's Empowerment, and Public Policy." December. Letort Papers. www.strategicstudiesinstitute.army.mil/Pubs/Display.Cfm?pubID=748.

Zunes, Stephen. 2006. "The United States: Belligerent Hegemon." In *The Iraq War: Causes and Consequences,* edited by Rick Fawn and Raymond Hinne - busch, 21–36. Boulder, CO: Lynne Rienner.

Index

Text: 10/13 Sabon
Display: Franklin Gothic
Compositor: Integrated Composition Systems
Printer and Binder: Thomson-Shore, Inc.